THE
COMMUNIST
MANIFESTO
and Other
Revolutionary Writings

DOVER·THRIFT·EDITIONS

THE COMMUNIST MANIFESTO
and Other Revolutionary Writings

Marx, Marat, Paine, Mao, Gandhi, and Others

Edited by
BOB BLAISDELL

DOVER PUBLICATIONS, INC.
Mineola, New York

DOVER THRIFT EDITIONS

GENERAL EDITOR: PAUL NEGRI

Copyright

Bibliographical Note

The Communist Manifesto and Other Revolutionary Writings: Marx, Marat, Paine, Mao, Gandhi, and Others is a new work, first published by Dover Publications, Inc., in 2003.

Library of Congress Cataloging-in-Publication Data

The Communist Manifesto and other revolutionary writings : Marx, Marat, Paine, Mao, Gandhi, and others / edited by Bob Blaisdell. — Dover thrift editions
    p. cm.
Includes bibliographical references.
ISBN-13: 978-0-486-42465-1
ISBN-10: 0-486-42465-0
    1. Revolutions. 2. Revolutionary literature. 3. Communism. I. Blaisdell, Robert.
JC491 .C6775 2002
303.6'4—dc21

2002031418

Manufactured in the United States by Courier Corporation
42465006
www.doverpublications.com

Contents

viii   Contents

Editor's Note

. . . revolution, that last resort of an indignant nation.
—Alexis de Tocqueville, *L'ancien regime et la Revolution*[1]

KARL MARX and Frederick Engels's *Communist Manifesto*, published in 1848, though chronologically almost equidistant between the French Revolution of 1789 and the Russian Revolution of 1917, is the document that links the two most earthshaking revolutions in history. In it Marx and Engels looked back to the French Revolution and analyzed their own Europe, about to boil over into revolution, in order to look forward; later, Trotsky and Lenin, the most important Russian revolutionaries of 1905 and 1917, sometimes saw themselves fulfilling the prophecies of what had become Socialism's most holy document. For more than a hundred and fifty years *The Communist Manifesto* has influenced our sense of history and helped promote social justice. The philosopher Karl Popper, though critical of many aspects of Marxism, recognizes Marx's contribution not only to ideas but to deeds: "One cannot do justice to Marx without recognizing his sincerity. His open-mindedness, his sense of facts, his distrust of verbiage, and especially of moralizing verbiage, made him one of the world's most influential fighters against hypocrisy and pharisaism. He had a burning desire to help the oppressed, and was fully conscious of the need for proving himself in deeds, and not only in words. His main talents being theoretical, he

---

1. Alexis de Tocqueville, *The Old Regime and the French Revolution*. Trans. Stuart Gilbert (New York: Doubleday Anchor Books, 1955), 101.

devoted immense labour to forging what he believed to be scientific weapons for the fight to improve the lot of the vast majority of men. His sincerity in his search for truth and his intellectual honesty distinguish him, I believe, from many of his followers."[2]

Idealism about human nature and hopefulness for social progress, less than any one ideology, characterize these thirty-six selections that begin with Rousseau's spirited analysis of social inequality in *Discourse on the Origins and Foundations of Inequality among Men* (1755) and continue through the Charter 77 manifesto of 1977. Necessarily, these selections are only a few of the thousands of eruptions from mountains of materials. All are famous and passionate outpourings by revolutionaries or revolutionary thinkers, even though in their time the ideas and the revolutionaries were at odds with each other or became so, sometimes to their own or their causes' destruction. "The men who rush into undertakings of vast change usually feel they are in possession of some irresistible power," observed Eric Hoffer. "The generation that made the French Revolution had an extravagant conception of the omnipotence of man's reason and the boundless range of his intelligence. . . . Lenin and the Bolsheviks who plunged recklessly into the chaos of the creation of a new world had blind faith in the omnipotence of Marxist doctrine."[3]

The greatest analyst of the ideas and history that created the French Revolution, Alexis de Tocqueville, simultaneously complicates and clarifies our understanding of social upheaval: ". . . it is not always when things are going from bad to worse that revolutions break out. On the contrary, it oftener happens that when a people which has put up with an oppressive rule over a long period without protest suddenly finds the government relaxing its pressure, it takes up arms against it. Thus the social order overthrown by a revolution is almost always better than the one immediately preceding it, and experience teaches us that, generally speaking, the most perilous moment for a bad government is one when it seeks to mend its ways. Only consummate statecraft can enable a King to save his throne when after a long spell of oppressive rule he sets to improving the lot of his subjects. Patiently endured so long as it seemed beyond redress, a grievance comes to appear intolerable once the possibility of removing it crosses men's minds."[4] Tocqueville's short book, *L'ancien regime et la Revolution*,

2. Karl Popper, *The Open Society and Its Enemies*, Volume 2 (New York: Harper Torchbooks, 1962), 82.
3. Eric Hoffer, *The True Believer: Thoughts on the Nature of Mass Movements* (New York: Harper and Row, 1951), 8.
4. Alexis de Tocqueville, *The Old Regime and the French Revolution*. Trans. Stuart Gilbert (New York: Doubleday Anchor Books, 1955), 176–177.

published in 1856, "contains more solid and incontrovertible historical criticism than hundreds of volumes of later date," writes an outstanding Italian historian of the French Revolution, Gaetano Salvemini.[5] As wonderful as *L'ancien regime et la Revolution* is, there are no end of analyses and histories of revolution and no shortage of biographies of the men and women who have stood at the forefront of revolution.

Other works consulted but *not* cited in the headnotes or as sources for individual selections include Hannah Arendt's *On Revolution* (1965), Crane Brinton's *The Anatomy of Revolution* (1965), Edmund Burke's *Reflections on the Revolution in France* (1790), E. H. Carr's *Studies in Revolution* (1964), Isaac Deutscher's *The Prophet Armed: Trotsky, 1879–1921* (1954), Alexander Herzen's *My Past and Thoughts* (1923), R. R. Palmer's *Twelve Who Ruled: The Year of the Terror in the French Revolution* (1941), Harold Rosenberg's *The Tradition of the New* (1960), Leon Trotsky's *1905* (1917), and Edmund Wilson's *To the Finland Station* (1940). I acknowledge a large debt to the editors of earlier anthologies, particularly Albert Fried and Ronald Sanders's *Socialist Thought: A Documentary History* (1964) and Robert V. Daniels's *A Documentary History of Communism* (1984). Also of guidance were James Bunyan and H. H. Fisher's *The Bolshevik Revolution, 1917–1918: Documents and Materials* (1934), Steven M. Cahn's *Classics of Modern Political Theory: Machiavelli to Mill* (1997), James E. Connor's *Lenin on Politics and Revolution: Selected Writings* (1968), Frank A. Golder's *Documents of Russian History, 1914–1917* (1928), Lawrence Kaplan's *Revolutions: A Comparative Study* (1973), Robert C. Tucker's *The Marx-Engels Reader* (1978), and George Woodcock's *A Hundred Years of Revolution: 1848 and After* (1948). Martin L. Van Creveld's *The Encyclopedia of Revolutions and Revolutionaries: From Anarchism to Zhou Enlai* (1996) and the websites of Marxists.org, the International Institute of Social History, and the Anarchy Archives helped provide me with biographical information. I thank Dover's executive editor, Paul Negri, for suggesting several of the selections and my friend Kia Penso for her advice on background readings.

BOB BLAISDELL

---

5. Gaetano Salvemini, *The French Revolution: 1788–1792* (New York: Norton, 1962), 337.

THE
COMMUNIST
MANIFESTO
and Other
Revolutionary Writings

JEAN-JACQUES ROUSSEAU
Preface and Part 2,

Discourse on the Origins and Foundations of Inequality among Men
[Discours sur l'origine et les fondements de l'inégalité parmi les hommes]

1755

"Our men of letters did not merely impart their revolutionary ideas to the French nation," writes Alexis de Tocqueville, reflecting on the causes of the French Revolution, "they also shaped the national temperament and outlook on life. In the long process of molding men's minds to their ideal pattern their task was all the easier since the French had had no training in the field of politics, and they thus had a clear field. The result was that our writers ended up giving the Frenchman the instincts, the turn of mind, the tastes, and even the eccentricities characteristic of the literary men. And when the time came for action, these literary propensities were imported into the political arena.

"When we closely study the French Revolution we find that it was conducted in precisely the same spirit as that which gave rise to so many books expounding theories of government in the abstract. Our revolutionaries had the same fondness for broad generalizations, cut-and-dried legislative systems, and a pedantic symmetry; the same contempt for hard facts; the same taste for reshaping institutions on novel, ingenious, original lines; the same desire to reconstruct the entire constitution according the rules of logic and a preconceived system instead of trying to rectify its faulty parts. The result was nothing short of disastrous; for what is a merit in the writer may well be a vice in the statesman and the very qualities which go to make great literature can lead to catastrophic revolutions."[1]

---

1. Alexis de Tocqueville, *The Old Regime and the French Revolution*. Trans. Stuart Gilbert (New York: Doubleday Anchor Books, 1955), 146.

Jean-Jacques Rousseau (1712–1778), born in Geneva, Switzerland, author of *The Confessions* (1781), the most extraordinary autobiography in literature, was, whether he would have liked it or not, one of the French Revolution's ideological forefathers. *Discourse on the Origins and Foundations of Inequality among Men* was a prize-winning essay that assured his fame among fellow *philosophes* and inspired those revolutionaries who followed with "the same fondness for broad generalizations, cut-and-dried legislative systems, and a pedantic symmetry; the same contempt for hard facts; the same taste for reshaping institutions on novel, ingenious, original lines; the same desire to reconstruct the entire constitution according the rules of logic and a preconceived system instead of trying to rectify its faulty parts."

Part philosophy, part sociology, the *Discourse* is an almost continuous flight of genius on the wing. In his Preface Rousseau introduces himself and the topic. (Part 1, not included in this selection, is speculative, compelling—if often fanciful—anthropology.) In Part 2, Rousseau discusses "the nature of the fundamental compact of all government . . . a contract by which both parties bind themselves to observe the laws therein expressed, which form the ties of their union."

SOURCE: Jean-Jacques Rousseau, "A Dissertation on the Origin and Foundation of the Inequality of Mankind." In *The Miscellaneous Works of Mr. J. J. Rousseau*, Volume 1. Anonymous translator (London: T. Becket and P. A. DeHondt, 1767), 153–161, 213–260.

Preface

Of all human sciences the most useful and most imperfect, appears to me that of mankind: and I will venture to say, the simple inscription on the Temple of Delphos contained a precept more difficult and important than is to be found in all the huge volumes of morality, that have been written. I consider the subject of the following discourse, as one of the most interesting questions philosophy can propose, and unhappily for us, one of the most perplexing for philosophers to solve. For how shall we know the source of the inequality subsisting among men, if we do not begin with the knowledge of mankind. And how shall man arrive at the prospect of himself, such as he was formed by nature, through all those changes which the succession of place and time must have produced in his original constitution? How shall he be able to separate and distinguish, that which is essential to his nature, from what accident and improvement may have added to, or diversified in, his primitive state.

As the statue of Glaucus, which was so disfigured by time, by the seas and tempests, that it bore the resemblance rather of a wild beast than a God; so the human soul, altered in the midst of society by a thousand causes perpetually recurring, by the acquisition of a multiplicity of truths and errors, by the changes happening to the constitution of the body, and by the continual jarring of the passions, hath, if I may so speak, lost its original appearance, so as to be hardly known for the same. Instead of a Being, acting constantly from fixed and invariable principles; instead of that celestial and majestic simplicity, impressed on it by its divine Author, we find in it only the frightful contrast of passion, mistaking itself for reason, and of understanding totally perverted.

It is still more cruel that, every improvement made by the human species removing it still farther from its primitive state, the more discoveries we make, the more we deprive ourselves of the means of making the most important of all. Thus it is, on one sense, from our very application to the study of man, that the knowledge of him is put out of our power.

It is easy to perceive that, it is in these successive changes, which have happened to the constitution of man, we are to look for the origin of those differences which now subsist among the several parts of our species; all which, it is allowed, are as equal among themselves as were the animals of every kind, before physical causes had introduced those varieties which are now observable among some of them.

It is, in fact, not to be conceived that these primary changes, to whatever causes they may be imputed, could have altered, all at once and in the same manner, every individual of the species. It is natural to think that, while the condition of some of them grew better or worse, and they were acquiring various good or bad qualities not inherent in their nature, there were others who continued a longer time in their first situation. Such was doubtless the first source of the inequality of mankind; which it is much easier to point out thus in general terms, than to assign with precision the true causes of particular distinctions.

Let not my readers, therefore, imagine that I flatter myself with having seen what it appears to me so difficult to discover. I have here opened some arguments, and risked a few conjectures; but less from the hope of being able to solve the difficulty, than with a view to throw some light upon it, and of giving a true state of the question. Others may easily proceed farther in the same route, without finding it very easy to reach the end of their career. For, it is, by no means, a slight undertaking to distinguish properly between what is originally natural, and what is artificial, in the actual constitution of man; to form a just notion of a state, which exists no longer, perhaps never did exist, and probably never will; and of which, it is, nevertheless, necessary to have just ideas, in order to form a proper judgment of our present state. It requires, indeed, more philosophy than may possibly be imagined, to enable any one to determine exactly, what precautions he ought to take, in order to make solid observations on this subject; it appearing to me that a good solution of the following problem is not unworthy of the Aristotles and Plinys of the present age. *What are the experiments necessary to be made, in order to discover the natural state of man? And how are those experiments to be made in a state of society!*

So far am I from undertaking to solve this problem, that I think I have sufficiently considered the subject, to venture to declare beforehand that, it would require all the sagacity of our greatest philosophers to direct how such experiments are to be made, and the influence of our most powerful sovereigns to make them. A concurrence of which, we have very little reason to expect, especially attended with that perseverance, or rather succession of science and zeal, necessary on both sides to reach the end proposed.

These researches, so difficult to make, and which have been hitherto so little thought of, are, nevertheless, the only means which remain to obviate a multitude of difficulties, which deprive us of the knowledge of the real foundations of human society.

It is this ignorance of the nature of man, which casts so much uncertainty and obscurity on the true definition of natural justice: for, the idea of justice, says Burlamaqui, and more particularly that of natural justice, are ideas manifestly relative to the nature of man. It is therefore from this very nature itself, continues he, from the constitution and state of man, that we are to deduce the first principles of natural law.

We cannot without surprize and disgust remark how little the different Authors agree, who have treated this important subject. There can hardly be found any two, among the most serious writers, that are of the same opinion concerning it. I shall not insist upon what the ancient philosophers have advanced on this head; as one would imagine they had purposely engaged to contradict one another, in respect to the most fundamental principles. The Roman civilians subjected man and all other animals indiscriminately to the same natural law, because they considered, under that appellation, rather that law which nature imposes on herself than what she hath prescribed to others; or perhaps because of the particular acceptation of the term, law, among those Civilians; who seem on this occasion to have understood nothing more by it than the general relations, established by nature, between all animated Beings, for their common preservation. The moderns, understanding only by the term, law, a rule prescribed to a moral Being, that is to say intelligent, free and considered as to the relations in which he stands to other beings, have consequently confined the jurisdiction of natural law to man as the only animal endowed with reason. But, as in defining this law, almost every one hath taken a different method, they have established it on such metaphysical principles, that there are very few persons among us capable of comprehending them, much less of originally discovering them themselves. So that the definitions of these learned men, all differing in every thing else, agree only in this, that it is impossible to comprehend the law of nature, and of course to obey it, without being a very subtil casuist, and a profound metaphysician. All which is exactly the same as to say that, mankind must have employed, in the establishment of society, that knowledge which is with great difficulty, and by very few persons, to be acquired even in a state of society.

Knowing so little, therefore, of nature, and so ill agreeing about the meaning of the word *law*, it would be difficult for us to fix upon a good definition of the law of nature. Thus all the definitions we meet with in books, setting aside their defect in point of uniformity, have yet another, in that they are derived from many kinds of knowledge, which men by nature do not possess, and from advantages of which they can have no idea when they have once departed from that state. Our modern civilians begin by enquiring, what rules it would be expedient for men to agree to, for their common interest; and then give the name of natural law to a system composed of these rules, without any other proof of their originality, than the utility which would result from their being universally practised. This is undoubtedly a commodious way of making definitions, and of explaining the origin and natural fitness of things, by the accidental and almost arbitrary convenience of them.

But so long as we are ignorant of the natural state of man, it is in vain for us to attempt to determine either the law originally prescribed to him, or that which is best adapted to his constitution. All we can know with any certainty respecting this law, is that, in order to its being a law, not only the will of those it obliges, must be sensible of its obligation in their submitting to it; but also that, in order to its being natural, it must come directly from the voice of nature.

Throwing aside, therefore, all those scientific books, which teach us only to look upon men, in the light wherein they have placed themselves, and contemplating the first and most simple operations of the human soul, I think I can perceive in it two distinct principles of action, prior to reason one of them deeply interesting us in our own welfare and preservation, and the other exciting a natural aversion to see any other sensible being, and particularly any of our own species, suffer pain or death. It is from the concurrence and combination, which the understanding is capable of forming between these two principles, without its being at all necessary to annex that of sociability, that all the rules of natural equity appear to me readily deducible; rules which our reason is afterwards obliged to re-establish on other foundations, when by its successive efforts to the improvements of science, it hath suppressed the voice of nature.

In proceeding thus, we shall not be obliged to make man a philosopher, before he is made a man. His obligations toward other Beings are not only dictated to him by the late and tedious lessons of wisdom; but so long as he does not resist the internal impulse of compassion, he will never hurt any other man, nor even any animate creature, except on those lawful occasions, in which his own preservation is concerned, and he is obliged to give himself the preference.

By this method, also, we may terminate the ancient disputes, concerning the participation of other animals in the law of nature: for it is clear that being destitute of knowledge and freewill, they are not recognizable to that law; as they partake, however, in some measure of our nature, in consequence of the sensibility with which they are endowed, they ought to partake equally of a right to natural justice; so that mankind are subjected to a kind of moral obligation even toward the brutes. It appears, in fact, that my natural obligation to do no injury to my fellow creatures is founded less on their being rational than sensible creatures: and this quality of sensibility, being common both to men and beasts, ought to entitle the latter at least to the privilege of not being wantonly abused by the former.

The very study of the origin of man, of his real wants, and the fundamental principles of his duty, is besides the only proper method we can take to obviate a number of difficulties, which present themselves on the origin of moral inequality, on the true foundations of the body politic, on the reciprocal rights of its members, and many other similar topicks equally important and obscure.

In taking a view of human society with a calm and disinterested eye, it seems, at first, to present us only with a prospect of the violence of the powerful and the oppression of the weak. The mind is shocked at the cruelty of the one, or is induced to lament the blindness of the other; and as nothing is less permanent in life than those external relations, which are more frequently produced by accident than wisdom, and which are called weakness or power, riches or poverty, all human establishments appear at first glance to be founded merely on moving banks of quick-sand. By taking a nearer survey of them, indeed, and removing the dust which surrounds the edifice; we may perceive the immoveable basis on which it is raised, and thence learn to respect their foundation.

Now, without a serious application to the study of man, his natural faculties and their successive developement, we shall never be able to make these necessary distinctions; or to separate, in the actual situation of things, that which is the effect of the divine will, from the improvements attempted by human art. The political and moral researches, therefore, to which the examination of the important question before me, leads us, are in every respect useful; while the hypothetical history of governments, affords a lesson equally instructive to mankind.

In considering what we should have been, if left to ourselves, we should learn to bless that Being, whose gracious hand, correcting our institutions, and giving them an immoveable basis, hath prevented those disorders which otherwise would have arisen from them, and caused our happiness to proceed from those means, which seemed calculated to involve us in misery.

> *quem te deus esse*
> *iussit et humana qua parte locatus es in re;*
> *disce.**

Part 2

The first person, who, having inclosed a piece of ground, bethought himself of saying *This is mine*, and found people simple enough to believe him, was the real founder of civil society. From how many crimes, battles and murders, from how many horrors and misfortunes would not that man have saved mankind, who should have pulled up the stakes, or filled up the ditch, crying out to his fellows, "Beware of listening to this impostor; you are undone if you once forget that the fruits of the earth belong to us all, and that the earth itself belongs to nobody." But there is great probability that things were arrived to such a pitch, that they could no longer continue in the same state: for this idea of property depends so much on prior ideas, which could only be successively acquired, that it could not be suggested all at once to the human mind. Mankind must have made a very considerable progress, they must have amassed a great stock of knowledge and industry; which they must also have transmitted and increased from age to age, before they arrived at this last term of a state of nature. Let us recur therefore still farther back, and endeavour to trace under one point of view that slow succession of events and discoveries, as they proceeded in their natural order.

Man's first sentiment was that of his own existence, and his first care that of self-preservation. The produce of the earth furnished him with the means, and instinct directed him in the use of them. Hunger and other appetites made him at various times experience various modes of

---

*(Learn) what part God has ordered you to play, and at what point in the human commonwealth you have been stationed. (Persius, *Satires*, iii. 71. Translation by G. G. Ramsay. Loeb Classical Library, 1918, 1940. Harvard University Press, 1979.)

existence: among these there was one which urged him to the propagation of his species; a blind propensity that having nothing to do with
the heart, produced only an act merely animal. This desire once grati-
fied, the two sexes had nothing farther to do with each other; even the
offspring of their embraces caring as little for its mother, as soon as it
could do without her.

Such was the condition of infant man; such the life of an animal limited at first to mere sensations, and hardly profiting by the gifts
bestowed on him by nature, much less capable of entertaining a
thought of forcing them from her. But difficulties soon presented themselves, and it became necessary to learn to surmount them: the height
of the trees, which prevented his gathering their fruits; the competition
of other animals desirous of the same fruits; the ferocity of those who
attacked his person; all these things obliged him to apply himself to
bodily exercises. It was necessary for him to be active, swift of foot, and
vigorous in flight. Those natural weapons, stones and sticks, were easily found. Thus surmounting the obstacles of nature, he learned to contend in cases of necessity, with other animals, and to dispute the means
of subsistence even with other men, or to indemnify himself for what
he was forced to give up to a stronger.

In proportion as the species grew more numerous, the cares of individuals would increase. The difference of soils, climates, and seasons,
would introduce some difference of course into their manner of living.
Barren years, from long and sharp winters, or scorching summers
parching the fruits of the earth, would require them to be more than
ordinarily industrious. On the sea-shore and the banks of rivers, they
would invent the hook and line, and become fishermen. In the forests
they would make bows and arrows, and become huntsmen and war-
riours. In cold countries they would clothe themselves with the skins of
the beasts they had slain. The lightning, a volcano, or some lucky incident brought them acquainted with fire; a new relief against the rigour
of winter: they next learned the way to preserve this element, then the
method to reproduce it when extinguished, and at length that of using
it to prepare the flesh of animals, which before they had been accustomed to devour raw.

This repeated application of different beings to himself, and of one
to the other, would naturally give rise in the human mind to the per-
ceptions of certain relations between them. Thus, for example, the
relations which we denote by the terms, great, little, strong, weak, swift,
slow, fearful, bold, and the like, being occasionally and almost insensibly compared, would at length produce in him a kind of reflection, or
rather a mechanical sort of prudence, which indicated to him the precautions most necessary to his security.

The new lights which would result from this developement, would augment his superiority over other animals, by making him sensible of it. He would now endeavour, therefore, to ensnare them; would play them a thousand tricks; and though many of them might surpass him in swiftness or in strength, he would in time become the master of some and the tyrant over others.

It is hence that man, when he first looked into himself, felt the first emotion of human pride; and this it was that, at a time when he scarce knew how to distinguish the different orders of beings, yet by looking upon himself as the first of animals, as one of the superior species, he prepared the way, at a distance, for assuming pre-eminence as an individual.

Other men, it is true, were not then to him what they now are to us, and he had hardly any greater intercourse with them, than he had with other animals; yet they were not neglected in his observations. The conformities, which he might in time discover between them, and between himself and his female, led him to form a judgment of others which might not then be perceptible; and finding that they all behaved as he himself would probably have done in like circumstances, he naturally inferred that their manner of thinking and acting was altogether conformable to his own. This important truth, being once impressed deeply on his mind, would induce him, from a presentiment more certain and much quicker than any kind of argument, to pursue the best rules of conduct, which he ought to observe towards them, for his own security and advantage.

Taught by experience that the love of happiness is the sole motive of all human actions, he now found himself in a capacity to distinguish the few cases, in which mutual interest might justify him in relying upon the assistance of his fellows; and also those, which are still fewer, wherein a concurrence of jarring interests might give cause to suspect it. In the former case, he joined in the same herd with them, or at farthest in some kind of loose association, that laid no tie or restraint on its members, and lasted no longer than the transitory occasion that formed it. In the latter case, every one sought his own private advantage, either by open force if he was strong enough, or by address and cunning, if he found himself the weakest.

In this manner, mankind might have insensibly acquired some gross ideas of mutual engagements, and the advantages of fulfilling them: that is, just so far as their present and apparent interest was concerned: for, with regard to foresight, they were perfect strangers to it, and were so far from troubling themselves about a futurity far distant, that they hardly entertained a thought of the morrow. If a deer was to be taken, every one saw that, in order to succeed, he must abide faithfully by his post: but if a hare happened to come within the reach of any one of them, it is not to be doubted that he pursued it without scruple; and, having seized his prey, cared very little, if by so doing he occasioned his companions to miss of catching the deer.

It is easy to conceive that such kind of intercourse would not require a language much more refined than that of rooks or monkeys, who associate together, much to the same purpose, and in the same manner. Inarticulate cries, a multiplicity of gestures and some imitative sounds, must have been for a long time the universal language of our species; by adding to which, in every country some conventional articulate sounds (of which, as I have already intimated, the first institution is not very easy to explain) particular languages were produced; but those rude and imperfect, and nearly such as are now to be found among several savage nations. Hurried on by the rapidity of time, by the abundance of things I have to say, and by the almost insensible progress of things in their beginnings, I pass over in an instant a multitude of ages; for the slower the events were in their succession, the quicker may I be allowed to be in their description.

These first improvements enable mankind, at length, to make others with greater success and rapidity. In proportion as they grew enlightened, they grew industrious. They ceased to fall asleep under the first tree, or in the first cave that afforded them casual shelter; but, lighting upon some flints, resembling spades and hatchets, they made use of them to dig up the earth, and to cut down trees; with the branches of which they built themselves huts; which they afterwards plaistered over with clay and dirt. This was the era of a first revolution, productive of the establishment and distinction of families; and introductive of a kind of property, the source perhaps of a thousand contests and quarrels. As the strongest, however, were very probably the first who made themselves cabins, as they were sensible they should be able to defend them, it may be concluded that the weak found it much easier and safer to imitate, than to attempt to dislodge them: and as to those who were once provided with cabins, none could have any great inducement to appropriate that of his neighbour; not indeed so much because it did not belong to him, as because it could be of no use to him, being already provided; and as besides he must expose himself to a desperate battle with the occupier, before he could make himself master of it.

The first expansions of the human heart, were the effects of a novel situation, which united husbands and wives, parents and children, under one roof. The habit of living thus together soon gave rise to the most delightful sentiments the human heart is capable of entertaining; viz. conjugal love and paternal affection. Every family became a little society, by so much the more intimately united as liberty and a reciprocal attachment were the only bonds of their union. The sexes, whose manner of life had been hitherto the same, began now to adopt different customs and manners. The women became more sedentary, and used to stay at home with their children, while the men went abroad in search of their common subsistence. By living also a little more at their ease, both sexes began to lose something of their strength and ferocity: but, if individuals became, on the one hand, less able to encounter separately the wild beasts, they were, on the other hand, more readily called together to make a general resistance.

The simplicity and solitude of man's life in this new situation, the paucity of his wants, and the implements he had invented to satisfy them, leaving him a great deal of leisure, he employed it to furnish himself with many conveniences unknown to his fathers: and this was the first yoke he inadvertently imposed on himself, and the first source of the evils he prepared for his descendants. For, besides continuing thus to enervate both body and mind, these conveniences losing by use almost all their fitness to please, and even degenerating into real conveniences, the want of them became far more disagreeable than the possession of them had been agreeable. They would have been unhappy to lose them, though the possession of them did not make them happy.

One may discover a little better here how the use of speech insensibly took place, and improved in each family, and may form a conjecture also concerning the manner in which various particular causes might have extended and accelerated the progress of language, by rendering it daily more necessary. Earthquakes or inundations caused inhabited districts to be surrounded with chasms or waters. The violent revolutions that have happened in the globe tore off portions from the continent, and constituted islands. It is readily conceived that among men thus collected and compelled to live together, a general idiom of speech must have took place much earlier, than among those who still wandered through the forests of the continent. Thus it is very possible, that after their first essays in navigation, the islanders brought over the use of speech to the continent: and it is at least very probable that communities and languages were first established in islands, and even came to some perfection there before either of them were known to the inhabitants of the continent.

Every thing began now to change its aspect. Mankind, heretofore vagrant in the woods, by taking to a more settled manner of life, flocked gradually together, formed separate bodies, and at length in every country a distinct nation, united by character and manners, not by any regulations or laws; but by an uniformity of life, a sameness of subsistence, and the common influence of the climate. A permanent vicinage could not fail of producing, at length, some kind of connection between different families. Among the young people of both sexes, living in contiguous cabins, the transient commerce required by nature, soon induced another kind not less agreeable, but from their mutual intercourse more permanent. Men began now to examine into the difference of objects, and to make comparisons; they acquired imperceptibly the ideas of beauty and merit, which soon gave rise to sentiments of preference and distinction. In consequence of seeing each other often, they could not do without seeing each other constantly. A tender and agreeable mode of sentiment insinuated itself into the soul, which the least opposition converted into an impetuous fury: love gave birth to jealousy; discord triumphed, and human blood was sacrificed to the gentlest of all the passions.

In proportion to the progress of ideas and sentiments, and as the head and the heart proceed in their exercise, mankind go on to lay aside their original wildness; their private connections becoming every day more intimate as their general limits grow extensive. They accustom themselves now to assemble round a large tree; while singing and dancing, the genuine offspring of love and leisure, become the amusement, or rather the occupation of men and women thus assembled together and having nothing else to do. Every one begins to respect another, and to be desirous of having respect paid him in turn; and thus a value becomes affixed to public esteem. Whoever sings or dances best; whoever is the handsomest, the strongest, the most dexterous, or the most eloquent, becomes the most distinguished; and this was the first step toward inequality, and at the same time toward vice. From these first distinctions arose on one side vanity and contempt; and on the other shame and envy: the fermentation, caused by which new leavens, produced at length combinations the most fatal to innocence and happiness.

As soon as men began to shew each other mutual esteem, and the idea of respect had got footing in the mind, every one of course put in his claim to it, and it became impossible to refuse it to any with impunity. Hence arose the first obligations of civility even among savages; and hence every intended injury became an affront; because, besides the hurt which might result from it, the party injured was certain to find in it a contempt for his person often more insupportable than the hurt itself.

Thus it is that every man, resenting the contempt shewn for him by others, in proportion to his opinion of himself, revenge became terrible, and mankind by degrees became sanguinary and cruel. Such was precisely the state to which most of the savage nations, which are known to us, were arrived: and it is for want of having made a proper distinction in our ideas, and remarking how very far they were from being in a state of nature, that so many writers have precipitately concluded that man is naturally cruel, and requires civil institutions to soften him; whereas nothing is more mild and gentle than man in his primitive state, when placed by nature at an equal distance from the stupidity of brutes, and the fatal ingenuity of civilized man. Equally confined by instinct and reason to the sole care of guarding against the mischiefs which threaten him, he is restrained by natural compassion from doing any injury to others; to which he has not the least inducement even in return for injuries received. For, according to the axiom of the sagacious Mr. Locke, *There can be no injury, where there is no property.*

But it must be remarked that the society thus formed, and the relations once established among mankind, required of them qualities different from those which they possessed from their primitive constitution. A sense of morality beginning now to introduce itself into human actions, and every one, before the institutions of laws, being his own judge and avenger of the injuries done him, that goodness which was suitable enough to a pure state of nature, was no longer that which agreed with an infant state of society. It was requisite that punishments should be made more severe, in proportion as the opportunities of offending became more frequent, and that the dread of vengeance should stand in the place of the terror of the law.

Thus, though men were become less patient, and their natural compassion had already suffered some diminution, this period of the expansion of the human faculties, keeping a just mean between the indolence of his primitive state and the present petulant activity of our self-love; it must have been the most happy and durable epoch of human life. The more we reflect on it, the more we shall find, that this state was the least subject of any other to change; the very best that could be, for mankind; and a state, out of which nothing could have drawn him, but some sinister accident, which it had been better for the publick good had never happened. The example of the savages, most of whom have been found in this state, seems indeed to prove that mankind were formed ever to remain in it; that this situation was the real youth and vigour of the world, and that all subsequent improvements have been apparently so many steps toward the perfection of the individual, but in reality to the decrepitude of the species.[1]

So long as men rested content with their rustic cabins; so long as they were satisfied with cloths made of the skins of other animals, and the use of thorns and fish-bones in sewing these skins together; so long as they considered feathers and shells as sufficient ornaments of dress; and continued to paint their bodies of different colours, to improve and adorn their bows and arrows, to form with sharp-edged stones their fishing boats or clumsey instruments of musick; in a word, so long as they undertook such performances only as a single person could execute, and abided by such arts, as did not require the joint labours of several hands, they lived free, healthy, honest and happy; at least so far as their nature would admit of, continuing to enjoy all the pleasures of a mutual and independent intercourse. But from the instant they began to stand in need of each other's assistance; from the moment in which it appeared advantageous to any one man to possess the quantity of provisions necessary for two, all equality disappeared, property introduced itself, industry became indispensible; vast forests became smiling fields, which it was found necessary for man to cultivate with the sweat of his brow, and in which slavery and misery were seen presently to germinate and grow up with the harvest.

Metallurgy and agriculture were the two arts, whose invention produced this grand revolution. The poets tell us it was gold and silver, but the philosophers assure us it was iron and corn, which first civilized man, and ruined human-kind. Thus both one and the other were unknown to the savages of America, who for that reason have still continued savage: there are nations also who seem to have continued in a state of barbarism while they exercised only one of these arts without the other. And one of the best reasons, perhaps, that can be given why Europe hath been, if not sooner, at least more constantly and better civilized than the other parts of the world, is, that it is at once the most abundant in iron and the most fertile in corn.

It is very difficult to conjecture how mankind came first to know the nature and use of iron; for it is impossible to suppose they should think of digging the ore out of the mine, and preparing it for smelting, before they knew what would be the consequence of the process. On the other hand, we have the less reason to suppose this discovery the effect of any accidental fire, as mines are only formed in barren places, bare of trees and plants; so that it looks as if nature had taken some pains to keep so hurtful a secret from us. There remains, therefore, only the extraordinary incident of some volcano; which, by ejecting metallic substances already fused, might suggest to the spectators a notion of imitating the process of nature in that operation. And we must even conceive them, after all, possessed of an uncommon share of fortitude as well as foresight, to undertake so laborious a work, with so distant a view to the advantages that might result from it; yet these qualities are rarely thus united in minds more improved than we can suppose those of these first discoverers.

With regard to agriculture, the principles of it were known long before they were put in practice; and it is indeed hardly possible that men, constantly employed in drawing their subsistence from plants and trees, should not readily acquire a knowledge of the means made use of by nature for the propagation of vegetables. It was in all probability very late, however, before their industry took that turn, either because trees, which together with their land and water game afforded them sufficient food, did not require their attention; or because they were ignorant of the use of corn, or destitute of instruments to cultivate it; or because they wanted foresight in respect to future exigencies; or lastly, because they were destitute of the means of preventing others robbing them of the fruit of their labours.

On their growing more industrious, it is natural to conceive that they began, by the help of sharp stones and pointed sticks, to cultivate a few pulse or roots, round about their cabins; though it was long before they knew the method of dressing corn, or were provided with the implements necessary to raise it in any large quantity; not to mention how requisite it is, in order to follow the business of husbandry, to consent to a present loss, in order to reap a future gain; a precaution very foreign to the turn of mind in a savage; who, as I before observed, hardly foresees in the morning what he shall have occasion for at night.

The invention of other arts must therefore have been necessary to compel mankind to apply to that of agriculture. No sooner were artificers wanted to smelt and forge iron, than other labourers were required to maintain them; while the more hands were employed in manufactures, the fewer were left to provide subsistence for all, though the number of mouths to be furnished with food continued the same: and as some required commodities in exchange for their iron, the rest at length discovered the method of making iron serve to the multiplication of commodities. By this means the arts of husbandry and agriculture were established on the one hand, and the art of working metals, and multiplying the uses of them, on the other.

As the earth was cultivated, it was necessarily distributed and parcelled out among the cultivators. Hence came property, and that once acknowledged, the first rules of justice: for, before every one could be secured in the enjoyment of his own, it was necessary for him to have something to enjoy. Besides, as men began to look forward into futurity, and were all in possession, more or less, of something capable of being lost, every one of them in particular had reason to apprehend that reprisals would be made on him, for any injury he might do to another. This origin is so much the more natural, as it is impossible to conceive how property can be deduced from any thing but manual labour: for what else can a man add to things which he does not originally create, to have any pretence to property in them? It is the husbandman's labour alone that, giving him a title to the produce of the ground he has tilled, gives him a claim also to the land itself, at least till he hath reaped the fruits of his labour; which claim, being continued from year to year, forms a constant possession which easily transforms itself into property.

When the ancients, says Grotius, gave to Ceres the title of Legislatrix, and to a festival celebrated in her honour the name of Thesmophoria, they gave the people by that to understand that the distribution of lands was productive of a new species of right: that is to say, a right of property different from that which is deducible from the law of nature.

Things being thus situated, an equality might have been kept up, had the talents of individuals been all equal, and if the use of iron, for example, and the consumption of commodities, had constantly held an exact proportion with each other: but as this proportion had nothing to support it, it was soon broken through: the strongest performed the most labour; the cunningest turned his labour to best account; the most ingenious devised methods to diminish his labour: the husbandman wanted more iron, or the smith more corn, and while both laboured equally, the one gained a great deal by his work, while the other could hardly support himself. Thus it is that natural inequality displays itself insensibly with that of combination, and that the difference of mankind, unfolded by that of circumstances, becomes more sensible in its effects, and begins to have an influence, in the same proportion, over the lot of individuals.

Things once arrived at this pitch, it is easy to conceive the rest. I shall not detain the reader with a description of the successive inventions of other arts, the improvements of language, the trail and employment of talents, the inequality of fortunes, the use and abuse of wealth, nor of all those particulars which attend on these, and which are easily suggested. I shall confine myself to the taking a slight view of mankind, placed in this new situation of things.

Behold, then, all the human faculties developed; the memory and imagination in full play; self-love become interested; reason rendered active; and the mind arrived almost at the highest point of its perfection. Behold all the natural qualities put in action; the rank and condition of every man assigned him; not merely as to his share of property and his power to serve or injure others, but also as to genius, beauty, strength or address, merit or talents: and these being the only qualities capable of commanding respect, it of course presently becomes necessary to possess, or to affect them.

It became now the interest of men to appear what they really were not. To be and to seem, became two things totally different; and thus from this necessary distinction sprung insolent pomp and artful knavery, with all the numerous vices that compose their train. On the other hand, free and independent as mankind were before, they were now, in consequence of a multiplicity of new wants, brought under subjection, as it were, to every thing in nature, and particularly to one another; each becoming in some degree a slave even in becoming a master: if rich, they stood in need of the services of others; if poor, of their assistance; even mediocrity itself not enabling them to do without each other. Man must, now, therefore, have been perpetually employed in getting others to interest themselves in his happiness, and in making them apparently at least, if not really, find their advantage in promoting his own. Thus he must have been sly and artful in his behaviour to some, and imperious and cruel to others; being laid under a kind of necessity to use all those persons ill of whom he stood in need, when he could not awe them into a compliance with his will, and did not judge it his interest to purchase such compliance at the expence of being really useful to them.

In fine, insatiable ambition, the thirst of raising their respective fortunes, not so much from real want as from the desire of surpassing others, must inspire all mankind with a vile propensity to injure each other, and with a secret jealousy, by so much the more dangerous, as it puts on the face of benevolence, to carry its point with the greater security. In a word, rivalry and competition on the one hand, jarring and opposite interests on the other, together with a secret desire on both of profiting at the expence of others, universally prevailed. All these evils were the first effects of property, and the inseparable retinue of growing inequality.

Before the invention of signs to represent riches, wealth could hardly consist in any thing but lands and cattle, the only genuine property men can possess. But, when inheritances were so much increased as to occupy whole countries, and border on each other, it became impossible for one man to aggrandize himself but at the expence of some other; at the same time the supernumeraries, who had been too weak or too indolent to make such acquisitions, and were grown poor without sustaining any loss, because while they saw every thing changed around them, they remained still the same; these, I say, were obliged to receive their subsistence, or steal it, from the rich; whence there soon appeared, according to the different characters of each, dominion and slavery, or violence and rapine. The wealthy, on their part, had hardly begun to taste the pleasure of command, before they disdained all others, and, making use of their old slaves to acquire new, thought of nothing but subduing and enslaving their neighbours; just like those ravenous wolves, which, having once tasted of human flesh, despise every other food, and seek only to devour men for ever after.

It is thus that the most powerful or the most miserable, considering their respective might or misery as a kind of claim to the possessions of others, equivalent, in their opinion, to that of property; the equality being once broken through, the breach of it was attended with the most terrible disorders. It is thus that the usurpations of the rich, the thefts of the poor, and the unbridled passions of both suppressing the cries of natural compassion and the feeble voice of justice, rendered mankind avaricious, ambitious and vicious. Between the title of the strongest and that of the first occupier, there arose perpetual conflicts, which never ended but in battles and bloodshed.[2] The infant state of society thus admitted a horrid state of war; while mankind thus harrassed and depraved, were no longer capable of retreat or renouncing the fatal acquisitions they had made; but, labouring, in short, by the abuse of those faculties which do them so much honour, merely to their own confusion, brought themselves to the very brink of ruin.

> *Attonitus novitate mali, divesque miserque,*
> *Effugere optat opes; et quae modo voverat odit.**

It is impossible that men should not at length, reflect on a situation so wretched, and on the calamities that overwhelmed them. The rich must, in particular, have presently been made sensible how much they suffered by a constant state of war, of which they bore all the expence; and in which, though all risked their lives, they alone risked their properties. Besides, however speciously they might colour over their usurpations, they knew in fact that they were founded on precarious and false titles; so that others might deprive them by force, of what they by force acquired, without their having any room to complain of injustice. Nay, even those who were enriched by their own industry, could scarce found their property on better claims. It was in vain any one repeated, "I built this well; I gained this spot by my "industry." Who gave you the limits, it might be objected, and what right have you to demand payment of us, for doing what we did not require you? Are you ignorant that numbers of your fellow-creatures are starving, for want of what you possess in superfluity? You ought to have had the express and universal consent of mankind, to appropriate to yourself more of their common subsistence than comes to your own private share. Destitute of valid reasons to justify and sufficient force to defend himself; capable of crushing individuals with ease, but easily crushed himself by a troop of

---

*Astonished at his new misfortune, / Rich man and poor man, [he] tries to flee his riches / Hating the favor he had lately prayed for. (Ovid, *Metamorphoses*, xi. 127. Translation by Rolfe Humphries. Indiana University Press, 1955.)

banditti; one against all, and incapable, on account of mutual jealousy, to join with his equals against numerous enemies united by the common hopes of plunder, the rich man, thus urged by necessity, conceived at length the profoundest project that ever entered the mind: this was to employ in his favour, the forces even of those who attacked him, to make allies of his adversaries, to inspire them with different maxims, and induce them to adore other institutions as favourable to him as the law of nature was prejudicial.

With this view, after having represented to his neighbours the honour of a situation, which armed every man against another, rendering their possessions as burthensome as their wants were insufferable; and in which no safety could be expected either for the rich or the poor, he readily devised plausible arguments to make them close with his design. "Let us join," said he, "to guard the weak from oppression, to lay a restraint on the ambitious, and secure to every man the possession of what belongs to him: let us institute rules of justice and peace, to which all may be obliged to conform without exception of persons; rules that may in some measure make amends for the caprices of fortune, by subjecting equally the powerful and the weak to the observance of obligations that shall be reciprocal. Let us, in a word, instead of turning our forces against ourselves, collect them in a supreme power; which may govern us by wife laws, may protect and defend all the members of the association, repulse their common enemies, and maintain a constant harmony among us."

A much shorter harangue to this purpose would have been sufficient to impose on men so little cultivated, and easily seduced; especially as they had too many disputes among themselves to live without arbiters, and too much ambition and avarice to subsist long without masters. All ran headlong into the yoke, in hopes of securing their liberty; for, they had just wit enough to perceive the conveniences of a political establishment, they had not experience enough to enable them to foresee the dangers of it. The most capable among them to discern these dangers were the very persons who expected to benefit by them; and even the most prudent of them judged it not inexpedient to sacrifice one part of their freedom to ensure the other; even as a man, dangerously wounded in his arm, parts with it, tho' reluctantly, to save the rest of his body.

Such was, or it is natural to suppose, might have been the origin of society and laws; which added to the fetters of the poor, and gave new power of dominion to the rich;[3] which brought irretrievable destruction on natural liberty, fixed eternally the law of property and inequality, converted an artful usurpation into unalterable right, and for the advantage of a few ambitious individuals, subjected all mankind to perpetual labour, slavery, and wretchedness.

It is easy to see how the establishment of one community rendered that of all the rest indispensibly necessary, and how, in order to make head against such united forces, it behoved the rest of mankind to unite in turn. Societies being thus once formed, presently multiplied and diffused themselves over the face of the earth; in so much that scarce a corner of the world was left, in which a man could throw off the yoke, and withdraw his head from beneath the sword which he saw perpetually suspended, and that often on a breaking thread, over him. The civil law being thus become the common rule of conduct among the members of each community, the law of nature maintained its place only among different communities; where, under the name of the law of nations, it was qualified by certain tacit connections to render their mutual commerce practicable, and serve as a substitute to natural compassion; which, losing, when applied to societies, almost all that influence it had over individuals, exists no longer except in some great minds, some true cosmopolites, who, breaking through those imaginary barriers that separate different people, copy the example of our supreme Creator, and include the whole human race within the circle of their benevolence. But bodies politic, remaining thus in a state of nature among themselves, presently experienced the inconveniences which had obliged individuals to forsake it; this state becoming still more fatal to these great bodies than it had before been to the individuals of which they were composed. Hence those national wars, those battles, murders, and reprisals, which are so shocking both to nature and reason; together with all those horrid prejudices which place the honour of shedding human blood among the virtues. The most worthy men hence learned to consider the practice of cutting each others throats as a moral duty; at length they massacred their fellow-creatures by thousands without even so much as knowing for what; committing more murders in a single fight, and more violent outrages in the sacking of a single town, than were committed in a state of nature, for a succession of ages over the face of the whole earth. Such were the first effects, which we may conceive from the division of mankind into different communities. But to return to their institution. I know that many have imputed another origin to political societies, such as the conquest of the powerful, or the associations of the weak. It is, indeed, no matter which of these causes we adopt in regard to what I would establish. That which I have just laid down, however, appears to me the most natural for the following reasons.

Firstly: Because, in the first case, the right of conquest being no right in itself, it could not serve as a foundation on which to build another; the victor and the vanquished ever remaining with respect to each other in a state of war, unless the vanquished being restored to the full possession of their liberty, they should voluntarily make choice of the victor for their chief. For till then whatever truce or capitulation may have been made between them, as such capitulations were founded in violence, and of course *ipso facto* void, there could not have subsisted in this hypothesis either a real society or body politic, or any other law than that of the strongest.

Secondly: Because these words *strong* and *weak* are, in the second case, ambiguous; for during the interval between the establishment of a right of property, or prior occupancy, and that of political government, the intent of these words is better expressed by the terms *rich* and *poor:* because, in fact, before the institution of laws, men had no other way to reduce their equals to submission, than by invading their property, or by parting with some of their own property to them.

Thirdly: Because the poor, having nothing but their freedom to lose, it would have been to the highest degree absurd in them to resign voluntarily the only blessing they enjoyed, without receiving any compensation for it: whereas the rich, being sensible, if I may so express myself, in every part of their possessions, it was much easier to do them a mischief, and therefore more necessary for them to guard against it, and in short, because it is more reasonable to suppose any thing to have been invented by a person to whom it could be of service, rather than by one to whom it must have proved prejudicial.

Government had, in its infancy, no regular and constant form. The want of a competent fund of experience and philosophy preventing mankind from seeing any but present inconveniences, they thought not of providing against the future till they presented themselves. In spite of the endeavours of their wisest legislators, the political state remained imperfect, because it was little more than the work of chance; and, being ill begun, tho' time sufficiently discovered its mistakes, it could never remove its original defects. The work of reparation was constantly repeating, instead of the area being cleared and the old materials removed, as was done by Lycurgus at Sparta, to erect a solid and lasting edifice. Civil society consisted at first merely of a few general terms of convention, which every member bound himself to observe, and for his performance of covenants the whole body became security to the respective individuals. Experience only could shew the weakness of such a constitution, and how easily it might be infringed with impunity, from the difficulty of being convicted of faults, in which the publick alone were to be both witness and judge: hence the laws could not fail of being variously eluded; disorders and inconveniences could not fail of being multiplied, till it became at length necessary to commit the dangerous trust of public authority to the hands of private persons, and the care of enforcing obedience to the deliberations of the people to the magistrate. For to pretend that chiefs were chosen before social confederacies were formed, and that the administrators of the laws subsisted before the laws themselves, is a supposition too absurd to merit a serious confutation. It would be as little reasonable to suppose that mankind at first threw themselves at the feet of an absolute master, without making any conditions with him, or that the first expedient which proud and uncivilized men should hit upon for their common security, was to run precipitately into slavery. For what reason, in fact, did they take to themselves superiors at all, if it was not in order that they might by their means be defended from oppression, and protected in their lives, liberties and properties, which are in a manner the constitutional elements of their being? Now, in the relations between individuals, the worst that can happen to one man being to find himself subjected to another, it would have been inconsistent with common-sense to commence by bestowing on a chief the only things, which they wanted his assistance to preserve. What equivalent was it in his power to offer them in return for so ample a grant? And if he had presumed to exact it under pretence of defending them, would he not have received the answer recorded in the fable; What can we grant more to the enemy? It is therefore beyond dispute, and indeed a fundamental maxim in politics, that people have preferred chiefs to protect not to enslave them. If we have a prince, said Pliny to Trajan, it is in order that he may prevent our having a master.

Politicians are guilty of the same sophistry in regard to the love of liberty, as philosophers are in respect to a state of nature. They judge by what they see, of things very different, which they have not seen; imputing to man a natural propensity to servitude, because the slaves within their observation are seen to bear their yoke without impatience; without reflecting that the case of liberty is the same with that of innocence or virtue; the value is not known except by those who possess them, and that a taste for them is forfeited when they are forfeited themselves. I know the charms of your country, said Brasidas to a Satrape, who was comparing the manner of life at Sparta with that at Persepolis, but it is out of your power to taste the pleasures of mine.

An unbroken horse erects his mane, paws the ground and starts back at the sight of the bridle; while that which is properly trained suffers patiently even the whip and spur: so savage man bends not his neck to that yoke, to which civilized man submits without murmuring; but prefers the most turbulent state of liberty to the most peaceful slavery. It is not therefore, from the servility of nations already enslaved, that we must form our judgment of the natural dispositions of mankind either for or against slavery; but rather from the prodigious efforts of every free people to prevent oppression. I am sensible that the former are perpetually declaiming in praise of that tranquility they enjoy in their chains, and that they call a state of wretched servitude a state of peace: *miserrimam servitutempacem appellant*: But when I observe the latter sacrificing pleasure, peace, wealth, power and even life itself to the preservation of that only treasure, which is so much disdained by those who have lost it; when I see free-born animals dash their brains out against the bars of their cage, out of an innate impatience of captivity; when I behold numbers of naked savages, that despise European pleasures, braving hunger, fire, the sword, and even death itself, to preserve their independency; I feel that it belongs not to slaves to argue about liberty.

With regard to paternal authority, from which absolute government and indeed all kinds of society have been deduced by many writers; it will suffice, without recurring to the contrary arguments of Locke and Sidney, to remark that nothing is farther from the ferocious spirit of despotism, than the mildness of that authority which regards more the advantage of him who obeys than that of him who commands; that by the law of nature, the father is the master over the child no longer than his paternal assistance is necessary; that after that time they become both equal, the son being perfectly independent of the father, and owing him no obedience but only respect. For, as to gratitude; it is a duty which ought to be paid, but which none hath a right to exact. Instead of saying that civil society derives its origin from paternal authority, we ought to say rather that the latter derives its principal influence from the former. No individual was ever acknowledged as the father of many, till his sons and daughters settled about him. The goods of the father, of which he is really the master, are the ties of his children's dependence, and he may bestow on them, if he pleases, a share of his property, in proportion as they may have merited it of him, by paying a constant obedience to his will. Now the subjects of an arbitrary despot, are so far from having the like favour to expect from their chief, that they themselves and every thing they possess are his property, or at least are considered by him as such; so that they are forced to receive, as a favour, the little he is pleased to let them enjoy of their own. When he strips them he does them but justice, and is merciful that he permits them to live.

By proceeding to compare, in this manner, the matter of fact with the matter of right, we should discover full as little reason as truth in the voluntary establishment of tyranny. It would also be no easy matter to prove the validity of a contract, binding only on one of the contracting parties; who should at the same time stake every thing, and the other party nothing: so that none could suffer by such contract but he who had bound himself by it. This hateful system is indeed, even in modern times, very different from that of wife and good monarchs, and especially of the kings of France; as may be seen by several passages in their edicts; particularly by that celebrated one published in 1667 in the name and by the orders of Lewis XIV; which contains the following passage.

"Let it not, therefore, be said that the sovereign is not subject to the laws of his realm; since the contrary proposition is a maxim in the law of nations; which tho' flattery hath sometimes attacked, good princes have always defended, as the tutelary divinity of their dominions. How much more just and rational is it to say, with the wife Plato, that the perfect felicity of a kingdom consists in the obedience of subjects to their prince, that of the prince to the laws, and in the laws being just and constantly directed to the public good!"

I shall not stay here to enquire whether, as free-will is the noblest faculty of man, it be not degrading our very nature; reducing ourselves to a level with the brutes, the mere slaves of instinct; and even an affront to the Author of our being, to renounce without reserve the most precious of all his gifts, and to subject ourselves to the commission of all the crimes he has forbidden us, merely for the gratification of a mad or cruel master; or if this sublime artist ought not to be less irritated at seeing his workmanship entirely destroyed than thus dishonoured. I shall ask only, what right those, who were not afraid thus to debase themselves, could have to subject their posterity to the same ignominy; and to renounce for them those blessings which they do not owe to the liberality of their progenitors, and without which life itself must be a burthen to all those who are worthy of it?

Puffendorf says, that we may divest ourselves of our liberty in favour of other men, in the same manner as we transfer our property from one to another by contracts and agreements. But this seems to be a very weak argument. For in the first place, the property I alienate becomes quite foreign to me, nor can I suffer from the abuse of it; but it very nearly concerns me that my liberty is not abused; and I cannot without incurring in a great degree the guilt of what crimes I may be compelled to commit, expose myself to become the instrument of any. Besides, the right of property being only of human institution, men may dispose of what they possess just as they please: but it is not the same with the essential blessings of nature, such as life and liberty; which every man is permitted to enjoy, and of which it is at least dubious whether any have a right to divest themselves. By giving up the one, we degrade our being; by giving up the other, we do all in our power to annihilate it; and, as no temporal enjoyment can indemnify us for the loss of either, it would be an offence at once to reason and nature to renounce them upon any account whatever.

But, tho' it were in our power to transfer our liberty, as we do our property, yet there would be a wide difference with regard to our children, who enjoy our substance only by virtue of a cession of our right; whereas, liberty being a gift frankly bestowed on them by nature, their parents have no right whatever to divest them of it. Hence, to establish slavery, it was evidently necessary to do violence to nature, and thus it became necessary to alter nature, in order to perpetuate such a right. In the mean time, the civilians who have gravely determined that the child of a slave comes into the world a slave, have decided, in other words, that a man does not come into the world a man.

It appears hence to me incontestable, that governments did not commence with arbitrary power; but that this is the depravation, the extreme term of government; bringing to back, at length, to the law of the strongest; against which it was at first designed as a remedy. Admitting, however, that they had begun in this manner, such power, as it was illegal in itself, could not have served as a basis to the laws of society, nor of consequence to the inequality of its institution.

Without entering at present upon the discussion, that still remains to be made, of the nature of the fundamental compact of all government; I content myself with adopting the common opinion concerning it, and confine myself here to the establishment of the political body as a real contract between the people and the chiefs elected by them: a contract by which both parties bind themselves to observe the laws therein expressed, which form the ties of their union. The people having in respect to the social relations subsisting between them, concentrated all their wills in one person, the several articles, concerning which this will is explained, become so many fundamental laws, obligatory on all the members of the state without distinction: at the same time, that one of these laws regulates the choice, and the power, of the magistrates, appointed to observe the execution of the whole.

This power extends to every thing relative to the support and maintenance of the constitution; but not to any thing that may tend to alter it. It is accordingly accompanied by honours, in order to render the laws and the administrators of them respectable. These ministers are also distinguished by certain personal prerogatives, in order to make them some recompense for the cares and fatigues, inseparable from a good administration. The magistrate, on his side, obliges himself to use the power he is entrusted with, conformably to the design of his constituents; to maintain them all in the peaceable possession of their property; and to prefer on every occasion the public to his own particular interest. Before experience had shewn, or a knowledge of the human heart enabled us to foresee the unavoidable abuses of such a constitution, it must have appeared so much the more compleat, as those persons who were charged with the care of its preservation found themselves interested in it; for the office and privileges of magistracy being solely built on the fundamental laws of the constitution, the magistrates would cease to be lawful as soon as ever these ceased to exist; the people would no longer owe them obedience; and as the laws, not the magistrates, are essential to the being of a state, the several members of it would become entitled to their natural liberty.

If we reflect with ever so little attention on this subject, we shall find new arguments suggest themselves in confirmation of its truth, and that we might be convinced alone from the very nature of the contract that it cannot be irrevocable: for, if there were no superior power capable of ensuring the fidelity of the contracting parties, and of obliging them to perform their reciprocal engagements, they would be sole judges in their own cause, and each of them have a right to renounce his contract, as soon as he found that the other had violated the terms of it, or that those terms no longer suited his private convenience. It is upon this principle that the right of abdication may possibly be founded. Now, to consider only what is merely human in this institution, it is certain that, if the magistrate, who has all the power in his own hands, and appropriates to himself all the advantages of the contract, hath a right to divest himself of his authority; the people, who suffer for all the faults of their chief, have a much better right to renounce their dependence on him. But the terrible and innumerable disorders that would necessarily arise from so dangerous a privilege, sufficiently demonstrate how much human governments stood in need of a more solid basis than that of mere human reason, and how expedient it was for the public tranquility that providence should interpose to invest the sovereign authority with a sacred and inviolable character; which might deprive subjects of the pernicious right of disposing of it to whomsoever they pleased. If the world had received no other advantages from religion, this alone would be sufficient to induce mankind to adopt and cultivate it, as it hath been the means of saving more blood than fanaticism hath caused to be spilt. But to follow the clue of our hypothesis.

The different forms of government owe their origin to the inequalities subsisting between individuals at the time of their forming themselves into a community. If there happened to be any one man among them greatly pre-eminent in power, in virtue, in riches or personal influence, he became sole magistrate, and the state assumed the form of monarchy. If several nearly equal in point of eminence stood above the rest, they were elected jointly, and formed an aristocracy. Again, among a people who had deviated less from a state of nature, and between whose fortune or talents there was no such disproportion, they retained the supreme administration in common, and formed a democracy. It was discovered in process of time, which of these forms suited mankind the best. Some people remained altogether subject to the laws; others soon became slaves to their magistrates. The former laboured to preserve their liberty; the latter, irritated to see others enjoy a blessing they had lost, employed their thoughts solely in making slaves of their neighbours. In fine, the one possessed themselves of wealth and conquest, and the other of happiness and virtue.

In these different governments, the offices were at first elective; and when the influence of wealth was out of the question, the preference was allowed to merit, which gives a natural ascendant; and to age possessed of experience in business sedateness and deliberation in council. The Elders among the Hebrews, the Geronts at Sparta, and the Senate at Rome, nay the very etymology of our word Seigneur, serve to shew how much grey hairs were formerly held in veneration. But the more frequently the choice fell upon old men, the more frequently it was of course to be repeated, and the more the trouble of such repetitions were felt; the intrigues of electioneering took place; factions were formed; parties grew inveterate; civil wars arose; the lives of individuals were sacrificed to the pretended welfare of the state; and at length matters were carried so far as to be on the point of relapsing into their primitive state of anarchy and confusion. The ambition of the chiefs induced them to profit by these circumstances, to perpetuate their respective offices in their several families: at the same time the people, accustomed to dependence, to ease, the conveniences of life, and already incapable of breaking their fetters, agreed to augment their slavery, in order to secure their tranquility. Thus it was, that magistrates became hereditary, contracting the habit of considering their offices as a family estate, and themselves as proprietors of those communities, of which they were at first but the officers; to regard their fellow-citizens as their slaves, and to look upon them as part of their stock of cattle; stiling themselves equal to the Gods and Kings of kings.

If we follow the progress of inequality in these different revolutions, we shall find that the establishment of laws and the right of property was the first term of it; the institution of magistrates the second; and the conversion of legal into arbitrary power the third and last; so that the difference between rich and poor were authorized by the first; that between the powerful and the weak by the second; and that between master and slave by the third; the last being the ultimate degree of inequality, and that term at which all the rest having at length arrived remain, till the government is entirely dissolved by new revolutions, or brought back again to a legal constitution.

To comprehend the necessity of this progress, we are not to consider so much the motives for the establishment of bodies politic, as the forms they assume in their administration, and the inconveniences that necessarily attend them: for the vices which render social institutions necessary are the very same which render the abuse of them unavoidable. If we except, also, Sparta alone, whose laws chiefly regarded education, and where Lycurgus established such customs and manners, as in a great measure rendered laws needless; the laws in general, being less forcible than the passions, restrain mankind without altering them; so that it would not be difficult to prove that every government, which should scrupulously comply with the ends of its institution, carefully guarding against change and corruption, hath been unnecessarily instituted; for a country, in which no one should either evade the laws or make an ill use of magisterial power, could require neither laws nor magistrates. Political distinctions necessarily induce social distinctions. The inequality increasing between the chiefs and the people, soon becomes perceptible among individuals, and receives various modifications according to passions, talents and circumstances. The magistrate cannot usurp any illegal power, without distinguishing his creatures, with whom he must share it. Add to this, that individuals suffer themselves to be oppressed only in proportion as they are hurried on by a blind ambition; and looking rather below than above them, they come in time to love authority more than independence. When they submit to slavery, it is only that they may enslave others in turn. It is no easy matter to make him obey, who has no ambition to command; nor would the most refined policy find it possible to enslave a people who should only desire to be independent. But inequality easily makes its way among base and ambitious minds, ever ready to run any risk, and almost indifferent whether they command or obey, as fortune is favourable or adverse. Thus, there must have been a time, in which the senses of the people were fascinated to such a degree, that their rulers had only to say to the most pitiful wretch, "Be great, you and all your posterity," to make him immediately appear great in the eyes of every one as well as his own. His descendents took still more upon them, and that in proportion to their distance; the more obscure and uncertain the cause, the greater the effect: the greater number of idlers any family had produced, the more illustrious it was accounted.

If this were a place to descend to minute particulars, I could readily explain how inequalities in point of credit and authority became unavoidable among private persons,[4] as soon as ever their union obliged them to compare themselves one with another, and to remark the differences which they find by the continual use every man must make of his neighbour. These differences are of several kinds; but riches, rank, power and personal merit, being the principal distinctions, by which men form an estimate of each other, in a state of society, I could prove that the harmony or incongruity of these different forces, is the surest indication of the good or bad original constitution of any state. I could shew that among these four kinds of inequality, personal qualities being the origin of all the others, wealth is that in which they all terminate; because tending most immediately to the prosperity of individuals, and being the most easy of communication, riches are made use of to purchase every other distinction.

We are enabled to judge, by this observation, pretty exactly, how far a people may have deviated from their primitive institution, and how far they have still to go, ere they arrive at the extreme term of corruption. I could explain how much this universal desire of reputation, honour and preference, with which we are all inflamed, exercises our faculties and powers; how much it excites and multiplies our passions; and, by creating an universal competition, or rather enmity among mankind, occasions numberless disappointments, and catastrophies among the innumerable pretenders whom it engages to enter on the same career. I could shew that it is to this desire of being talked of, to this unremitting rage of distinguishing ourselves, that we owe the very best, and the worst things among us, our virtues and our vices; our sciences and our errours, our heroes and our philosophers; that is to say, a great many bad things, and a very few good ones. In a word, I could prove that, if we have a few rich and powerful men placed on the pinnacle of fortune and grandeur, while the groveling croud are in want and obscurity, it is because the former prize what they enjoy only in the degree that others are destitute of it; and that, without changing their condition, they would cease to be happy the moment the people ceased to be miserable.

These particulars alone, however, would furnish matter for a more considerable performance; in which might be estimated the advantages and disadvantages of every species of government, relatively to man in a state of nature, and at the same time might be unveiled all the different appearances which inequality hath at times put on to this day, and may hereafter put on, even to the end of time, according to the nature of those several governments, and those alterations in them which must unavoidably be occasioned by time. We should then behold the multitude oppressed by domestic tyrants, in consequence of the very precautions taken to guard against foreign tyrants. We should see oppression continually gain ground without its being possible for the oppressed to know where it would stop, or what lawful means might be left them to check its progress. We should see the rights of individuals, and the freedom of nations by slow degrees extinguished, and the complaints, protests and appeals of the weak neglected as seditious murmurings. We should see the honour of defending the common cause confined by policy, to a mercenary part of the people. We should see imposts and taxes rendered necessary by such means; and the disheartened husbandman leave his fields even in the midst of peace, and quit the plough to take up the sword. We should see fatal and capricious maxims established with regard to points of honour; the champions of their country sooner or later becoming her enemies, and perpetually pointing their swords to the breasts of their fellow-citizens. The time would even come when they might be heard to say to the oppressor of their country,

> *Pectore si fratris gladium iuguloque parentis*
> *Condere me iubeas, gravidaeque in viscera partu*
> *Coniugis, invita peragam tamen omnia dextra.**

From the great inequality of fortunes and conditions, from the vast variety of passions and of talents, of useless and pernicious arts, of frivolous sciences, would arise a multitude of prejudices equally contrary to reason, happiness and virtue. We should see the magistrates foment every thing that might serve to weaken men united in society, by promoting divisions among them; every thing that sows in it the seeds of actual division, while it breathes the air of apparent harmony; every thing that can inspire the different ranks of people with mutual hatred and distrust, by an opposition of their rights and interests, and of course strengthen that power which comprehends them all.

It is from the midst of this disorder and these revolutions, that despotism, gradually rearing up its frightful head, and devouring every thing that remained sound and untainted in any part of the state, would at length trample both on the laws and the people, and establish herself on the ruins of the republick. The times which should immediately precede this last change, would be times of trouble and calamity; but at length the monster would swallow up every thing, and the people would no longer have either chiefs or laws; but merely tyrants. From this instant there would be no longer any regard paid to virtue or morals: for despotism *cui ex honesto nulla est spes*, wherever it prevails, admits of no other master; it no sooner speaks than probity and duty lose their influence; the most implicit obedience being the only virtue which slaves can practise.

This is the last term of inequality, the point that closes the circle, and meets that from which we set out. Here it is that private persons return

---

*If you bid me bury my sword in my brother's breast or my father's throat or the body of my pregnant wife, I will perform it all, even if my hand be reluctant. (Lucan, *The Civil War*, i. 376. Translation [slightly altered] by J.D. Duff. Loeb Classical Library, 1928. Harvard University Press, 1957.)

to their primitive equality, because they are no longer of importance; and that, subjects having no longer any law but the will of their master, nor their master any other restraint than his passions, all notions of moral good and all principles of equity vanish. It is here that every thing returns to the law of the strongest, and of course to a new state of nature, differing from what we set out from; as that was a state of nature in its first purity, and this the consequence of excessive corruption. There is so little difference between the two states in other respects, and the contract of government is so far dissolved by despotism, that the despot is no longer master than while he remains the strongest; but as soon as he can be expelled, he may be so without having any right to complain of injustice. The popular insurrection, that ends in the death or deposition of a sultan, is as lawful an act as those by which he might, the day before, dispose of the lives and fortunes of his subjects. As he was supported alone by force, so is he by the same force subverted. Thus every thing takes place according to natural order; and whatever may be the event of such frequent and precipitate revolutions, no one man has reason to complain of the injustice of another, but only of his own ill-fortune or indiscretion.

In thus pursuing the almost obliterated traces, by which man hath passed from a state of nature, to a state of society; by restoring with the intermediate situations which I have pointed out, those which want of time hath obliged me to suppress, or my imagination hath not suggested; the attentive reader cannot fail to be struck at the vast distance which separates the two states. It is in tracing this slow succession of things he may find the solution of a number of problems in politics and morals, which philosophers find it very difficult to solve.

He will perceive that, mankind being different in different ages, the reason why Diogenes could not find out a man, was that he sought among his contemporaries the man of an earlier period. He will see that Cato fell with Rome and liberty, because he did not suit the age in which he lived; the greatest of men serving only to astonish that world, which would have readily obeyed him, had he lived five hundred years sooner. In a word, he will find himself in a condition to comprehend how the soul, and the passions of men change as it were by insensible alterations, their very nature; how our wants and pleasures in the end change their objects; and how the original man vanishing by degrees, society offers to our inspection only an assemblage of artificial men and factitious passions; the work of these several new relations, and without any foundation in nature. We are taught nothing on this subject, by reflection, but what is entirely confirmed by experience. The savage and the civilized man differ so much with regard to their passions and inclinations, that those things which constitute the happiness of the one, would reduce the other to despair. The first requires nothing but sustenance, liberty and rest; he desires only to live and be exempt from labour; nay the apathy of the stoic falls short of his consummate indifference for every other object.

Civilized man is, on the contrary, perpetually in motion, sweating, toiling and racking his brains to find out occupations still more laborious: he continues drudging to his last moment, and even seeks death to put himself in a situation to live, or renounces life to acquire immortality. He pays his court to men in power, whom he hates; and to the wealthy, whom he despises; he stops at nothing in order to have the honour of serving them; he is not ashamed to value himself on his own meanness and their protection; while, proud of his chains, he speaks with disdain of those, who have not the honour of wearing them as well as himself.

What a sight would the perplexing and envied labours of an European minister of state, present to the eyes of a Carribean! What a cruel death would not this indolent savage prefer to such a horrid life, the labours of which are seldom even sweetened by the pleasure of doing good! But, to see into the motives of all this solicitude, it is requisite that the words *power* and *reputation*, should have some meaning affixed to them in his mind; it is requisite he should know that there are men who set a value on the looks of the rest of mankind: who can be made happy and satisfied with themselves rather on the testimony of other people than on their own. In reality, the source of all these differences is, that the savage lives within himself; while the citizen constantly lives beside himself, studying only how to live in the opinion of others; insomuch that he seems to receive the consciousness of his own existence merely from the judgment of others concerning him. It is not to my present purpose to insist on the great indifference of good and evil, which takes rise from this disposition, in spite of our many fine discourses of morality; or to shew how every thing of this kind being reduced to appearances, all is mere art and mummery, including even honour, friendship, virtue, and often even vice itself, of which we at length learn the secret to make our boast; to shew, in short, how being ever on the inquiry of others what we are, and never daring to ask ourselves so delicate a question, in the midst of so many sublime maxims of philosophy, humanity and politeness, we have nothing to shew for ourselves but a frivolous and deceitful external appearance; honour without virtue, reason without wisdom, and pleasure without happiness.

It is sufficient that I have proved this not to be the original state of man; but that it is merely the spirit of society, and the inequality which society produces, that thus transform and diversify all our natural inclinations.

Thus have I endeavoured to trace the origin and display the progress of the inequality of mankind; with the institution and abuse of political societies, as far as these things are capable of being deduced from the nature of man merely by the light of reason, and independent of those sacred tenets which give the sanction of divine right to sovereign authority. The inferences which may be drawn from a view of this exhibition, are, *first*, that as there is hardly any inequality among men in a state of nature, all the inequality which now prevails, owes its strength and growth to the development of our faculties and the improvement of our understanding; becoming at length permanent and lawful by the establishment of property and the institution of laws. *Secondly*, it follows that a moral inequality, authorized by any right merely arbitrary, clashes with natural right, as often as it does not combine in the same proportion as physical inequality; a distinction which determines sufficiently what we ought to think of that species of inequality which prevails in all civilized countries; since it is plainly contrary to the law of nature, that infants should command old men, fools conduct philosophers, and that the privileged few should gorge themselves with superfluities, while the starving multitude are in want of the common necessaries of life.

Notes

1. It is a thing very remarkable, that, although the Europeans have been endeavouring, for so many years past, to bring over the savages of different parts of the world to our manner of living, we have not been able as yet to prevail on one of them; not even with the assistance of the motives of christianity, for it is certain that though our missionaries have converted savages into Christians, they never have been able to civilize them. There is no possibility of surmounting their invincible reluctance to our customs and manners. But if these poor people are really so unhappy as some represent them, by what unaccountable depravity is it that they so obstinately refuse to submit to our government, or to live happy among us? Whereas we read frequently of Frenchmen and other Europeans, who have voluntarily taken refuge and spent the remainder of their lives among savages, without being able to quit them. Nay, we have instances of very sensible missionaries, that have with tears regretted the calm and innocent days they had spent among the simple mortals we so much despise. If it be objected that they have not understanding enough to judge properly of the difference of conditions, I reply that happiness is not so properly estimated by the understanding as by the heart. Besides, this objection may be retorted with greater force on ourselves; for our notions are far more remote from the disposition of mind necessary for us to taste the relish, which the savages find in their way of life, than their notions are from those by which they may enter into the relish we find in ours. In fact, it is easy for them to see, after a very few observations, that all our endeavours are employed on two objects, viz. on the conveniences of life, and the respect paid us by others. But, how shall we be able to conceive that kind of pleasure, which a savage finds in spending his time in solitude, in the woods, in fish-

ing, or in blowing into a wretched flute, without being able to make it sound a note, or taking any trouble to learn better?

There have been savages frequently brought to Paris, London, and other places; and no pains spared to instill into them sublime ideas of our luxury, our wealth, and useful and curious arts; they were never seen, however, to express any thing more than a stupid admiration of those things without the least appearance of coveting them. I remember, among other circumstances, related of the chief of some American Indians who was about thirty years ago in London, a number of things were shewn him, in order to see what present might be acceptable to him, but without fixing upon any thing he happened to like. Our arms seemed clumsy and inconvenient; our shoes hurt his feet; our cloaths incumbered his limbs; he would in short accept of nothing; at length, however, he was observed to fix his eye on a blanket, which he wrapped with a seeming pleasure over his shoulders. On this, the people about him remarked that he must allow this to be an useful piece of furniture.

Yes, replied the Indian, it seems to me almost as good as the skin of a beast. Not that he would have allowed even this, had he compared the different wear of both in a shower of rain. It may perhaps be said it is from habit that different people liking their own way of life best, the savages are hindered from perceiving the pleasures of ours. Upon this footing, however, it must appear at least very extraordinary, that habit should have more influence to preserve in savages a relish for their misery, than in the Europeans a taste for the enjoyment of their felicity. But to make an unanswerable reply to this objection; and that without taking notice of the many young savages, whom no endeavours have been able to civilize; or the natives of Greenland and Iceland, whom it has been several times attempted to educate in Denmark, and who have either pined away with grief ashore, or perished at sea in attempting to swim back to their own country; I shall content myself with the citation of one well attested example, and leave it to the determination of those who so greatly admire the police of European states.

"The Dutch missionaries have not been able, with all their endeavours, to convert a single Hottentot. Vander Stel, their governor at the Cape, having procured an Hottentot child, had him educated in the principles of the Christian religion, and the manners and customs of Europe. He had him richly cloathed, and instructed in various languages; while the boy's improvement was equal to the pains bestowed on him. The governor, full of expectations from his pupil's capacity, sent him to the Indies with a commissary general, who employed him in transacting the company's business. On his return, however, to the Cape, after the death of the commissary, he made a visit to his Hottentot relations; in which he took a resolution to throw off all his European finery, and to cloathe himself again in a sheep's-skin. Thus equipped, he returned to the fort, bringing with him his other clothes in a bundle, and presenting them to the governor, addressed him in the following words. 'Be so good, Sir, as to take notice that I renounce for ever this dress. I renounce, likewise, for ever the Christian religion; my resolution being to live and die in the religion, the manners and customs of my ancestors. The only favour I ask of you, is to permit me to wear this collar and hanger. I will keep them for your sake.' Having said this, without waiting for an answer from the governor, he disappeared in an instant, and was never after seen at the Cape." *Histoire des Voyages,* Tom. 5, *p.* 175.

2. It might be objected here, that in such a state of turbulence and disorder, mankind would have dispersed, instead of obstinately cutting each others throats, had their dispersion been limited. But, in the first place, their limits would only have been those of the whole earth; and if we reflect on the great population resulting from a state of nature, we shall find that in such a state the earth would have been covered, in a very short time, with men, thus forced to keep close together. Besides, had the progress of the evil been rapid, they would have dispersed, or had it been a change suddenly effected.

But they brought their fetters with them into the world; they were even in their infancy too much inured by custom to the weight of them, to feel them troublesome ever after. In fine, they were accustomed to a variety of conveniences, which obliged them to herd together: it was not so easy for them to disperse now as in those early times, when no man standing in need of any other, every one did what he liked best, without waiting for any other's consent.

3. Marshal de V— used to relate that the frauds of one of the contractors for the army, in one of his campaigns, having occasioned a very general complaint among the troops, he sent for the offender, and, after rating him pretty handsomely, threatened him with the gallows. To all which the hardened rascal calmly replied, that such threats did not at all affect him, but that he was glad of an occasion of telling the Marshal, that a man is not so readily hanged who has an hundred thousand crowns at his disposal. And I know not how it happened, added the Marshal ingenuously, but so it was, the scoundrel escaped hanging, notwithstanding he had deserved it an hundred times.

4. Distributive justice, indeed, would oppose this rigorous equality of a state of nature, even were it practicable in civil society; and as all the members of the state owe it their services in proportion to their talents and abilities, so they ought, on their part, to be distinguished and favoured in the same proportion to the services they have actually rendered it. It is in this sense we must understand that passage of Isocrates, in which he extols the primitive Athenians, for having determined which of the two kinds of equality was the most useful, viz. that which consists in dividing the same advantages indiscriminately among all the citizens in common, or that which consists in distributing them to each according to his merit. These able politicians, adds the orator, banishing that unjust inequality which makes no distinction between bad men and men of probity, adhered inviolably to that which rewards and punishes every man according to his desert.

But in the first place, there never existed a society, to whatever degree of corruption some have arrived, wherein no difference was made between the good and bad: and with regard to manners wherein no measures can be prescribed by law exact enough to serve as a practical rule to magistrates, it is with great prudence that, in order not to leave the fortune or quality of the citizens to their discretion, she prohibits their passing judgment on persons and confines it to actions. There are no manners, unless such as are pure as were those of the ancient Romans, that can bear with the office of censors, such a tribunal among us would throw every thing into confusion. The difference between good and bad men is determined by publick esteem; the magistrate being only a judge of what is strictly just and right; whereas the publick is the truest judge of manners, a judge of such integrity and penetration, although it may be sometimes deceived, it can never be corrupt. The rank of citizens ought, therefore, to be regulated, not according to their personal merit; as this method would put in the power of the magistrate to make an almost arbitrary application of the law, but according to the actual services they do the state, which are capable of being subjected to a more exact estimate.

VOLTAIRE
"Policy" ["*Politique*"]
from *Dictionnaire Philosophique*
1764

Born Francois-Marie Arouet (1694–1778), Voltaire was the free-thinking philosopher, poet, playwright, and author of tales (*Candide*, 1759) who wittily skewered the repressive measures of the Church and State in France and Europe. He challenged didactic religious beliefs and repeatedly called into question the literal truths of the Bible, which made him one of the most reviled and influential writers of intellectual and bourgeois France. "Policy" is one of the hundreds of essays he composed for the *Dictionnaire Philosophique* (a compendium first published in 1764, to which he continually added until his death). "How to procure for himself subsistence and accommodation, and protect himself from evil," he tells us, "comprises the whole object and business of man."

Voltaire has been made something of a scapegoat for the French Revolution's "excesses of reason," but more reasonable people have continued to appreciate his sense, his wit, and his advocacy of religious and ideological tolerance. "Certainly the *philosophes* did not destroy the old social order, for it was disintegrating of itself. Nor did they bring about the Revolution, the roots of which lay deep in the preceding centuries," writes Gaetano Salvemini. "But in their writings the future revolutionaries found not only moral justification for sweeping away the past but the materials they needed in setting up a new society. It was through the works of the *philosophes* that they learned, rightly or wrongly, the causes of their troubles and a possibility of better things."

SOURCE: Voltaire, *Philosophical Dictionary*, Volume VIII. Trans. William F. Fleming (Paris: E. R. DuMont, 1901), 225–232.

Policy

The policy of man consists, at first, in endeavoring to arrive at a state equal to that of animals, whom nature has furnished with food, clothing, and shelter. To attain this state is a matter of no little time and difficulty. How to procure for himself subsistence and accommodation, and protect himself from evil, comprises the whole object and business of man.

This evil exists everywhere; the four elements of nature conspire to form it. The barrenness of one-quarter part of the world, the numberless diseases to which we are subject, the multitude of strong and hostile animals by which we are surrounded, oblige us to be constantly on the alert in body and in mind, to guard against the various forms of evil.

No man, by his own individual care and exertion, can secure himself from evil; he requires assistance. Society therefore is as ancient as the world. This society consists sometimes of too many, and sometimes of too few. The vicissitudes of the world have often destroyed whole races of men and other animals, in many countries, and have multiplied them in others.

To enable a species to multiply, a tolerable climate and soil are necessary; and even with these advantages, men may be under the necessity of going unclothed, of suffering hunger, of being destitute of everything, and of perishing in misery.

Men are not like beavers, or bees, or silk-worms; they have no sure and infallible instinct which procures for them necessaries. Among a hundred men, there is scarcely one that possesses genius; and among women, scarcely one among five hundred.

It is only by means of genius that those arts are invented, which eventually furnish something of that accommodation which is the great object of all policy.

To attempt these arts with success, the assistance of others is requisite; hands to aid you, and minds sufficiently acute and unprejudiced to comprehend you, and sufficiently docile to obey you. Before, however, all this can be discovered and brought together, thousands of years roll on in ignorance and barbarism; thousands of efforts for improvement terminate only in abortion. At length, the outlines of an art are formed, but thousands of ages are still requisite to carry it to perfection.

Foreign Policy

When any one nation has become acquainted with metallurgy, it will certainly beat its neighbors and make slaves of them. You possess arrows and sabres, and were born in a climate that has rendered you robust. We are weak, and have only clubs and stones. You kill us, or if you permit us to live, it is that we may till your fields and build your houses. We sing some rustic ditty to dissipate your spleen or animate your languor, if we have any voice; or we blow on some pipes, in order to obtain from you clothing and bread. If our wives and daughters are handsome, you appropriate them without scruple to yourselves. The young gentleman, your son, not only takes advantage of the established policy, but adds new discoveries to this growing art. His servants proceed, by his orders, to emasculate my unfortunate boys, whom he then honors with the guardianship of his wives and mistresses. Such has been policy, the great art of making mankind contribute to individual advantage and enjoyment; and such is still policy throughout the largest portion of Asia.

Some nations, or rather hordes, having thus by superior strength and skill brought into subjection others, begin afterwards to fight with one another for the division of the spoil. Each petty nation maintains and pays soldiers. To encourage, and at the same time to control these soldiers, each possesses its gods, its oracles, and prophecies; each maintains and pays its soothsayers and slaughtering priests. These soothsayers or augurs begin with prophesying in favor of the heads of the nation; they afterwards prophesy for themselves and obtain a share in the government. The most powerful and shrewd prevail at last over the others, after ages of carnage which excite our horror, and of impostures which excite our laughter. Such is the regular course and completion of policy.

While these scenes of ravage and fraud are carried on in one portion of the globe, other nations, or rather clans, retire to mountain caverns, or districts surrounded by inaccessible swamps, marshes, or some verdant and solitary spot in the midst of vast deserts of burning sand, or some peninsular and consequently easily protected territory, to secure themselves against the tyrants of the continent. At length all become armed with nearly the same description of weapons; and blood flows from one extremity of the world to the other.

Men, however, cannot forever go on killing one another; and peace is consequently made, till either party thinks itself sufficiently strong to recommence the war. Those who can write draw up these treaties of peace; and the chiefs of every nation, with a view more successfully to impose upon their enemies, invoke the gods to attest with what sincerity they bind themselves to the observance of these compacts. Oaths of the most solemn character are invented and employed, and one party engages in the name of the great Somonocodom, and the other in that of Jupiter the Avenger, to live forever in peace and amity; while in the same names of Somonocodom and Jupiter, they take the first opportunity of cutting one another's throats.

In times of the greatest civilization and refinement, the lion of Æsop made a treaty with three animals, who were his neighbors. The object was to divide the common spoil into four equal parts. The lion, for certain incontestable and satisfactory reasons which he did not then deem it necessary to detail, but which he would be always ready to give in due time and place, first takes three parts out of the four for himself, and then threatens instant strangulation to whoever shall dare to touch the fourth. This is the true sublime of policy.

Internal Policy

The object here is to accumulate for our own country the greatest quantity of power, honor, and enjoyment possible. To attain these in any extraordinary degree, much money is indispensable. In a democracy it is very difficult to accomplish this object. Every citizen is your rival; a democracy can never subsist but in a small territory. You may have wealth almost equal to your wishes through your own mercantile dealings, or transmitted in patrimony from your industrious and opulent grandfather; your fortune will excite jealousy and envy, but will purchase little real co-operation and service. If an affluent family ever bears sway in a democracy, it is not for a long time.

In an aristocracy, honors, pleasures, power, and money, are more easily obtainable. Great discretion, however, is necessary. If abuse is flagrant, revolution will be the consequence. Thus in a democracy all the citizens are equal. This species of government is at present rare, and appears to but little advantage, although it is in itself natural and wise. In artistocracy, inequality or superiority makes itself sensibly felt; but the less arrogant its demeanor, the more secure and successful will be its course.

Monarchy remains to be mentioned. In this, all mankind are made for one individual: he accumulates all honors with which he chooses to decorate himself, tastes all pleasures to which he feels an inclination, and exercises a power absolutely without control; provided, let it be remembered, that he has plenty of money. If he is deficient in that, he will be unsuccessful at home as well as abroad, and will soon be left destitute of power, pleasures, honors, and perhaps even of life.

While this personage has money, not only is he successful and happy himself, but his relations and principal servants are flourishing in full enjoyment also; and an immense multitude of hirelings labor for them the whole year round, in the vain hope that they shall themselves, some time or other, enjoy in their cottages the leisure and comfort which their sultans and pashas enjoy in their harems. Observe, however, what will probably happen.

A jolly, full-fed farmer was formerly in possession of a vast estate, consisting of fields, meadows, vineyards, orchards, and forests. A hundred laborers worked for him, while he dined with his family, drank his wine, and went to sleep. His principal domestics, who plundered him, dined next, and ate up nearly everything. Then came the laborers, for whom there was left only a very meagre and insufficient meal. They at first murmured, then openly complained, speedily lost all patience, and at last ate up the dinner prepared for their master, and turned him out of his house. The master said they were a set of scoundrels, a pack of undutiful and rebellious children who assaulted and abused their own father. The laborers replied that they had only obeyed the sacred law of nature, which he had violated. The dispute was finally referred to a soothsayer in the neighborhood, who was thought to be actually inspired. The holy man takes the farm into his own hands, and nearly famishes both the laborers and the master; till at length their feelings counteract their superstition, and the saint is in the end expelled in his turn. This is domestic policy.

There have been more examples than one of this description; and some consequences of this species of policy still subsist in all their strength. We may hope that in the course of ten or twelve thousand ages, when mankind become more enlightened, the great proprietors of estates, grown also more wise, will on the one hand treat their laborers rather better, and on the other take care not to be duped by soothsayers.

THOMAS JEFFERSON

"A Summary View of the Rights of British America: Set Forth
in Some Resolutions Intended for the Inspection of the Present
Delegates of the People of Virginia, Now in Convention"

JULY 1774

As a member of Virginia's revolutionary convention, Thomas Jefferson (1743–
1826) composed "A Summary View of the Rights of British America." The
young, brilliant future President's arguments were forceful and clear. The
American Revolution, long simmering, was now near boiling-point.

SOURCE: Thomas Jefferson, *The Works of Thomas Jefferson*. Ed. Paul Leicester
Ford (New York: G. P. Putnam's Sons, 1904), 63–89.

A Summary View of the Rights of British America

Resolved, that it be an instruction to the said deputies, when assembled
in general congress with the deputies from the other states of British
America, to propose to the said congress that an humble and dutiful
address be presented to his Majesty, begging leave to lay before him, as
Chief Magistrate of the British empire, the united complaints of his
Majesty's subjects in America; complaints which are excited by many
unwarrantable encroachments and usurpations, attempted to be made
by the Legislature of one part of the empire, upon those rights which
God and the laws have given equally and independently to all. To represent to his Majesty that these his states have often individually made
humble application to his imperial throne to obtain, through its intervention, some redress of their injured rights, to none of which was ever
even an answer condescended; humbly to hope that this their joint

41

address, penned in the language of truth, and divested of those expressions of servility which would persuade his Majesty that we were asking favours, and not rights, shall obtain from his Majesty a more respectful acceptance. And this his Majesty will think we have reason to expect when he reflects that he is no more than the chief officer of the people, appointed by the laws, and circumscribed with definite powers, to assist in working the great machine of government, erected for their use, and consequently subject to their superintendance. And in order that these our rights, as well as the invasions of them, may be laid more fully before his Majesty, to take a view of them from the origin and first settlement of these countries.

To remind him that our ancestors, before their emigration to America, were the free inhabitants of the British dominions in Europe, and possessed a right which nature has given to all men, of departing from the country in which chance, not choice, has placed them, of going in quest of new habitations, and of there establishing new societies, under such laws and regulations as to them shall seem most likely to promote public happiness. That their Saxon ancestors had, under this universal law, in like manner left their native wilds and woods in the north of Europe, had possessed themselves of the island of Britain, then less charged with inhabitants, and had established there that system of laws which has so long been the glory and protection of that country. Nor was ever any claim of superiority or dependence asserted over them by that mother country from which they had migrated; and were such a claim made, it is believed that his Majesty's subjects in Great Britain have too firm a feeling of the rights derived to them from their ancestors, to bow down the sovereignty of their state before such visionary pretensions. And it is thought that no circumstance has occurred to distinguish materially the British from the Saxon emigration. America was conquered, and her settlement made, and firmly established, at the expense of individuals, and not of the British public. Their own blood was spilt in acquiring lands for their settlements, their own fortunes expended in making that settlement effectual; for themselves they fought, for themselves they conquered, and for themselves alone they have right to hold. Not a shilling was ever issued from the public treasures of his Majesty, or his ancestors, for their assistance, till, of very late times, after the colonies had become established on a firm and permanent footing. That then, indeed, having become valuable to Great Britain for her commercial purposes, his Parliament was pleased to lend them assistance against the enemy, who would fain have drawn to herself the benefits of their commerce, to the great aggrandizement of herself, and danger of Great Britain. Such assistance, and in such circumstances, they had often before given to Portugal, and other allied states, with whom they carry on a commercial intercourse; yet these states never supposed, that by calling in her aid, they thereby submitted themselves to her sovereignty. Had such terms been proposed, they would have rejected them with disdain, and trusted for better to the moderation of their enemies, or to a vigorous exertion of their own force. We do not, however, mean to under-rate those aids, which to us were doubtless valuable, on whatever principles granted; but we would shew that they cannot give a title to that authority which the British Parliament would arrogate over us, and that they may amply be repaid by our giving to the inhabitants of Great Britain such exclusive privileges in trade as may be advantageous to them, and at the same time not too restrictive to ourselves. That settlements having been thus effected in the wilds of America, the emigrants thought proper to adopt that system of laws under which they had hitherto lived in the mother country, and to continue their union with her by submitting themselves to the same common Sovereign, who was thereby made the central link connecting the several parts of the empire thus newly multiplied.

But that not long were they permitted, however far they thought themselves removed from the hand of oppression, to hold undisturbed the rights thus acquired, at the hazard of their lives, and loss of their fortunes. A family of princes was then on the British throne, whose treasonable crimes against their people brought on them afterwards the exertion of those sacred and sovereign rights of punishment reserved in the hands of the people for cases of extreme necessity, and judged by the constitution unsafe to be delegated to any other judicature. While every day brought forth some new and unjustifiable exertion of power over their subjects on that side the water, it was not to be expected that those here, much less able at that time to oppose the designs of despotism, should be exempted from injury.

Accordingly that country, which had been acquired by the lives, the labours, and the fortunes of individual adventurers, was by these princes, several times, parted out and distributed among the favourites and followers of their fortunes, and, by an assumed right to the crown alone, were erected into distinct and independent governments; a measure which it is believed his Majesty's prudence and understanding would prevent him from imitating at this day, as no exercise of such power, of dividing and dismembering a country, has ever occurred in his Majesty's realm of England, though now of very ancient standing; nor could it be justified or acquiesced under there, or in any other part of his Majesty's empire.

That the exercise of a free trade with all parts of the world, possessed by the American colonists, as of natural right, and which no law of their own had taken away or abridged, was next the object of unjust encroachment. Some of the colonies having thought proper to continue the administration of their government in the name and under the authority of his Majesty King Charles the First, whom, notwithstanding his late deposition by the commonwealth of England, they continued in the sovereignty of their state; the Parliament for the commonwealth took the same in high offence, and assumed upon themselves the power of prohibiting their trade with all other parts of the world, except the island of Great Britain. This arbitrary act, however, they soon recalled, and by solemn treaty, entered into on the 12th day of March, 1651, between the said commonwealth by their commissioners, and the colony of Virginia by their house of burgesses, it was expressly stipulated, by the 8th article of the said treaty, that they should have "free trade as the people of England do enjoy to all places and with all nations, according to the laws of that commonwealth." But that, upon the restoration of his majesty king Charles the second, their rights of free commerce fell once more a victim to arbitrary power; and by several acts of his reign, as well as of some of his successors, the trade of the colonies was laid under such restrictions as shew what hopes they might form from the justice of a British Parliament, were its uncontrouled power admitted over these states. History has informed us that bodies of men, as well as individuals, are susceptible of the spirit of tyranny. A view of these acts of parliament for regulation, as it has been affectedly called, of the American trade, if all other evidence were removed out of the case, would undeniably evince the truth of this observation. Besides the duties they impose on our articles of export and import, they prohibit our going to any markets northward of Cape Finisterre, in the kingdom of Spain, for the sale of commodities which Great Britain will not take from us, and for the purchase of others, with which she cannot supply us, and that for no other than the arbitrary purposes of purchasing for themselves, by a sacrifice of our rights and interests, certain privileges in their commerce with an allied state, who in confidence that their exclusive trade with America will be continued, while the principles and power of the British parliament be the same, have indulged themselves in every exorbitance which their avarice could dictate, or our necessities extort; have raised their commodities called for in America, to the double and treble of what they sold for before such exclusive privileges were given them, and of what better commodities of the same kind would cost us elsewhere, and at the same time give us much less for what we could carry thither than might be had at more convenient ports. That these acts prohibit us from carrying in quest of other purchasers the surplus of our tobaccoes remaining after the consumption of Great Britain is supplied; so that we must leave them with the British merchant for whatever he will please to allow us, to be by him reshipped to foreign markets, where he will reap the benefits of making sale of them for full value. That to heighten still the idea of parliamentary justice, and to shew with what moderation they are like to exercise power, where themselves are to feel no part of its weight, we take leave to mention to his majesty certain other acts of British parliament, by which they would prohibit us from manufacturing for our own use the articles we raise on our own lands with our own labour. By an act passed in the fifth year of the reign of his late majesty king George the second, an American subject is forbidden to make a hat for himself of the fur which he has taken perhaps on his own soil; an instance of despotism to which no parallel can be produced in the most arbitrary ages of British history. By one other act passed in the twenty-third year of the same reign, the iron which we make we are forbidden to manufacture, and heavy as that article is, and necessary in every branch of husbandry, besides commission and insurance, we are to pay freight for it to Great Britain, and freighth for it back again, for the purpose of supporting not men, but machines, in the island of Great Britain. In the same spirit of equal and impartial legislation is to be viewed the act of parliament passed in the fifth year of the same reign, by which American lands are made subject to the demands of British creditors, while their own lands were still continued unanswerable for their debts; from which one of these conclusions must necessarily follow, either that justice is not the same in America as in Britain, or else that the British parliament pay less regard to it here than there. But that we do not point out to his majesty the injustice of these acts, with intent to rest on that principle the cause of their nullity; but to shew that experience confirms the propriety of those political principles which exempt us from the jurisdiction of the British parliament. The true ground on which we declare these acts void is, that the British parliament has no right to exercise its authority over us.

That these exercises of usurped power have not been confined to instances alone, in which themselves were interested, but they have also intermeddled with the regulation of the internal affairs of the colonies. The act of the ninth of Anne for establishing a post office in America seems to have had little connection with British convenience, except that of accommodating his majesty's ministers and favourites with the sale of a lucrative and easy office.

That thus we have hastened through the reigns which preceded his majesty's during which the violations of our rights were less alarming, because repeated at more distant intervals than that rapid and bold succession of injuries which is likely to distinguish the present from all other periods of American story. Scarcely have our minds been able to emerge from the astonishment into which one stroke of parliamentary thunder had involved us, before another more heavy, and more alarming, is fallen on us. Single acts of tyranny may be ascribed to the accidental opinion of a day; but a series of oppressions begun at a distinguished period, and pursued, unalterably through every change of ministers, too plainly prove a deliberate and systematical plan of reducing us to slavery.

That the act, passed in the fourth year of his majesty's reign, entitled "An act for granting certain duties in the British colonies and plantations in America, etc."

One other act, passed in the fifth year of his reign, entitled "An act for granting and applying certain stamp duties and other duties in the British colonies and plantations in America, etc."

One other act, passed in the sixth year of his reign, entitled "An act for the better securing the dependency of his majesty's dominions in America upon the crown and parliament of Great Britain"; and one other act, passed in the seventh year of his reign, entitled "An act for granting duties on paper, tea, etc." form that connected chain of parliamentary usurpation, which has already been the subject of frequent applications to his majesty, and the houses of lords and commons of Great Britain; and no answers having yet been condescended to any of these, we shall not trouble his majesty with a repetition of the matters they contained.

But that one other act, passed in the same seventh year of the reign, having been a peculiar attempt, must ever require peculiar mention; it is entitled "An act for suspending the legislature of New York." One free and independent legislature hereby takes upon itself to suspend the powers of another, free and independent as itself; this exhibiting a phœnomenon unknown in nature, the creator and creature of his own power. Not only the principles of common sense, but the common feelings of human nature, must be surrendered up before his majesty's subjects here can be persuaded to believe that they hold their political existence at the will of a British parliament. Shall these governments be dissolved, their property annihilated, and their people reduced to a state of nature, at the imperious breath of a body of men, whom they never saw, in whom they never confided, and over whom they have no powers of punishment or removal, let their crimes against the American public be ever so great? Can any one reason be assigned why 160,000 electors in the island of Great Britain should give law to four millions in the states of America, every individual of whom is equal to every individual of them, in virtue, in understanding, and in bodily strength? Were this to be admitted, instead of being a free people, as we have hitherto supposed, and mean to continue ourselves, we should suddenly be found the slaves not of one but of 160,000 tyrants, distinguished too from all others by this singular circumstance, that they are removed from the reach of fear, the only restraining motive which may hold the hand of a tyrant.

That by "an act to discontinue in such manner and for such time as they are therein mentioned, the landing and discharging, lading or shipping, of goods, wares, and merchandize, at the town and within the harbour of Boston, in the province of Massachusetts Bay, in North America" which was passed at the last session of British parliament; a large and populous town, whose trade was their sole subsistence, was deprived of that trade, and involved in utter ruin. Let us for a while suppose the question of right suspended, in order to examine this act on principles of justice: An act of parliament had been passed imposing duties on teas, to be paid in America, against which act the Americans had protested as inauthoritative. The East India Company, who till that time had never sent a pound of tea to America on their own account, step forth on that occasion the assertors of parliamentary right, and send hither many ship loads of that obnoxious commodity. The masters of their several vessels, however, on their arrival to America, wisely attended to admonition, and returned with their cargoes. In the province of New England alone the remonstrances of the people were disregarded, and a compliance, after being many days waited for, was flatly refused. Whether in this the master of the vessel was governed by his obstinacy, or his instructions, let those who know say. There are extraordinary situations which require extraordinary interposition. An exasperated people, who feel that they possess power, are not easily restrained within limits strictly regular. A number of them assembled in the town of Boston, threw the tea into the ocean, and dispersed without doing any other act of violence. If in this they did wrong, they were known and were amenable to the laws of the land, against which it could not be objected that they had ever, in any instance, been obstructed or diverted from their regular course in favour of popular offenders. They should therefore not have been distrusted on this occasion. But that ill fated colony had formerly been bold in their enmities against the house of Stuart, and were now devoted to ruin by that unseen hand which governs the momentous affairs of this great empire. On the partial representations of a few worthless ministerial dependants, whose constant office it has been to keep that government embroiled, and who, by their treacheries, hope to obtain the dignity of the British knighthood, without calling for the party accused, without asking a proof, without attempting a distinction between the guilty and the innocent, the whole of that ancient and wealthy town is in a moment reduced from opulence to beggary. Men who had spent their lives in extending the British commerce, who had invested in that place the wealth their honest endeavors had merited, found themselves and their families thrown at once on the world for subsistence by its charities. Not the hundredth part of the inhabitants of that town had been concerned in the act complained of, many of them were in Great Britain and in other parts beyond sea, yet all were involved in one indiscriminate ruin, by a new executive power unheard of till then, that of a British Parliament. A property, of the value of many millions of money, was sacrificed to revenge, not repay, the loss of a few thousands. This is administering justice with a heavy hand indeed! and when is this tempest to be arrested in its course? Two wharfs are to be opened again when his Majesty shall think proper. The residue, which lined the extensive shores of the bay of Boston, are forever interdicted the exercise of commerce. This little exception seems to have been thrown in for no other purpose than that of setting a precedent for investing his majesty with legislative powers. If the pulse of his people shall beat calmly under this experiment, another and another shall be tried, till the measure of despotism be filled up. It would be an insult on common sense to pretend that this exception was made in order to restore its commerce to that great town. The trade which cannot be received at two wharfs alone must of necessity be transferred to some other place; to which it will soon be followed by that of the two wharfs. Considered in this light, it would be insolent and cruel mockery at the annihilation of the town of Boston.

By the act for the suppression of riots and tumults in the town of Boston, passed also in the last session of parliament, a murder committed there is, if the governor pleases, to be tried in a court of King's Bench, in the island of Great Britain, by a jury of Middlesex. The witnesses, too, on receipt of such a sum as the governor shall think it reasonable for them to expend, are to enter into recognizance to appear at the trial. This is, in other words, taxing them to the moment of their recognizance, and that amount may be whatever a governor pleases; for who does his majesty think can be prevailed on to cross the Atlantic for the sole purpose of bearing evidence to a fact? His expences are to be borne, indeed, as they shall be estimated by a governor; but who are to feed the wife and children whom he leaves behind and who have had no other subsistence but his daily labour? Those epidemical disorders too, so terrible in a foreign climate, is the cure of them to be estimated among the articles of expence, and their danger to be warded off by the almighty power of parliament? And the wretched criminal, if he happen to have offended on the American side, stripped of his privilege of trial by peers of his vicinage, removed from the place where alone full evidence could be obtained, without money, without council, without friends, without exculpatory proof, is tried before judges predetermined to condemn. The cowards who would suffer a countryman to be torn from the bowels of their society, in order to be thus offered a sacrifice to parliamentary tyranny, would merit that everlasting infamy now fixed on the authors of the act! A clause for a similar purpose had been introduced into an act passed in the twelfth year of his majesty's reign, entitled "An act for the better securing and preserving his majesty's dockyards, magazines, ships, ammunition and stores," against which, as meriting the same censures, the several colonies have already protested.

That these are acts of power, assumed by a body of men, foreign to our constitutions, and unacknowledged by our laws, against which we do, on behalf of the inhabitants of British America, enter this our solemn and determined protest; and we do earnestly entreat his majesty, as yet the only mediatory power between the several states of the British empire, to recommend to his parliament of Great Britain the total revocation of these acts, which, however nugatory they may yet prove the cause of further discontents and jealousies among us.

That we next proceed to consider the conduct of his majesty, as holding the executive powers of the laws of these states, and mark out his deviations from the line of duty. By the constitution of Great Britain, as well of the several American states, his majesty professes the power of refusing to pass into a law any bill which has already passed the other two branches of legislature. His majesty, however, and his ancestors, conscious of the impropriety of opposing their single opinion to the united wisdom of two houses of parliament, while their proceedings were unbiassed by interested principles, for several ages past have modestly declined the exercise of this power in that part of his empire called Great Britain. But by change of circumstances, other principles than those of justice simply obtained an influence on their determinations; the addition of new states to the British empire has produced an addition of new, and sometimes opposite interests. It is now, therefore, the great office of his majesty, to resume exercise of his negative power, and to prevent the passage of laws by any one legislature of the empire, which might bear injuriously on the rights and interests of another. Yet this will not excuse the wanton exercise of this power which we have seen his Majesty practise on the laws of the American legislatures. For the most trifling reasons, and sometimes for no conceivable reason at all, his majesty has rejected laws of the most salutary tendency. The abolition of domestic slavery is the great object of desire in those colonies, where it was unhappily introduced in their infant state. But previous to the enfranchisement of the slaves we have, it is necessary to exclude all further importations from Africa; yet our repeated attempts to effect this by prohibitions, and by imposing duties which might amount to a prohibition, have been hitherto defeated by his majesty's negative: Thus preferring the immediate advantages of a few African corsairs to the lasting interests of the American states, and to the rights of human nature deeply wounded by this infamous practice. Nay, the single interposition of an interested individual against a law was scarcely ever known to fail of success, though in the opposite scale were placed the interests of the whole country. That this is so shameful an abuse of a power trusted with his majesty for other purposes, as if not reformed, would call for some legal restrictions.

With equal inattention to the necessities of his people here has his Majesty permitted our laws to lie neglected in England for years, neither confirming them by his assent, nor annulling them by his negative; so that such of them as have no suspending clause we hold on the most precarious of all tenures, his majesty's will and such of them as suspend themselves till his majesty's assent be obtained, we have feared, might be called into existence at some future and distant period, when the time and change of circumstances shall have rendered them destructive to his people here. And to render this aggrievance still more oppressive, his majesty by his instructions has laid his governors under such restrictions that they can pass no law of any moment unless it have such suspending clause; so that, however immediate may be the call for legislative interposition, the law cannot be executed till it has twice crossed the Atlantic, by which time the evil may have spent its whole force.

But in what terms, reconcileable to majesty, and at the same time to truth, shall we speak of a late instruction to his majesty's governor of the colony of Virginia, by which he is forbidden to assent to any law for the division of a county, unless the new county will consent to have no representative in assembly? That colony has as yet fixed no boundary to the westward. Their westward counties, therefore, are of indefinite extent; some of them are actually seated many hundred miles from their eastward limits. Is it possible, then, that his majesty can have bestowed a single thought on the situation of those people, who, in order to obtain justice for injuries, however great or small, must, by the laws of that colony, attend their county court, at such a distance, with all their witnesses, monthly, till their litigation be determined? Or does his majesty seriously wish, and publish it to the world, that his subjects should give up the glorious right of representation, with all the benefits derived from that, and submit themselves the absolute slaves of his sovereign will? Or is it rather meant to confine the legislative body to their present numbers, that they may be the cheaper bargain whenever they shall become worth a purchase.

One of the articles of impeachment against Trestlain, and the other judges of Westminister-Hall, in the reign of Richard the second, for which they suffered death, as traitors to their country, was, that they had advised the king that he might dissolve his parliament at any time; and succeeding kings have adopted the opinion of these unjust judges. Since the establishment, however, of the British constitution, at the glorious revolution, on its free and antient principles, neither his majesty, nor his ancestors, have exercised such a power of dissolution in the island of Great Britain; and when his majesty was petitioned, by the united voice of his people there, to dissolve the present parliament, who had become obnoxious to them, his ministers were heard to declare in open parliament, that his majesty possessed no such power by the constitution.* But how different their language and his practice here! To declare, as their duty required, the known rights of their country, to oppose the usurpations of every foreign judicature, to disregard the imperious mandates of a minister or governor, have been the avowed causes of dissolving houses of representatives in America. But if such powers be really vested in his majesty, can he suppose they are there placed to awe the members from such purposes as these? When the representative body have lost their confidence of their constituents, when they have notoriously made sale of their most valuable rights, when they have assumed to themselves powers which the people never put into their hands, then indeed their continuing in office becomes dangerous to the state, and calls for an exercise of the power of dissolution. Such being the causes for which the representative body should, and should not be dissolved, will it not appear strange to an unbiased observer, that that of Great Britain was not dissolved, while those of the colonies have repeatedly incurred that sentence?

But your majesty, or your governors, have carried this power beyond every limit known, or provided for, by the laws: After dissolving one house of representatives, they have refused to call another, so that for a great length of time, the legislature provided by the laws has been out of existence. From the nature of things, every society must at all times possess within itself the sovereign powers of legislation. The feelings of human nature revolt against the supposition of a state so situated as that it may not in any emergency provide against dangers which perhaps

---

*"Since this period the king has several times dissolved the parliament a few weeks before its expiration, merely as an assertion of right."—MS. note in author's copy. "On further inquiry I find two instances of dissolutions before the Parliament would, of itself, have been at an end: viz., the Parliament called to meet August 24, 1698, was dissolved by King William, December 19, 1700, and a new one called, to meet February 6, 1701, which was also dissolved November 11, 1701, and a new one met December 30, 1701."—Additional note by author, in MS. copy, Department of State Archives.

threatened immediate ruin. While those bodies are in existence to whom the people have delegated the powers of legislation, they alone possess and may exercise those powers; but when they are dissolved by the lopping off one or more of their branches, the power reverts to the people, who may exercise it to unlimited extent, either assembling together in person, sending deputies, or in any other way they may think proper. We forbear to trace consequences further; the dangers are conspicuous with which this practice is replete.

That we shall at this time take notice of an error in the nature of our land holdings, which crept in at a very early period of our settlement. The introduction of the feudal tenures into the kingdom of England, though ancient, is well enough understood to set this matter in a proper light. In the earlier ages of the Saxon settlement feudal holdings were certainly altogether unknown; and very few, if any, had been introduced at the time of the Norman conquest. Our Saxon ancestors held their lands, as they did their personal property, in absolute dominion, disencumbered with any superior, answering nearly to the nature of those possessions which the feudalists term allodial. William, the Norman, first introduced that system generally. The land which had belonged to those who fell in the battle of Hastings, and in the subsequent insurrections of his reign, formed a considerable proportion of the lands of the whole kingdom. These he granted out, subject to feudal duties, as did he also those of a great number of his new subjects, who, by persuasions or threats, were induced to surrender them for that purpose. But still much was left in the hands of his Saxon subjects; held of no superior and not subject to feudal conditions. These, therefore, by express laws, enacted to render uniform the system of military defence, were made liable to the same military duties as if they had been feuds; and the Norman lawyers soon found means to saddle them also with all the other feudal burthens. But still they had not been surrendered to the king, they were not derived from his grant, and therefore they were not holden of him. A general principle indeed, was introduced, that "all lands in England were held either mediately or immediately of the crown," but this was borrowed from those holdings, which were truly feudal, and only applied to others for the purposes of illustration. Feudal holdings were therefore but exceptions out of the Saxon laws of possession, under which all lands were held in absolute right. These, therefore, still form the basis, or groundwork, of the common law, to prevail wheresoever the exceptions have taken place. America was not conquered by William the Norman, nor its lands surrendered to him, or any of his successors. Possessions there are undoubtedly of the allodial nature. Our ancestors, however, who emigrated hither, were farmers, not lawyers. The fictitious principle that all lands belong originally to the king, they were early persuaded to believe real; and accordingly took grants of their own lands from the crown. And while the crown continued to grant for small sums, and on reasonable rents, there was no inducement to arrest the error, and lay it open to the public view. But his majesty has lately taken on him to advance the terms of purchase, and of holding to the double of what they were, by which means the acquisition of lands being rendered difficult, the population of our country is likely to be checked. It is time, therefore, for us to lay this matter before his majesty, and to declare that he has no right to grant lands of himself. From the nature and purpose of civil institutions, all the lands within the limits which any particular society has circumscribed around itself are assumed by that society, and subject to their allotment only. This may be done by themselves assembled collectively, or by their legislature, to whom they may have delegated sovereign authority; and if they are alloted in either of these ways, each individual of the society may appropriate to himself such lands as he finds vacant, and occupancy will give him title.

That in order to force the arbitrary measures before complained of, his majesty has from time to time sent among us large bodies of armed forces, not made up of the people here, nor raised by the authority of our laws. Did his majesty possess such a right as this, it might swallow up all our other rights whenever he should think proper. But his majesty has no right to land a single armed man on our shores, and those whom he sends here are liable to our laws made for the suppression and punishment of riots, and unlawful assemblies; or are hostile bodies, invading us in defiance of the law. When in the course of the late war it became expedient that a body of Hanoverian troops should be brought over for the defence of Great Britain, his majesty's grandfather, our late sovereign, did not pretend to introduce them under any authority he possessed. Such a measure would have given just alarm to his subjects in Great Britain, whose liberties would not be safe if armed men of another country, and of another spirit, might be brought into the realm at any time without the consent of their legislature. He therefore applied to parliament, who passed an act for that purpose, limiting the number to be brought in, and the time they were to continue. In like manner is his majesty restrained in every part of the empire. He possesses, indeed, the executive power of the laws in every state, but they are the laws of the particular state which he is to administer within that state, and not those of any one within the limits of another. Every state must judge for itself the number of armed men which they may safely trust among them, of whom they are to consist, and under what restrictions they shall be laid.

To render these proceedings still more criminal against our laws, instead of subjecting the military to the civil powers, his majesty has expressly made the civil subordinate to the military. But can his majesty thus put down all law under his feet? Can he erect a power superior to that which erected himself? He has done it indeed by force, but let him remember that force cannot give right.

That these are our grievances which we have thus laid before his majesty, with that freedom of language and sentiment which becomes a free people claiming their rights, as derived from the laws of nature, and not as the gift of their chief magistrate: Let those flatter who fear, it is not an American art. To give praise which is not due might be well from the venal, but would ill beseem those who are asserting the rights of human nature. They know, and will therefore say, that kings are the servants, not the proprietors of the people. Open your breast, sire, to liberal and expanded thought. Let not the name of George the third be a blot in the page of history. You are surrounded by English counsellors, but remember that they are parties. You have no minister for American affairs, because you have none taken up from among us, nor amenable to the laws on which they are to give you advice. It behooves you, therefore, to think and to act for yourself and your people. The great principles of right and wrong are legible to every reader; to pursue them requires not the aid of many counsellors. The whole art of government consists in the art of being honest. Only aim to do your duty, and mankind will give you credit where you fail. No longer persevere in sacrificing the rights of one part of the empire to the inordinate desires of another; but deal out to all equal and impartial right. Let no act be passed by any one legislature which may infringe on the rights and liberties of another. This is the important post in which fortune has placed you, holding the balance of a great, if a well poised empire. This, sire, is the advice of your great American council, on the observance of which may perhaps depend your felicity and future fame, and the preservation of that harmony which alone can continue both in Great Britain and America the reciprocal advantages of their connection. It is neither our wish nor our interest to separate from her. We are willing, on our part, to sacrifice everything which reason can ask to the restoration of that tranquillity for which all must wish. On their part, let them be ready to establish union and a generous plan. Let them name their terms, but let them be just. Accept of every commercial preference it is in our power to give for such things as we can raise for their use, or they make for ours. But let them not think to exclude us from going to other markets to dispose of those commodities which they cannot use, or to supply those wants which they cannot supply. Still less let it be proposed that our properties within our own territories shall be taxed or regulated by any power on earth but our own. The

God who gave us life gave us liberty at the same time; the hand of force may destroy, but cannot disjoin them. This, sire, is our last, our determined resolution; and that you will be pleased to interpose with that efficacy which your earnest endeavors may ensure to procure redress of these our great grievances to quiet the minds of your subjects in British America, against any apprehensions of future encroachment, to establish fraternal love and harmony through the whole empire, and that these may continue to the last ages of time, is the fervent prayer of all British America.

Thomas Paine
Appendix to *Common Sense*
January 1776

The English-born working man Thomas Paine (1737–1809) well knew the
misery of poverty. He left England for the American colonies in 1774 and
shortly thereafter began his career as a journalist. He became one of the most
powerful voices in the American Revolution. His pamphlet *Common Sense*
helped persuade multitudes that the independence of America was simply
"common sense." He tells us that "He who takes nature for his guide is not easily beaten out of his argument, and on that ground I answer generally that
independence being a single simple line, contained within ourselves, and reconciliation a matter exceedingly perplexed and complicated, and in which a
treacherous capricious court is to interfere, gives the answer without a doubt."

Source: Thomas Paine, *Common Sense and Other Political Writings*. Ed.
Nelson F. Adkins (New York: Liberal Arts Press, 1953).

Appendix

Since the publication of the first edition of this pamphlet, or rather, on
the same day on which it came out, the King's speech made its appearance in this city.* Had the spirit of prophecy directed the birth of this
production, it could not have brought it forth at a more seasonable
juncture or at a more necessary time. The bloody-mindedness of the
one shows the necessity of pursuing the doctrine of the other. Men read
by way of revenge. And the speech, instead of terrifying, prepared a way
for the manly principles of independence.

Ceremony, and even silence, from whatever motive they may arise,
have a hurtful tendency when they give the least degree of countenance to base and wicked performances; wherefore, if this maxim be

---

*Philadelphia.

admitted, it naturally follows that the King's speech, as being a piece of
finished villainy, deserved and still deserves a general execration, both
by the Congress and the people. Yet, as the domestic tranquillity of a
nation depends greatly on the *chastity* of what may properly be called
"national manners," it is often better to pass some things over in silent
disdain than to make use of such new methods of dislike as might introduce the least innovation on that guardian of our peace and safety. And
perhaps it is chiefly owing to this prudent delicacy that the King's
speech has not before now suffered a public execution. The speech, if
it may be called one, is nothing better than a willful audacious libel
against the truth, the common good, and the existence of mankind;
and is a formal and pompous method of offering up human sacrifices
to the pride of tyrants. But this general massacre of mankind is one of
the privileges and the certain consequence of kings; for as nature knows
them *not* they know *not her,* and although they are beings of our *own*
creating they know not *us,* and are become the gods of their creators.
The speech has one good quality, which is that it is not calculated to
deceive; neither can we, even if we would, be deceived by it. Brutality
and tyranny appear on the face of it. It leaves us at no loss. And every
line convinces, even in the moment of reading, that he who hunts the
woods for prey, the naked and untutored Indian, is less savage than the
king of Britain.

Sir John Dalrymple, the putative father of a whining jesuitical piece,
fallaciously called *"The address of the people* of England *to the inhabitants* of America," has, perhaps from a vain supposition that the people
here were to be frightened at the pomp and description of a king, given
(though very unwisely on his part) the real character of the present one.
"But," says this writer, "if you are inclined to pay compliments to an
administration which we do not complain of (meaning the Marquis of
Rockingham's at the repeal of the Stamp Act), it is very unfair in you to
withhold them from that prince *by whose nod alone they were permitted to do anything."* This is toryism with a witness! Here is idolatry even
without a mask, and he who can calmly hear and digest such doctrine
has forfeited his claim to rationality—an apostate from the order of
manhood—and ought to be considered as one who has not only given
up the proper dignity of man, but sunk himself beneath the rank of animals, and contemptibly crawls through the world like a worm.

However, it matters very little now what the King of England either
says or does; he has wickedly broken through every moral and human
obligation, trampled nature and conscience beneath his feet, and by a
steady and constitutional spirit of insolence and cruelty procured for
himself a universal hatred. It is *now* the interest of America to provide
for herself. She has already a large and young family, whom it is more

her duty to take care of than to be granting away her property to support a power who is become a reproach to the names of men and Christians—ye whose office it is to watch over the morals of a nation, of whatsoever sect or denomination ye are of, as well as ye who are more immediately the guardians of the public liberty, if ye wish to preserve your native country uncontaminated by European corruption, ye must in secret wish a separation. But leaving the moral part to private reflection, I shall chiefly confine my farther remarks to the following heads:

First, that it is the interest of America to be separated from Britain.

Secondly, which is the easiest and most practicable plan, reconciliation or independence? with some occasional remarks.

In support of the first, I could, if I judged it proper, produce the opinion of some of the ablest and most experienced men on this continent, and whose sentiments on that head are not yet publicly known. It is in reality a self-evident position; for no nation in a state of foreign dependence, limited in its commerce and cramped and fettered in its legislative powers, can ever arrive at any material eminence. America does not yet know what opulence is; and although the progress which she has made stands unparalleled in the history of other nations, it is but childhood compared with what she would be capable of arriving at had she, as she ought to have, the legislative powers in her own hands. England is at this time proudly coveting what would do her no good were she to accomplish it, and the continent hesitating on a matter which will be her final ruin if neglected. It is the commerce and not the conquest of America by which England is to be benefited, and that would in a great measure continue were the countries as independent of each other as France and Spain, because in many articles neither can go to a better market. But it is the independence of this country of Britain, or any other, which is now the main and only object worthy of contention, and which, like all other truths discovered by necessity, will appear clear and stronger every day.

First, because it will come to that one time or other.

Secondly, because the longer it is delayed, the harder it will be to accomplish.

I have frequently amused myself, both in public and private companies, with silently remarking the specious errors of those who speak without reflecting. And among the many which I have heard, the following seems the most general, viz., that had this rupture happened forty or fifty years hence, instead of now, the continent would have been more able to have shaken off the dependence. To which I reply that our military ability, *at this time*, arises from the experience gained in the last war, and which in forty or fifty years' time would have been totally extinct. The continent would not, by that time, have had a general or even a military officer left, and we, or those who may succeed us, would have been as ignorant of martial matters as the ancient Indians; and this single position, closely attended to, will unanswerably prove that the present time is preferable to all others. The argument turns thus: At the conclusion of the last war, we had experience but wanted numbers, and forty or fifty years hence we shall have numbers without experience; wherefore the proper point of time must be some particular point between the two extremes, in which a sufficiency of the former remains and a proper increase of the latter is obtained. And that point of time is the present time.

The reader will pardon this digression, as it does not properly come under the head I first set out with and to which I again return by the following position, viz.:

Should affairs be patched up with Britain and she to remain the governing and sovereign power of America (which, as matters are now circumstanced, is giving up the point entirely), we shall deprive ourselves of the very means of sinking the debt we have or may contract. The value of the back lands, which some of the provinces are clandestinely deprived of by the unjust extension of the limits of Canada, valued only at five pounds sterling per hundred acres, amount to upward of twenty-five millions, Pennsylvania currency; and the quit-rents, at one penny sterling per acre, to two millions yearly.

It is by the sale of those lands that the debt may be sunk, without burden to any, and the quit-rent reserved thereon will always lessen and in time will wholly support the yearly expense of government. It matters not how long the debt is in paying, so that the lands when sold be applied to the discharge of it and for the execution of which the Congress for the time being will be the continental trustees.

I proceed now to the second head, viz., which is the easiest and most practicable plan, reconciliation or independence; with some occasional remarks.

He who takes nature for his guide is not easily beaten out of his argument, and on that ground I answer *generally that independence being a single simple line, contained within ourselves, and reconciliation a matter exceedingly perplexed and complicated, and in which a treacherous capricious court is to interfere, gives the answer without a doubt.*

The present state of America is truly alarming to every man who is capable of reflection. Without law, without government, without any other mode of power than what is founded on and granted by courtesy. Held together by an unexampled occurrence of sentiment, which is nevertheless subject to change and which every secret enemy is endeavoring to dissolve. Our present condition is legislation without law, wisdom without a plan, a constitution without a name, and, what is strangely astonishing, perfect independence contending for dependence. The instance is without a precedent, the case never existed before; and who can tell what may be the event? The property of no man is secure in the present unbraced system of things. The mind of the multitude is left at random, and seeing no fixed object before them, they pursue such as fancy or opinion presents. Nothing is criminal, there is no such thing as treason; wherefore, everyone thinks himself at liberty to act as he pleases. The Tories dared not have assembled offensively had they known that their lives, by that act, were forfeited to the laws of the state. A line of distinction should be drawn between English soldiers taken in battle and inhabitants of America taken in arms. The first are prisoners, but the latter traitors. The one forfeits his liberty, the other his head.

Notwithstanding our wisdom, there is a visible feebleness in some of our proceedings which gives encouragement to dissensions. The continental belt is too loosely buckled, and if something is not done in time, it will be too late to do anything and we shall fall into a state in which neither reconciliation nor independence will be practicable. The king and his worthless adherents are got at their old game of dividing the continent, and there are not wanting among us printers who will be busy in spreading specious falsehoods. The artful and hypocritical letter which appeared a few months ago in two of the New York papers, and likewise in two others, is an evidence that there are men who want either judgment or honesty.

It is easy getting into holes and corners and talking of reconciliation; but do such men seriously consider how difficult the task is, and how dangerous it may prove should the continent divide thereon? Do they take within their view all the various orders of men whose situation and circumstances, as well as their own, are to be considered therein? Do they put themselves in the place of the sufferer whose *all* is *already* gone, and of the soldier who has quitted *all* for the defense of his country? If their ill-judged moderation be suited to their own private situations only, regardless of others, the event will convince them that "they are reckoning without their host."

Put us, says some, on the footing we were on in sixty-three, to which I answer the request is not now in the power of Britain to comply with, neither will she propose it; but if it were and even should be granted I ask, as a reasonable question, By what means is such a corrupt and faithless court to be kept to its engagements? Another Parliament, nay, even the present, may hereafter repeal the obligation, on the pretense of its being violently obtained or unwisely granted, and in that case where is our redress? No going to law with nations; cannon are the barristers of crowns; and the sword, not of justice but of war, decides the suit. To be on the footing of sixty-three, it is not sufficient that the laws only be put in the same state but that our circumstances likewise be put in the same state; our burnt and destroyed towns repaired or built up, our private losses made good, our public debts (contracted for defense) discharged; otherwise we shall be millions worse than we were at that enviable period. Such a request, had it been complied with a year ago, would have won the heart and soul of the continent, but now it is too late. "The Rubicon is passed."

Besides, the taking up arms merely to enforce the repeal of a pecuniary law seems as unwarrantable by the divine law and as repugnant to human feelings as the taking up arms to enforce obedience thereto. The object, on either side, does not justify the means, for the lives of men are too valuable to be cast away on such trifles. It is the violence which is done and threatened to our persons, the destruction of our property by an armed force, the invasion of our country by fire and sword which conscientiously qualifies the use of arms; and the instant in which such a mode of defense became necessary all subjection to Britain ought to have ceased, and the independence of America should have been considered as dating its era from and published by *the first musket that was fired against her*. This line is a line of consistency, neither drawn by caprice nor extended by ambition, but produced by a chain of events of which the colonies were not the authors.

I shall conclude these remarks with the following timely and well-intended hints. We ought to reflect that there are three different ways by which an independence may hereafter be effected; and that *one* of those *three* will, one day or other, be the fate of America, viz., by the legal voice of the people in Congress, by a military power, or by a mob. It may not always happen that our soldiers are citizens and the multitude a body of reasonable men; virtue, as I have already remarked, is not hereditary, neither is it perpetual. Should an independence be brought about by the first of those means, we have every opportunity and every encouragement before us to form the noblest, purest constitution on the face of the earth. We have it in our power to begin the world over again. A situation similar to the present has not happened since the days of Noah until now. The birthday of a new world is at hand, and a race of men, perhaps as numerous as all Europe contains, are to receive their portion of freedom from the event of a few months. The reflection is awful; and in this point of view how trifling, how ridiculous, do the little paltry cavilings of a few weak or interested men appear when weighed against the business of a world.

Should we neglect the present favorable and inviting period, and independence be hereafter effected by any other means, we must charge the consequence to ourselves, or to those rather whose narrow and prejudiced souls are habitually opposing the measure, without either inquiring or reflecting. There are reasons to be given in support of independence which men should rather privately think of than be publicly told of. We ought not now to be debating whether we shall be independent or not, but anxious to accomplish it on a firm, secure, and honorable basis, and uneasy rather that it is not yet begun upon. Every day convinces us of its necessity. Even the Tories (if such beings yet remain among us) should, of all men, be the most solicitous to promote it; for as the appointment of committees at first protected them from popular rage, so a wise and well-established form of government will be the only certain means of continuing it securely to them. Wherefore, if they have not virtue enough to be Whigs, they ought to have prudence enough to wish for independence.

In short, independence is the only bond that can tie and keep us together. We shall then see our object, and our ears will be legally shut against the schemes of an intriguing as well as a cruel enemy. We shall then, too, be on a proper footing to treat with Britain; for there is reason to conclude that the pride of that court will be less hurt by treating with the American states for terms of peace than with those whom she denominates "rebellious subjects" for terms of accommodation. It is our delaying it that encourages her to hope for conquest, and our backwardness tends only to prolong the war. As we have, without any good effect therefrom, withheld our trade to obtain a redress of our grievances, let us now try the alternative, by independently redressing them ourselves and then offering to open the trade. The mercantile and reasonable part of England will be still with us, because peace with trade is preferable to war without it. And if this offer be not accepted, other courts may be applied to.

On these grounds I rest the matter. And as no offer has yet been made to refute the doctrine contained in the former editions of this pamphlet, it is a negative proof that either the doctrine cannot be refuted or that the party in favor of it are too numerous to be opposed. Wherefore, instead of gazing at each other with suspicious or doubtful curiosity, let each of us hold out to his neighbor the hearty hand of friendship and unite in drawing a line which, like an act of oblivion, shall bury in forgetfulness every former dissension. Let the names of Whig and Tory be extinct, and let none other be heard among us than those of *a good citizen, an open and resolute friend, and a virtuous supporter of the rights of mankind and of the free and independent states of America.*

REPRESENTATIVES OF THE UNITED STATES OF AMERICA
(SECOND CONTINENTAL CONGRESS)
Declaration of Independence
JULY 4, 1776

This most famous American document was drafted by Thomas Jefferson and revised in committee, then agreed upon and signed by fifty-six men on July 4, 1776. The "unanimous Declaration of the thirteen United States of America" inspired many of the ideas and ideals of the French "Declaration of the Rights of Man and of the Citizen" (see p. 79). The Revolutionary War continued until 1783, when the British renounced their sovereignty over the United States.

SOURCE: John Grafton, ed., *The Declaration of Independence and Other Great Documents of American History, 1775–1864* (Mineola, N.Y.: Dover Publications, Inc., 2000).

In CONGRESS, July 4, 1776

The unanimous Declaration of the thirteen united States of America,
When in the Course of human events, it becomes necessary for one people to dissolve the political bands which have connected them with another, and to assume among the powers of the earth, the separate and equal station to which the Laws of Nature and of Nature's God entitle them, a decent respect to the opinions of mankind requires that they should declare the causes which impel them to the separation.
—We hold these truths to be self-evident, that all men are created equal, that they are endowed by their Creator with certain unalienable

Rights, that among these are Life, Liberty and the pursuit of Happiness.—That to secure these rights, Governments are instituted among Men, deriving their just powers from the consent of the governed,—That whenever any Form of Government becomes destructive of these ends, it is the Right of the People to alter or to abolish it, and to institute new Government, laying its foundation on such principles and organizing its powers in such form, as to them shall seem most likely to effect their Safety and Happiness. Prudence, indeed, will dictate that Governments long established should not be changed for light and transient causes; and accordingly all experience hath shewn, that mankind are more disposed to suffer, while evils are sufferable, than to right themselves by abolishing the forms to which they are accustomed. But when a long train of abuses and usurpations, pursuing invariably the same Object evinces a design to reduce them under absolute Despotism, it is their right, it is their duty, to throw off such Government, and to provide new Guards for their future security.—Such has been the patient sufferance of these Colonies; and such is now the necessity which constrains them to alter their former Systems of Government. The history of the present King of Great Britain is a history of repeated injuries and usurpations, all having in direct object the establishment of an absolute Tyranny over these States. To prove this, let Facts be submitted to a candid world.

—He has refused his Assent to Laws, the most wholesome and necessary for the public good.

—He has forbidden his Governors to pass Laws of immediate and pressing importance, unless suspended in their operation till his Assent should be obtained; and when so suspended, he has utterly neglected to attend to them.

—He has refused to pass other Laws for the accommodation of large districts of people, unless those people would relinquish the right of Representation in the Legislature, a right inestimable to them and formidable to tyrants only.

—He has called together legislative bodies at places unusual, uncomfortable, and distant from the depository of their public Records, for the sole purpose of fatiguing them into compliance with his measures.

—He has dissolved Representative Houses repeatedly, for opposing with manly firmness his invasions on the rights of the people.

—He has refused for a long time, after such dissolutions, to cause others to be elected; whereby the Legislative powers, incapable of Annihilation, have returned to the People at large for their exercise; the State remaining in the mean time exposed to all the dangers of invasion from without, and convulsions within.

—He has endeavoured to prevent the population of these States; for that purpose obstructing the Laws for Naturalization of Foreigners; refusing to pass others to encourage their migrations hither, and raising the conditions of new Appropriations of Lands.

—He has obstructed the Administration of Justice, by refusing his Assent to Laws for establishing Judiciary powers.

—He has made Judges dependent on his Will alone, for the tenure of their offices, and the amount and payment of their salaries.

—He has erected a multitude of New Offices, and sent hither swarms of Officers to harrass our people, and eat out their substance.

—He has kept among us, in times of peace, Standing Armies without the Consent of our legislatures.

—He has affected to render the Military independent of and superior to the Civil power.

—He has combined with others to subject us to a jurisdiction foreign to our constitution, and unacknowledged by our laws; giving his Assent to their Acts of pretended Legislation:

—For Quartering large bodies of armed troops among us:

—For protecting them, by a mock Trial, from punishment for any Murders which they should commit on the Inhabitants of these States:

—For cutting off our Trade with all parts of the world:

—For imposing Taxes on us without our Consent:

—For depriving us in many cases, of the benefits of Trial by Jury:

—For transporting us beyond Seas to be tried for pretended offences.

—For abolishing the free System of English Laws in a neighbouring Province, establishing therein an Arbitrary government, and enlarging its Boundaries so as to render it at once an example and fit instrument for introducing the same absolute rule into these Colonies:

—For taking away our Charters, abolishing our most valuable Laws, and altering fundamentally the Forms of our Governments:

—For suspending our own Legislatures, and declaring themselves invested with power to legislate for us in all cases whatsoever.

—He has abdicated Government here, by declaring us out of his Protection and waging War against us.

—He has plundered our seas, ravaged our Coasts, burnt our towns, and destroyed the lives of our people.

—He is at this time transporting large Armies of foreign Mercenaries to compleat the works of death, desolation and tyranny, already begun with circumstances of Cruelty & perfidy scarcely paralleled in the most barbarous ages, and totally unworthy the Head of a civilized nation.

—He has constrained our fellow Citizens taken Captive on the high Seas to bear Arms against their Country, to become the executioners of their friends and Brethren, or to fall themselves by their Hands.

—He has excited domestic insurrections amongst us, and has endeavoured to bring on the inhabitants of our frontiers, the merciless Indian Savages, whose known rule of warfare, is an undistinguished destruction of all ages, sexes and conditions.

In every stage of these Oppressions We have Petitioned for Redress in the most humble terms: Our repeated Petitions have been answered only by repeated injury. A Prince whose character is thus marked by every act which may define a Tyrant, is unfit to be the ruler of a free people.

Nor have We been wanting in attentions to our British brethren. We have warned them from time to time of attempts by their legislature to extend an unwarrantable jurisdiction over us. We have reminded them of the circumstances of our emigration and settlement here. We have appealed to their native justice and magnanimity, and we have conjured them by the ties of our common kindred to disavow these usurpations, which would inevitably interrupt our connections and correspondence. They too have been deaf to the voice of justice and of consanguinity. We must, therefore, acquiesce in the necessity, which denounces our Separation, and hold them, as we hold the rest of mankind, Enemies in War, in Peace Friends.

We, therefore, the Representatives of the United States of America, in General Congress, Assembled, appealing to the Supreme Judge of the world for the rectitude of our intentions, do, in the Name, and by Authority of the good People of these Colonies, solemnly publish and declare, That these United Colonies are, and of Right ought to be Free and Independent States; that they are Absolved from all Allegiance to the British Crown, and that all political connection between them and the State of Great Britain, is and ought to be totally dissolved; and that as Free and Independent States, they have full Power to levy War, conclude Peace, contract Alliances, establish Commerce, and to do all other Acts and Things which Independent States may of right do. And for the support of this Declaration, with a firm reliance on the protection of divine Providence, we mutually pledge to each other our Lives, our Fortunes and our sacred Honor.

CAMILLE DESMOULINS
"Live Free or Die"
FEBRUARY 1788

Lucie Simplice Camille Benoist Desmoulins (1760–1794) was born in the French province of Picardy. His speech "Live Free or Die" is a formal address, unlike the one he gave July 14, 1789, that inspired the taking of the Bastille, the event usually taken as the beginning of the French Revolution. He published a series of influential pamphlets on "Revolutions de France et de Brabant" from November 1789 to July 1792. A deputy to the Convention of 1792, he served as Secretary General to the Minister of Justice, Georges Jacques Danton. Both men became opponents of the Committee of Public Safety's Maximilien Robespierre, who had them arrested, "guilty of demanding the cessation of this mad race of blood."[1] They were guillotined in the revolution's Year of Terror, 1794.

SOURCE: Mayo W. Hazeltine, ed., *Orations: From Homer to William McKinley* (New York: P. F. Collier and Son, 1902), 3463–3466.

Live Free or Die

One difference between the monarchy and the republic, which alone should suffice to make the people reject with horror all monarchical rule and make them prefer the republic regardless of the cost of its establishment, is that in a democracy, though the people may be deceived, yet, at least, they love virtue. It is merit that they believe they put in power in place of the rascals who are the very essence of monar-

---

1. R. W. Postgate, ed., *Revolution from 1789 to 1906* (London: Grant Richards, 1920), 23.

chies. The vices, the concealments, and the crimes which are the diseases of republics are the very health and existence of monarchies. Cardinal Richelieu avowed openly in his political principles, that "the king should always avoid using the talents of thoroughly honest men." Long before him Sallust said: "Kings cannot get along without rascals. On the contrary, they should fear to trust the honest and the upright."

It is, therefore, only under a democracy that the good citizen can reasonably hope to see a cessation of the triumphs of intrigue and crime; and to this end the people need only to be enlightened.

There is yet this difference between a monarchy and the republic; the reigns of Tiberius, of Claudius, of Nero, of Caligula, of Domitian, had happy beginnings. In fact, all reigns make a joyous entry, but only as a delusion. Therefore the Royalists laugh at the present state of France as if its violent and terrible entry under the republic must always last.

Everything gives umbrage to a tyrant. If a citizen have popularity, he is becoming a rival to the prince. Consequently, he is stirring up civil strife, and is a suspect. If, on the contrary, he flee popularity and seclude himself in the corner of his own fireside, this retired life makes him remarked, and he is a suspect. If he is a rich man, there is an imminent peril that he corrupt the people with his largesses, and he is a suspect. Are you poor? How then! Invincible emperors, this man must be closely watched; no one so enterprising as he who has nothing. He is a suspect! Are you in character sombre, melancholy, or neglectful? You are afflicted by the condition of public affairs, and are a suspect.

If, on the contrary, the citizen enjoy himself and have resultant indigestion, he is only seeking diversion because his ruler has had an attack of gout, which made his Majesty realize his age. Therefore he is a suspect. Is he virtuous and austere in his habits? Ah! he is a new Brutus with his Jacobin severity, censuring the amiable and well-groomed court. He is a suspect. If he be a philosopher, an orator, or a poet, it will serve him ill to be of greater renown than those who govern, for can it be permitted to pay more attention to the author living on a fourth floor than to the emperor in his gilded palace? He is a suspect.

Has one made a reputation as a warrior—he is but the more dangerous by reason of his talent. There are many resources with an inefficient general. If he is a traitor he cannot so quickly deliver his army to the enemy. But an officer of merit like an Agricola—if he be disloyal, not one can be saved. Therefore, all such had better be removed and promptly placed at a distance from the army. Yes, he is a suspect.

Tacitus tells us that there was anciently in Rome a law specifying the crimes of "lèse-majesté." That crime carried with it the punishment of death. Under the Roman republic treasons were reduced to but four kinds, viz., abandoning an army in the country of an enemy; exciting sedition; the maladministration of the public treasury; and the impairment by inefficiency of the majesty of the Roman people. But the Roman emperors needed more clauses, that they could place cities and citizens under proscription.

Augustus was the first to extend the list of offences that were "lèse-majesté" or revolutionary, and under his successors the extensions were made until none was exempt. The slightest action was a state offence. A simple look, sadness, compassion, a sigh, even silence was "lèse-majesté" and disloyalty to the monarch. One must needs show joy at the execution of their parent or friend lest they would perish themselves. Citizens, liberty must be a great benefit, since Cato disembowelled himself rather than have a king. And what king can we compare in greatness and heroism to the Cæsar whose rule Cato would not endure? Rousseau truly says: "There is in liberty as in innocence and virtue a satisfaction one only feels in their enjoyment and a pleasure which can cease only when they are lost."

EMMANUEL JOSEPH SIEYÈS
Preface and Chapter 1,
What Is the Third Estate? [Qu'est que le Tiers-État?]
JANUARY 1789

Emmanuel Joseph Sieyès (1748–1836) was often referred to as "Abbé Sieyès" because of his clerical status. His emphatic and dramatic *What Is the Third Estate?* was "the great manifesto against privilege in the early days of the Revolution."[1] "'What is the tiers état?' demanded the Abbé Sieyès in a pamphlet that had a tremendous sale. 'Everything. What has it been until now in the political sphere? Nothing. What does it desire? To count for something.'"[2] Sieyès' ideas helped the Third Estate assert itself in the coming months and years. Sieyès himself had a long and tangled career in French politics, including helping Napoleon overthrow the very Directory on which Sieyès was serving in 1799.

SOURCE: Emmanuel Joseph Sieyès, *What Is the Third Estate?* Trans. M. Blondel. Ed. S. E. Finer (New York: Frederick A. Praeger, 1963), 51–52, 142–155, 166–174.

Preface

The plan of this book is fairly simple. We must ask ourselves three questions.

1) What is the Third Estate? *Everything.*

---

1. John McManners, *European History, 1789–1914: Men, Machines and Freedom* (New York: Harper Torchbooks, 1969), 50.
2. Gaetano Salvemini, *The French Revolution: 1788–1792.* Trans. I. M. Rawson. (New York: Norton, 1962), 115.

2) What has it been until now in the political order? *Nothing*.

3) What does it want to be? *Something*.

We are going to see whether the answers are correct. Meanwhile, it would be improper to say these statements are exaggerated until the supporting evidence has been examined. We shall next examine the measures that have been tried and those that must still be taken for the Third Estate really to become something. Thus, we shall state:

4) What the Ministers have attempted and what even the privileged orders propose to do for it.

5) What ought to have been done.

6) Finally, what remains to be done in order that the Third Estate should take its rightful place.

Chapter I. The Third Estate is a Complete Nation

What does a nation require to survive and prosper? It needs *private* activities and *public* services.

These private activities can all be comprised within four classes of persons:

1) Since land and water provide the basic materials for human needs, the first class, in logical order, includes all the families connected with work on the land.

2) Between the initial sale of goods and the moment when they reach the consumer or user, goods acquire an increased value of a more or less compound nature through the incorporation of varying amounts of labour. In this way human industry manages to improve the gifts of nature and the value of the raw material may be multiplied twice, or ten-fold, or a hundred-fold. Such are the activities of the second class of persons.

3) Between production and consumption, as also between the various stages of production, a variety of intermediary agents intervene, to help producers as well as consumers; these are the dealers and the merchants. Merchants continually compare needs according to place and time and estimate the profits to be obtained from warehousing and transportation; dealers undertake, in the final stage, to deliver the goods on the wholesale and retail markets. Such is the function of the third class of persons.

4) Besides these three classes of useful and industrious citizens who deal with *things* fit to be consumed or used, society also requires a vast number of special activities and of services *directly* useful or pleasant to the *person*. This fourth class embraces all sorts of occupations, from the

most distinguished liberal and scientific professions to the lowest of menial tasks.

Such are the activities which support society. But who performs them? The Third Estate.

Public services can also, at present, be divided into four known categories, the army, the law, the Church and the bureaucracy. It needs no detailed analysis to show that the Third Estate everywhere constitutes nineteen-twentieths of them, except that it is loaded with all the really arduous work, all the tasks which the privileged order refuses to perform. Only the well-paid and honorific posts are filled by members of the privileged order. Are we to give them credit for this? We could do so only if the Third Estate was unable or unwilling to fill these posts. We know the answer. Nevertheless, the privileged have dared to preclude the Third Estate. 'No matter how useful you are,' they said, 'no matter how able you are, you can go so far and no further. Honours are not for the like of you.' The rare exceptions, noticeable as they are bound to be, are mere mockery, and the sort of language allowed on such occasions is an additional insult.

If this exclusion is a social crime, a veritable act of war against the Third Estate, can it be said at least to be useful to the commonwealth? Ah! Do we not understand the consequences of monopoly? While discouraging those it excludes, does it not destroy the skill of those it favours? Are we unaware that any work from which free competition is excluded will be performed less well and more expensively?

When any function is made the prerogative of a separate order among the citizens, has nobody remarked how a salary has to be paid not only to the man who actually does the work, but to all those of the same caste who do not, and also to the entire families of both the workers and the non-workers? Has nobody observed that as soon as the government becomes the property of a separate class, it starts to grow out of all proportion and that posts are created not to meet the needs of the governed but of those who govern them? Has nobody noticed that while on the one hand, we basely and I dare say *stupidly* accept this situation of ours, on the other hand, when we read the history of Egypt or stories of travels in India, we describe the same kind of conditions as despicable, monstrous, destructive of all industry, as inimical to social progress, and above all as debasing to the human race in general and intolerable to Europeans in particular . . . ? But here we must leave considerations which, however much they might broaden and clarify the problem, would nevertheless slow our pace.

It suffices to have made the point that the so-called usefulness of a privileged order to the public service is a fallacy; that, without help from this order, all the arduous tasks in the service are performed by the Third Estate; that without this order the higher posts could be infinitely better filled; that they ought to be the natural prize and reward of recognised ability and service, and that if the privileged have succeeded in usurping all well-paid and honorific posts, this is both a hateful iniquity towards the generality of citizens and an act of treason to the commonwealth.

Who is bold enough to maintain that the Third Estate does not contain within itself everything needful to constitute a complete nation? It is like a strong and robust man with one arm still in chains. If the privileged order were removed, the nation would not be something less but something more. What then is the Third Estate? All; but an 'all' that is fettered and oppressed. What would it be without the privileged order? It would be all; but free and flourishing. Nothing will go well without the Third Estate; everything would go considerably better without the two others.

It is not enough to have shown that the privileged, far from being useful to the nation, can only weaken and injure it; we must prove further that the nobility is not part of our society at all: it may be a *burden* for the nation, but it cannot be part of it.

First, it is impossible to find what place to assign to the caste of nobles among all the elements of a nation. I know that there are many people, all too many, who, from infirmity, incapacity, incurable idleness or a collapse of morality, perform no functions at all in society. Exceptions and abuses always exist alongside the rule, and particularly in a large commonwealth. But all will agree that the fewer these abuses, the better organised a state is supposed to be. The most ill-organised state of all would be the one where not just isolated individuals but a complete class of citizens would glory in inactivity amidst the general movement and contrive to consume the best part of the product without having in any way helped to produce it. Such a class, surely, is foreign to the nation because of its *idleness*.

The nobility, however, is also a foreigner in our midst because of its *civil and political* prerogatives.

What is a nation? A body of associates living under *common* laws and represented by the same *legislative assembly*, etc.

Is it not obvious that the nobility possesses privileges and exemptions which it brazenly calls its rights and which stand distinct from the rights of the great body of citizens? Because of these special rights, the nobility does not belong to the common order, nor is it subjected to the common laws. Thus its private rights make it a people apart in the great nation. It is truly *imperium in imperio*.

As for its *political* rights, it also exercises these separately from the nation. It has its own representatives who are charged with no mandate from the People. Its deputies sit separately, and even if they sat in the same chamber as the deputies of ordinary citizens they would still constitute a different and separate representation. They are foreign to the nation first because of their origin, since they do not owe their powers to the People; and secondly because of their aim, since this consists in defending, not the general interest, but the private one.

The Third Estate then contains everything that pertains to the nation while nobody outside the Third Estate can be considered as part of the nation. What is the Third Estate? *Everything!*

THIRD ESTATE (ESTATES GENERAL OF FRANCE)
Decree upon the National Assembly
JUNE 17, 1789

"The States-General of France met May 5, 1789. It contained approximately twelve hundred members—three hundred nobles, three hundred clergy, six hundred deputies of the Third Estate. As King Louis XVI had failed to provide regulations respecting its organization and method of voting, a controversy immediately developed over these questions. The nobles and clergy desired separate organization and vote by order; the Third Estate demanded a single order and vote by head. This decree was finally adopted by the Third Estate alone, after an invitation to the other two orders had met with no general response. The document indicates the method by which the Third Estate proposed to proceed, the arguments by which the method was justified, and the general temper which characterized the proceedings."[1]

By this decree, the Third Estate of the Estates General effectively began its transformation from a component of a largely symbolic, subordinate body of a feudal state into a recognizably modern representative legislature, a National Assembly.

See also "The Tennis Court Oath" of three days later, p. 77.

SOURCE: Frank Maloy Anderson, ed., *The Constitutions and Other Select Documents Illustrative of the History of France, 1789–1907* (Minneapolis: H. W. Wilson, 1908), 1–2.

Decree upon the National Assembly

The Assembly, deliberating after the verification of its credentials, recognizes that this assembly is already composed of the representatives sent directly by at least ninety-six per cent of the nation.

---

1. Frank Maloy Anderson, ed., *The Constitutions and Other Select Documents Illustrative of the History of France, 1789–1907* (Minneapolis: H. W. Wilson, 1908), 1.

Such a body of deputies cannot remain inactive owing to the absence of the deputies of some bailliages and some classes of citizens; for the absentees, who have been summoned, cannot prevent those present from exercising the full extent of their rights, especially when the exercise of these rights is an imperious and pressing duty.

Furthermore, since it belongs only to the verified representatives to participate in the formation of the national opinion and since all the verified representatives ought to be in this assembly, it is still more indispensable to conclude that the interpretation and presentation of the general will of the nation belong to it, and belong to it alone, and that there cannot exist between the throne and this assembly any *veto*, and negative power.—The assembly declares then that the common task of the national restoration can and ought to be commenced without delay by the deputies present and that they ought to pursue it without interruption as well as without hindrance.—The denomination of NATIONAL ASSEMBLY is the only one which is suitable for the Assembly in the present condition of things; because the members who compose it are the only representatives lawfully and publicly known and verified; because they are sent directly by almost the totality of the nation; because, lastly, the representation being one and indivisible, none of the deputies, in whatever class or order he may be chosen, has the right to exercise his functions apart from the present assembly.—The Assembly will never lose the hope of uniting within its own body all the deputies absent today; it will not cease to summon them to fulfil the obligation laid upon them to participate in the holding of the States-General. At any moment when the absent deputies present themselves in the course of the session which is about to open, it declares in advance that it will hasten to receive them and to share with them, after the verification of their credentials, the remainder of the great labors which are bound to effect the regeneration of France.—The National Assembly orders that the motives of the present decision be immediately drawn up in order to be presented to the king and the nation.

NATIONAL ASSEMBLY OF FRANCE
The Tennis Court Oath [*Le serment du jeu de paume*]
JUNE 20, 1789

"When the deputies of the Third Estate went to their hall on June 20, 1789, they found it closed to them and placards posted announcing a royal session two days later. Fearing that this foreshadowed a command from the king for separate organization and vote by order, they met in a neighboring tennis court and with practical unanimity formulated the resolution embodied in this document."[1]

With the Tennis Court Oath, the Third Estate—now the National Assembly—asserted its authority as the representative body of the nation and affirmed its determination to function in the interest of the people, challenging the feudal right of the monarchy to unimpeded rule.

SOURCE: Frank Maloy Anderson, ed., *The Constitutions and Other Select Documents Illustrative of the History of France, 1789–1907* (Minneapolis: H. W. Wilson, 1908), 3.

The Tennis Court Oath

The National Assembly, considering that it has been summoned to determine the constitution of the kingdom, to effect the regeneration of public order, and to maintain the true principles of the monarchy; that nothing can prevent it from continuing its deliberations in what-

---

1. Frank Maloy Anderson, ed., *The Constitutions and Other Select Documents Illustrative of the History of France, 1789–1907* (Minneapolis: H. W. Wilson, 1908), 3.

ever place it may be forced to establish itself, and lastly, that wherever its members meet together, there is the National Assembly.

Decrees that all the members of this assembly shall immediately take a solemn oath never to separate, and to reassemble wherever circumstances shall require, until the constitution of the kingdom shall be established and consolidated upon firm foundations; and that, the said oath being taken, all the members and each of them individually shall ratify by their signatures this steadfast resolution.

NATIONAL ASSEMBLY OF FRANCE
The Declaration of the Rights of Man and of the Citizen
[*La declaration des droits de l'homme et du citoyen*]

AUGUST 26, 1789

About the feverish first months of the French Revolution, Alexis de Tocqueville observes: "No nation had ever before embarked on so resolute an attempt as that of the French in 1789 to break with the past, to make, as it were, a scission in their life line and to create an unbridgeable gulf between all they had hitherto been and all they now aspired to be. With this in mind they took a host of precautions so as to make sure of importing nothing from the past into the new regime, and saddled themselves with all sorts of restrictions in order to differentiate themselves in every possible way from the previous generation; in a word, they spared no pains in their endeavor to obliterate their former selves."[1]

The historian Gaetano Salvemini narrates the composition of "The Declaration of the Rights of Man and of the Citizen": "On the afternoon of August 4th, the Assembly, before proceeding to discuss the feudal regime, rejected by 570 votes to 433 the proposal for a declaration of duties; it decided almost unanimously to draw up a declaration of human rights; and from August 20th to August 26th it drafted the text, in which proposals by Lafayette, Sieyès, Mounier, Traget and other deputies were merged, according to the inspiration of the moment, with suggestions that rained in from every side. Spurred on by shouts and applause, they improvised formulae and emendments, embodying in concise, forceful, and clear-cut maxims the whole of eighteenth-century revolutionary thought."[2] Right II, for example, reads: "The end of all political associations is the preservation of the natural and imprescriptible rights of man; and these rights are Liberty, Property, Security, and Resistance of Oppression."

SOURCE: Thomas Paine, *The Rights of Man* (New York: Dutton, 1915), 94–97.

1. Alexis de Tocqueville, *The Old Regime and the French Revolution*. Trans. Stuart Gilbert (New York: Doubleday Anchor Books, 1955), vii.
2. Gaetano Salvemini, *The French Revolution: 1788–1792*. Trans. I. M. Rawson. (New York: Norton, 1962), 144.

Declaration of the Rights of Man and of the Citizen

The representatives of the people of France, formed into a National Assembly, considering that ignorance, neglect, or contempt of human rights, are the sole causes of public misfortunes and corruptions of Government, have resolved to set forth in a solemn declaration, these natural, imprescriptible, and inalienable rights; that this declaration being constantly present to the minds of the members of the body social, they may be ever kept attentive to their rights and their duties; that the acts of the legislative and executive powers of Government, being capable of being every moment compared with the end of political institutions, may be more respected; and also, that the future claims of the citizens, being directed by simple and incontestable principles, may always tend to the maintenance of the Constitution, and the general happiness.

For these reasons the National Assembly doth recognise and declare, in the presence of the Supreme Being, and with the hope of his blessing and favour, the following *sacred* rights of men and of citizens:

I. Men are born, and always continue, free and equal in respect of their rights. Civil distinctions, therefore, can be founded only on public utility.

II. The end of all political associations is the preservation of the natural and imprescriptible rights of man; and these rights are Liberty, Property, Security, and Resistance of Oppression.

III. The Nation is essentially the source of all sovereignty; nor can any individual, or any body of men, be entitled to any authority which is not expressly derived from it.

IV. Political Liberty consists in the power of doing whatever does not injure another. The exercise of the natural rights of every man, has no other limits than those which are necessary to secure to every *other* man the free exercise of the same rights; and these limits are determinable only by the law.

V. The law ought to prohibit only actions hurtful to society. What is not prohibited by the law should not be hindered; nor should any one be compelled to that which the law does not require.

VI. The law is an expression of the will of the community. All citizens have a right to concur, either personally or by their representatives, in its formation. It should be the same to all, whether it protects or punishes; and all being equal in its sight, are equally eligible to all honours, places, and employments, according to their different abilities, without any other distinction than that created by their virtues and talents.

VII. No man should be accused, arrested, or held in confinement, except in cases determined by the law, and according to the forms which it has prescribed. All who promote, solicit, execute, or cause to be executed, arbitrary orders, ought to be punished, and every citizen called upon, or apprehended by virtue of the law, ought immediately to obey, and renders himself culpable by resistance.

VIII. The law ought to impose no other penalties but such as are absolutely and evidently necessary; and no one ought to be punished, but in virtue of a law promulgated before the offence, and legally applied.

IX. Every man being presumed innocent till he has been convicted, whenever his detention becomes indispensable, all rigour to him, more than is necessary to secure his person, ought to be provided against by the law.

X. No man ought to be molested on account of his opinions, not even on account of his religious opinions, provided his avowal of them does not disturb the public order established by the law.

XI. The unrestrained communication of thoughts and opinions being one of the most precious Rights of Man, every citizen may speak, write, and publish freely, provided he is responsible for the abuse of this liberty, in cases determined by the law.

XII. A public force being necessary to give security to the Rights of Men and of citizens, that force is instituted for the benefit of the community and not for the particular benefit of the persons with whom it is intrusted.

XIII. A common contribution being necessary for the support of the public force, and for defraying the other expenses of Government, it ought to be divided equally among the members of the community, according to their abilities.

XIV. Every citizen has a right, either by himself or his representative, to a free voice in determining the necessity of public contributions, the appropriation of them, and their amount, mode of assessment, and duration.

XV. Every community has a right to demand of all its agents an account of their conduct.

XVI. Every community in which a separation of powers and a security of rights is not provided for, wants a Constitution.

XVII. The right to property being inviolable and sacred, no one ought to be deprived of it, except in cases of evident public necessity, legally ascertained, and on condition of a previous just indemnity.

JEAN PAUL MARAT
"Are We Undone?"
From *The Friend of the People* [*L'ami du peuple*]
JULY 26, 1790

Jean Paul Marat (1743–1793) was a Swiss-born, Scottish-trained London-prac-
ticing doctor and author of scientific books before he became one of France's
most strident revolutionaries. From September 1789 he used his influential
journal, *L'ami du peuple*, as a clarion call to apply the "principles" and achieve
the "goals" of the French Revolution. He was instrumental in the establishment of the Committee of Public Safety and became (with Robespierre and
Danton) a member of it as well as of the National Convention. Marat the
physician has become a notorious historical figure because of his advocacy of
terror. He asked rhetorically in an issue of *L'ami du peuple*: "Do you really
believe that you can change the inclinations and habits, the manners and passions, of the ruling class, by the preaching of moral principles?"[1] In "Are We
Undone?" he rues the recent "mistaken humanity" of his readers that prevented them from "cutting off of five or six hundred heads," a deed which
"would have guaranteed you peace, liberty and happiness."

Marat's death has become almost as famous as his life. On July 13, 1793, he
was stabbed to death in his bathtub by a twenty-five-year-old Royalist sympa-
thizer named Charlotte Corday.

SOURCE: Jean Paul Marat, *Writings of Jean Paul Marat*. Introduction and notes
by Paul Friedlander (New York: International Publishers, 1927), 33–36.

Are We Undone?

An Appeal to All Citizens!
 Citizens, our enemies stand without the gates, the masters have had
the frontiers opened to them under the pretext of granting them free

---

1. Jean Paul Marat, *Writings of Jean Paul Marat*. Introduction and notes by Paul
    Friedlander (New York: International Publishers, 1927), 24.

passage through our country. Perhaps, at this very moment, they are advancing in our direction with great speed. The King will go to Compiègne, where the apartments for his reception have already been prepared; the road from Compiègne to Toul or Metz can easily be traveled incognito. Who will prevent him from joining with the Austrian army and with the troops of the line which have remained faithful to him? Soon he will be surrounded by hosts of army officers who are hastening to him from all sides, the malcontents, and particularly his faithful retainers, de Bezenval, d'Autichamps, Lambesc, de Broglio. Already one of the ministers, the vile Guignard [the Count of Saint-Priest], who has been unmasked as head of the conspirators, and whose arrest was demanded by me, has taken to flight; his colleagues will soon follow his example and repair to some town of Lorraine in order to constitute a "government" there. The King, this "good King," who disdained to swear allegiance to you on the altar of our country, has observed the profoundest silence concerning all these facts. The National Committee of Investigation did not open its mouth until the mine had been sprung; the local Committee of Investigation, who had sold out to the Court, has refused to take any steps to ascertain the instigators of this infernal attempt.

In order to prevent you from deliberating on the dangers that threaten, they have not ceased to overwhelm you with festivities, and to keep you in a constant state of intoxication in order that you may not see the disaster that is about to engulf you. Can you believe it—your General, who has neglected not a single means of corruption, has just organized an entire battery of artillery, against the will of all the districts, in order to destroy you; the staff of your guard consists only of your enemies, who draw princely salaries; your heads of battalions have almost all been bribed; and, horror of horrors, the Militia of Paris consists now only of undependable or blind men, who have forgotten their country for all the flatteries of the General!

Citizens of every age and every station! The measures adopted by the National Assembly cannot save you from destruction; you are lost forever if you do not take arms speedily, if you do not again give evidence of your heroism, which has already saved France twice, namely, on July 14, and on October 5. Go to Saint-Cloud before it is too late; bring the King and the Dauphin back within your walls. Guard them well. They shall be your hostages in the events that are yet to come; shut in the Austrian* woman and her brother-in-law, so that they may not instigate further intrigues; seize all the ministers and their agents and put them

---

*Marie-Antoinette (1755–1793), daughter of Emperor Francis I and Maria-Theresa, wife of Louis XVI, later guillotined. (Note by Paul Friedlander.)

in irons; make sure you have the Mayor and the City Secretaries! Do not take your eyes away from the General; arrest the General Staff; remove the battery of artillery from the Rue Verte, take possession of all the magazines and powder mills; the pieces of artillery must be distributed to all the districts. All the districts must again meet and declare themselves in permanent session; they must rescind all counter-revolutionary decrees. Hurry, hurry, before it is too late, else soon the numerous legions of the enemy will be upon you; soon you will see the privileged classes again rising, and despotism, frightful despotism, will come to life more terribly than ever before.

The cutting off of five or six hundred heads would have guaranteed your peace, liberty and happiness. A mistaken humanity has crippled your arms and held back your blows; it will cost the lives of millions of your brothers. The soldiers of the National Guard shall escape death no more than the others! The French guards whom I have just mentioned, and all the soldiers who are deserting the King's flags and gathering under those of the nation, will be sacrificed first of all, in spite of all the pacifying sermons which the General is delivering to them. Your enemies need only to triumph for a moment, and blood will flow in torrents. They will murder you without compassion, they will rip open the bellies of your wives, and in order to choke within you the love of liberty, their bloody hands will explore the entrails of your children to find their hearts.

THOMAS PAINE

From Conclusion to Part 1,

The Rights of Man

1791

Thomas Paine, having helped to inspire the American drive for independence, returned to Europe, and occupied himself with various projects until he entered the fray in Revolutionary France. He countered Edmund Burke's *Reflections on the Revolution in France* (1790), an attack on the principles and evolution of the Revolution, with *The Rights of Man*. "As it is not difficult to perceive, from the enlightened state of mankind, that hereditary Governments are verging to their decline," Paine concludes, "and that Revolutions on the broad basis of national sovereignty and Government by representation, are making their way in Europe, it would be an act of wisdom to anticipate their approach, and produce Revolutions by reason and accommodation, rather than commit them to the issue of convulsions."

SOURCE: Thomas Paine, *The Rights of Man* (New York: Dutton, 1915), 130–138.

The Rights of Man

From the Revolutions of America and France, and the symptoms that have appeared in other countries, it is evident that the opinion of the world is changed with respect to systems of Government, and that Revolutions are not within the compass of political calculations.

The progress of time and circumstances, which men assign to the accomplishment of great changes, is too mechanical to measure the force of the mind, and the rapidity of reflection, by which Revolutions are generated: All the old Governments have received a shock from those that already appear, and which were once more improbable, and are a greater subject of wonder, than a general Revolution in Europe would be now.

When we survey the wretched condition of Man, under the monarchical and hereditary systems of Government, dragged from his home by one power, or driven by another, and impoverished by taxes more than by enemies, it becomes evident that those systems are bad, and that a general Revolution in the principle and construction of Governments is necessary.

What is Government more than the management of the affairs of a Nation? It is not, and from its nature cannot be, the property of any particular man or family, but of the whole community, at whose expence it is supported; and though by force and contrivance it has been usurped into an inheritance, the usurpation cannot alter the right of things. Sovereignty, as a matter of right, appertains to the Nation only, and not to any individual; and a Nation has at all times an inherent, indefeasible right to abolish any form of Government it finds inconvenient, and to establish such as accords with its interest, disposition, and happiness. The romantic and barbarous distinction of men into Kings and subjects, though it may suit the conditions of courtiers, cannot that of citizens; and is exploded by the principle upon which Governments are now founded. Every citizen is a member of the sovereignty, and, as such, can acknowledge no personal subjection: and his obedience can be only to the laws.

When men think of what Government is, they must necessarily suppose it to possess a knowledge of all the objects and matters upon which its authority is to be exercised. In this view of Government, the Republican system, as established by America and France, operates to embrace the whole of a Nation; and the knowledge necessary to the interest of all the parts, is to be found in the centre, which the parts by representation form; but the old Governments are on a construction that excludes knowledge as well as happiness; Government by monks, who know nothing of the world beyond the walls of a convent, is as inconsistent as Government by Kings.

What we formerly called Revolutions, were little more than a change of persons, or an alteration of local circumstances. They rose and fell like things of course, and had nothing in their existence or their fate that could influence beyond the spot that produced them. But what we now see in the world, from the Revolutions of America and France, are a renovation of the natural order of things, a system of principles as universal as truth and the existence of man, and combining moral with political happiness and national prosperity.

I. *Men are born, and always continue, free and equal in respect of their rights. Civil distinctions, therefore, can be founded only on public utility.*

II. *The end of all political associations is the preservation of the natural and imprescriptible rights of man; and these rights are liberty, property, security, and resistance of oppression.*

III. *The Nation is essentially the source of all sovereignty; nor can* ANY INDIVIDUAL, *or* ANY BODY OF MEN, *be entitled to any authority which is not expressly derived from it.*

In these principles there is nothing to throw a Nation into confusion by inflaming ambition. They are calculated to call forth wisdom and abilities, and to exercise them for the public good, and not for the emolument or aggrandisement of particular descriptions of men or families. Monarchical sovereignty, the enemy of mankind, and the source of misery, is abolished; and sovereignty itself is restored to its natural and original place, the Nation. Were this the case throughout Europe, the cause of wars would be taken away.

It is attributed to Henry the Fourth of France, a man of enlarged and benevolent heart, that he proposed, about the year 1610, a plan for abolishing war in Europe: the plan consisted in constituting an European Congress, or as the French authors stile it, a Pacific Republic, by appointing delegates from the several Nations who were to act as a Court of Arbitration in any disputes that might arise between Nation and Nation.

Had such a plan been adopted at the time it was proposed, the taxes of England and France, as two of the parties, would have been at least ten millions sterling annually to each nation less than they were at the commencement of the French Revolution.

To conceive a cause why such a plan has not been adopted (and that instead of a Congress for the purpose of *preventing* war, it has been called only to *terminate* a war, after a fruitless expense of several years), it will be necessary to consider the interest of Governments as a distinct interest to that of Nations.

Whatever is the cause of taxes to a Nation, becomes also the means of revenue to a Government. Every war terminates with an addition of taxes, and consequently with an addition of revenue; and in any event of war, in the manner they are now commenced and concluded the power and interest of Governments are increased. War, therefore, from its productiveness, as it easily furnishes the pretence of necessity for taxes and appointments to places and offices, becomes a principal part of the system of old Governments; and to establish any mode to abolish war, however advantageous it might be to Nations, would be to take from such Government the most lucrative of its branches. The frivolous matters upon which war is made shew the disposition and avidity of Governments to uphold the system of war, and betray the motives upon which they act.

Why are not Republics plunged into war, but because the nature of their Government does not admit of an interest distinct from that of the Nation? Even Holland, though an ill-constructed Republic, and with a commerce extending over the world, existed nearly a century without war; and the instant the form of Government was changed in France the republican principles of peace and domestic prosperity and economy arose with the new Government; and the same consequences would follow the same causes in other nations.

As war is the system of Government on the old construction, the animosity which Nations reciprocally entertain is nothing more than what the policy of their Governments excites to keep up the spirit of the system. Each Government accuses the other of perfidy, intrigue, and ambition, as a means of heating the imagination of their respective Nations, and incensing them to hostilities. Man is not the enemy of Man, but through the medium of a false system of Government. Instead, therefore, of exclaiming against the ambition of Kings, the exclamation should be directed against the principle of such Governments; and instead of seeking to reform the individual, the wisdom of a Nation should apply itself to reform the system.

Whether the forms and maxims of Governments which are still in practice were adapted to the condition of the world at the period they were established is not in this case the question. The older they are the less correspondence can they have with the present state of things.

Time, and change of circumstances and opinions, have the same progressive effect in rendering modes of Government obsolete as they have upon customs and manners. Agriculture, commerce, manufactures, and the tranquil arts, by which the prosperity of Nations is best promoted, require a different system of Government, and a different species of knowledge to direct its operations, than what might have been required in the former condition of the world.

As it is not difficult to perceive, from the enlightened state of mankind, that hereditary Governments are verging to their decline, and that Revolutions on the broad basis of national sovereignty and Government by representation, are making their way in Europe, it would be an act of wisdom to anticipate their approach, and produce Revolutions by reason and accommodation, rather than commit them to the issue of convulsions.

From what we now see, nothing of reform in the political world ought to be held improbable. It is an age of Revolutions, in which everything may be looked for.

The intrigue of Courts, by which the system of war is kept up, may provoke a confederation of Nations to abolish it; and an European Congress to patronize the progress of free Government, and promote the civilisation of Nations with each other, is an event nearer in probability than once were the Revolutions and Alliance of France and America.

GEORGES JACQUES DANTON
"Dare, Dare Again, Always Dare"
SEPTEMBER 2, 1792

Unlike the majority of the French revolutionaries, Georges Jacques Danton (1759–1794) delivered his speeches impromptu; they were recorded by witnesses and journalists.

Danton's energy, intelligence, and "daring" brought him fame and power as revolutionary France's Minister of Justice, but his opposition to Robespierre on the Committee of Public Safety brought him to the guillotine in 1794. "Danton will retain the distinction conferred upon him by Karl Marx," writes Paul Frolich, "the distinction of having been the greatest master of insurrectionary tactics in the bourgeois revolution."[1]

SOURCE: William Jennings Bryan and Francis W. Halsey, eds., *The World's Famous Orations*. Volume 7 (New York: Funk and Wagnalls, 1906), 130–131.

"Dare, Dare Again, Always Dare"

It is gratifying to the ministers of a free people to have to announce to them that their country will be saved. All are stirred, all are excited, all burn to fight. You know that Verdun is not yet in the power of our enemies. You know that its garrison swears to immolate the first who breathes a proposition of surrender.

One portion of our people will proceed to the frontiers, another will throw up intrenchments, and the third with pikes will defend the hearts

---

1. In Georges Jacques Danton, *Speeches of Georges Jacques Danton*. (New York: International Publishers, 1928), 15.

of our cities. Paris will second these great efforts. The commissioners of the Commune will solemnly proclaim to the citizens the invitation to arm and march to the defense of the country. At such a moment you can proclaim that the capital deserves well of all France.

At such a moment this National Assembly becomes a veritable committee of war. We ask that you concur with us in directing this sublime movement of the people, by naming commissioners who will second us in these great measures. We ask that any one refusing to give personal service or to furnish arms shall be punished with death. We ask that a set of instructions be drawn up for the citizens to direct their movements. We ask that couriers be sent to all the departments to notify them of the decrees that you proclaim here. The tocsin we are about to ring is not an alarm signal; it sounds the charge on the enemies of our country. To conquer them we must dare, dare again, always dare, and France is saved!

Manifesto of the Equals [*Manifeste des Egaux*]

APRIL 1796

Pierre-Sylvain Maréchal (1750–1803), a French anarchist who admired Rousseau, Voltaire, and Diderot, gained notoriety for his *L'Almanach des Honnêtes Gens* (1788), in which he argued for honoring history's wise men and authors with holidays rather than Christian figures and saints. After the downfall of Robespierre in 1794, he joined Babeuf's Society of the Equals and drafted *Manifesto of the Equals*, and challenged the new government. Its most controversial assertion ("What do we want more than equality in law? We want this equality written down in the Declaration of the Rights of Man and the Citizen: we want it in our midst, beneath the roofs of our houses. We will consent to everything for it; we will make a clean sweep to hold to it alone. Perish, if need be, all the arts as long as we have real equality") was too radical, even for such a radical group, and Babeuf's manifesto (see p. 96) was adopted instead. Unlike Babeuf, however, Maréchal did not sign his work, and escaped arrest and execution.

SOURCE: R. W. Postgate, ed., *Revolution from 1789 to 1906* (London: Grant Richards, 1920), 54–56.

Manifesto of the Equals

Equality of fact, final aim of the human art.
Condorcet, *Table of the Human Soul*

PEOPLE OF FRANCE!

For fifteen centuries you have lived slaves, and therefore unhappy. It is now scarcely six years since you have begun to revive in the hope of independence, happiness and equality.

Equality! First need of nature, first demand of man, and chief bond of all legitimate society! French people! you have not been more favoured than the other nations that vegetate on this wretched globe! Always and everywhere poor humanity, in the hands of more or less adroit cannibals is the tool of every ambition, the pasture of every tyranny. Always and everywhere men were lulled by fine phrases; never and nowhere did they receive the fulfilment with the promise. From time immemorial we have been hypocritically told: *Men are equal:* and from time immemorial the insolent weight of the most degrading and most monstrous inequality has weighed down the human race. Since civilised society began, this finest possession of humanity has been unanimously recognised, yet not once realised; equality was only a fair and sterile fiction of the law. To-day when it is more loudly claimed, we are answered: Silence, wretches! real equality is but a chimera: be content with constitutional equality: you are all equal before the law. *Canaille,* what more do you want?—What more do we want? Legislators, governors, rich proprietors, listen in your turn.

We are all equal, are we not? This principle is uncontested: for without being mad one cannot say it is night when it is day.

Well, henceforward we are going to live and die equal as we were born; we desire real equality or death: that is what we want.

And we shall have this real equality at all costs. Woe to those who stand between it and us! Woe to those who resist so strong a desire!

The French Revolution is but the precursor of another revolution, far greater, far more solemn, which will be the last.

The people marched over the corpses of the kings and priests who banded against them. They will do the same to the new tyrants and new political Tartuffes who sit in the seats of the others.

What do we want more than equality in law?

We want this equality nor merely written down in the Declaration of the Rights of Man and the Citizen: we want it in our midst, beneath the roofs of our houses. We will consent to everything for it; we will make a clean sweep to hold to it alone. Perish, if need be, all the arts as long as we have real equality!*

Legislators and governors who have neither intellect nor honesty, rich and heartless proprietors, you in vain try to neutralize our holy enterprise by saying: They only revive that agrarian law so often demanded before.

---

*Doubt over this sentence caused the Babouvists to reject this manifesto ultimately in favor of the "Analysis of the Doctrine of Babeuf." See next piece. [*Note by R. W. Postgate.*]

Slanderers, hold your peace in your turn, and in silent confusion, hear our demands, dictated by nature and based on justice.

An agrarian law, or the division of lands was the momentary wish of some unprincipled soldiers and some tribes moved by instinct rather than reason. We aim at something more sublime and more just, the COMMON good or the COMMUNITY OF GOODS! No more private property in land: *The earth is nobody's.* We claim, we will the common use of the fruits of the earth: *its fruits are everybody's.*

We declare that we can no longer permit that the huge majority of men toil and sweat for the service and at the pleasure of the tiny minority.

Long enough and too long have less than a million individuals disposed of what belongs to over twenty millions of their likes and their equals.

End at last this crying scandal, scandal our descendants will not credit! Vanish at last, revolting distinctions of rich and poor, great and little, masters and servants, governors and governed.

Let there be no difference now between human beings but in age and sex! Since all have the same needs and the same faculties, let there be for all one education and one standard of life! They are content with one sun and the same air for all, why should not the same portion and quality of food suffice for each?

But already the enemies of a state which is the most natural imaginable, declaim against us.

Disorganisers and factious men, they say to us, all you wish are massacres and booty.

PEOPLE OF FRANCE,

We shall not waste our time in answering them; we shall tell you: The holy enterprise which we are organizing has for its only aim to end civil dissension and the poverty of the people.

Never has more vast a design been conceived and executed. At long intervals some men of genius, some sages have spoken of it in a low and trembling voice. None of them have had the courage to tell the whole truth.

The moment for great measures has come. The evil is at its height, it covers the face of the earth. Chaos has reigned there under the name of politics too many centuries. Everything must be in order and resume its place. Let the elements of justice and happiness crystallize at the voice of Equality. The time has come to found the REPUBLIC OF EQUALS, that great guesthouse of all mankind. The days of restitution have arrived. Weeping families take your seats at the common table, nature spreads for all her children.

PEOPLE OF FRANCE,

For you, then, was reserved the purest of all glories. Yes, it is you that will first offer the world that touching sight!

Ancient habits, archaic prejudices again try to prevent the establishment of the *Republic of Equals*. The organising of real equality, the only state which answers all requirements without making victims or costing sacrifices, perhaps will not at first please everyone. The egoist and ambitious man will scream with rage. Those who possess unjustly will cry out, injustice! Their exclusive delights, their solitary pleasures, their personal ease will leave bitter longings in the hearts of some individuals who have grown effete by their neighbour's toil. Lovers of absolute power, and worthless tools of arbitrary authority, will find it hard to bring their proud chiefs to the level of equality. Their shortsight cannot penetrate into the near future of the common good; but what is the power of a few thousand malcontents against the mass of men, entirely happy and wondering that they sought so long for what was beneath their hand.

On the morrow of this true revolution they will say: What, was the common good so easy? We had but to will it. Ah, why did we not will it sooner? Was it necessary to repeat it to us so often? Yes, without doubt, but one man on earth more rich and powerful than his fellows, his equals, shatters the equilibrium; and crime and unhappiness arise on earth.

PEOPLE OF FRANCE,

By what sign in the future must you recognise the excellence of a constitution? . . . That which is entirely founded on real equality is the only one that can suit you and satisfy all your wishes.

The aristocratic Charters of 1791 and 1795 riveted your chains instead of breaking them. That of 1793 was a great step in fact toward real equality, it had never been approached so near before but it did not achieve the goal; or arrive at the common good, whose great principle it yet so solemnly consecrated.

PEOPLE OF FRANCE,

Open your eyes and hearts to the fulness of joy. Recognize and proclaim with us THE REPUBLIC OF EQUALS.

F. N. BABEUF

"Analysis of the Doctrine of Babeuf, Proscribed by the Executive Committee for Having Told the Truth"

1796

When Francois Noel ("Gracchus") Babeuf (1760–1797), one of the founders of French socialism, saw the revolution being betrayed by a government worse than the king's, he formed the Society of the Equals to demand France's renewed commitment to social justice and equality. "The Revolution is not terminated," reads doctrine 11, "because the rich absorb all valuable productions, and command exclusively. Whilst the poor toil like real slaves, pine in misery, and count for nothing in the State." Babeuf pointed out in his trial for conspiracy against the Republic that the "Analysis of the Doctrine of Babeuf" had not been composed by him as such, but had been collected and sorted by his followers from various of his statements. In 1797 he defended his "treasonous" actions against the government by quoting Rousseau at his judges. He was executed soon after.

SOURCE: R. W. Postgate, ed., *Revolution from 1789 to 1906* (London: Grant Richards, 1920), 56–57.

Analysis of the Doctrine of Babeuf

1. Nature has given to each individual an equal right to the enjoyment of all the goods of life.
2. The end of society is to defend this equality, often assailed by the strong and wicked in the state of nature and to augment, by the co-operation of all, the common enjoyments of all.
3. Nature has imposed on each person the obligation to work; nobody could, without crime, evade his share of the common labour.
4. Labour and enjoyments ought to be common.

5. There is oppression wherever one part of society is exhausted by labour and in want of everything, whilst the other part wallows in abundance without doing any work at all.

6. Nobody could, without crime, exclusively appropriate to himself the goods of the earth or of industry.

7. In a veritable society there ought to be neither rich nor poor.

8. The rich who are not willing to renounce their superfluities in favour of the indigent, are the enemies of the people.

9. No one can, by accumulating to himself all the means, deprive another of the instruction necessary for his happiness. Instruction ought to be common to all.

10. The end of the French Revolution is to destroy inequality, and to reestablish general prosperity.

11. The Revolution is not terminated, because the rich absorb all valuable productions, and command exclusively. Whilst the poor toil like real slaves, pine in misery, and count for nothing in the State.

12. The Constitution of 1793 is the veritable law of Frenchmen, because the people has solemnly accepted it; because the Convention had not the right to change it; because to succeed in superseding it, the Convention has caused the people to be shot for demanding its execution; because it has hunted and massacred the deputies, who performed their duty in defending it; because a system of terrorism against the people, and the influence of emigrants, have presided over the fabrication and pretended acceptation of the Constitution of 1795, which, nevertheless, had not a quarter of the number of suffrages in its favour that the Constitution of 1793 has obtained; because the Constitution of 1793 has consecrated the inalienable right of every citizen to consent to the laws, to exercise political rights, to meet in assembly, to propose what he deems useful, to receive instruction, and not to die of hunger; rights which the counter-revolutionary Act of 1795 has openly and completely violated.

13. Every citizen is bound to re-establish and defend, in the Constitution of 1793, the will and happiness of the people.

14. All the powers emanating from the pretended Constitution of 1795 are illegal and counter-revolutionary.

15. Those who have used violence against the Constitution of 1793 are guilty of high treason against the nation.

ROBERT OWEN
"The Legacy of Robert Owen to the Population of the World"
MARCH 29, 1834

The English cotton manufacturer Robert Owen (1771–1858), a "Utopian" socialist, organized cooperative communities and factories in England and America. He continually advocated for universal education for children and for workers' rights, and headed England's Revolutionary Trades Union movement in the 1830s. In this selection, he addresses members of the Grand National Consolidated Trades Union of Great Britain and Ireland on how "the greatest revolution ever effected in the history of the human race will be commenced, rapidly carried on and completed all over the world, without bloodshed, violence or evil of any kind, merely by an overwhelming moral influence . . ."

SOURCE: R. W. Postgate, ed., *Revolution from 1789 to 1906* (London: Grant Richards, 1920), 95–97.

The Legacy of Robert Owen

"Sacred to Truth, without Mystery, Mixture of Error or Fear of Man."

More than half a century ago I discovered that there was some grievous error deep in the foundations of society, which created evil, and prevented the good which man by his nature was evidently destined, in some stage of his progress, to attain and permanently to enjoy.

From that period to the present, I have never ceased honestly and fearlessly to search for that truth which should enable me to detect the error, remove the evil and forever establish the good.

Having found this truth, and proved it to be such by the only criterion of truth known to man; that is, by its undeviating consistency with ascertained facts, I now give it to you, that through its influence you may be regenerated, your minds born again, and your posterity be made partakers of the endless blessings which this truth, and this truth alone, can ensure permanently for the human race.

This great truth which I have now to declare to you, is, that "the system on which all the nations of the world are acting is founded in gross deception, in the deepest ignorance or in a mixture of both. That, under no possible modification of the principles on which it is based, can it ever produce good to man; but that, on the contrary, its practical results must ever be to produce evil continually"—and, consequently, that no really intelligent and honest individual can any longer support it; for, by the constitution of this system, it unavoidably encourages and upholds, as it ever has encouraged and upheld, hypocrisy and deception of every description, and discouraged and opposed truth and sincerity, whenever truth and sincerity were applied permanently to improve the condition of the human race. It encourages and upholds national vice and corruption to an unlimited extent; whilst to an equal degree it discourages national virtue and honesty. The whole system has not one redeeming quality; its very virtues, as they are termed, are vices of great magnitude. Its charities, so called, are gross acts of injustice and deception. Its instructions are to rivet ignorance in the mind and, if possible, render it perpetual. It supports, in all manner of extravagance, idleness, presumption and uselessness; and oppresses, in almost every mode which ingenuity can devise, industry, integrity and usefulness. It encourages superstition, bigotry and fanaticism; and discourages truth, commonsense and rationality. It generates and cultivates every inferior quality and base passion that human nature can be made to receive; and has so disordered all the human intellects, that they have become universally perplexed and confused, so that man has no just title to be called a reasonable or rational being. It generates violence, robbery and murder, and extols and rewards these vices as the highest of all virtues. Its laws are founded in gross ignorance of individual man and of human society; they are cruel and unjust in the extreme, and, united with all the superstitions in the world, are calculated only to teach men to call that which is preeminently true and good, false and bad; and that which is glaringly false and bad, true and good. In short, to cultivate with great care all that leads to vice and misery in the mass, and to exclude from them, with equal care, all that would direct them to true knowledge and real happiness, which alone, combined, deserve the name of virtue.

In consequence of the dire effects of this wretched system upon the whole of the human race, the population of Great Britain—the most advanced of modern nations in the acquirement of riches, power and happiness—has created and supports a theory and practice of government which is directly opposed to the real well-being and true interests of every individual member of the empire, whatever may be his station, rank or condition—whether subject or sovereign. And so enormous are the increasing errors of this system now become, that, to uphold it the government is compelled, day by day, to commit acts of the grossest cruelty and injustice, and to call such proceedings laws of justice and of Christian mercy.

Under this system, the idle, the useless and the vicious govern the population of the world; whilst the useful and the truly virtuous, as far as such a system will permit men to be virtuous, are by them degraded and oppressed.

Under this system, those who daily and hourly practise the act of poisoning the body, deranging the intellect, and reducing individuals to the lowest stage of human existence, are openly fostered and encouraged until they build palaces of temptations, to excite to every conceivable vice and crime, and at the same time teach almost a continued language of the vilest and most demoralizing oaths; while those who, to protect themselves and their helpless families, by their industry and good conduct, from these dire effects, meet together to aid and encourage each other in their wise and virtuous proceedings, and engage to do so by righteous oath, taken solely with a view to unite these, the producers of all good to society, in a virtuous bond of brotherhood and sisterhood, are hunted like beasts of prey, incarcerated in demoralizing prisons, subjected to a much worse than farcical trial, found guilty by ignorant and prejudiced individuals, and sentenced to a cruel, ignominious and grossly unjust punishment.

Men of industry, and of good and virtuous habits! This is the last state to which you ought to submit; nor would I advise you to allow the ignorant, the idle, the presumptuous and the vicious, any longer to lord it over the well-being, the lives and happiness, of yourselves and families, when by *three days* of such idleness as constitutes the whole of their lives, you would for ever convince each one of these mistaken individuals that you now possess the power to compel *them* at once to become the abject slaves, and the oppressed portion of society which they have hitherto made *you*.

But all the individuals now living are the suffering victims of this accursed system, and all are objects of pity: you will, therefore, effect this great and glorious revolution without, if possible, inflicting individual evil. You can easily accomplish this most-to-be-desired object. Proceed with your Union on the principles which you have latterly adopted; they are wise and just, and wisdom and justice, combined with your Union, will be sure to render them for ever legal.

Men of industry, producers of wealth and knowledge, and of all that is truly valuable in society! unite your powers now to create a wise and righteous state of human existence — a state in which the only contest shall be, who shall produce the greatest amount of permanent happiness for the human race. You have all the requisite materials awaiting your proper application of them to effect this change, and circumstances have arisen within the last week to render delay a dereliction of the highest duty which you have to perform to yourselves, to your families, and to the population of the world.

Men of industrious habits, you who are the most honest, useful and valuable portion of society, by producing for it all its wealth and knowledge, you have formed and established the Grand National Consolidated Trades Union of Great Britain and Ireland, and it will prove the palladium of the world. All the intelligent, well-disposed and superior minds among all classes of society, male and female, will now rally round the Consolidated Union and become members of it; and, if the irrationality of the present degraded and degrading system should render it necessary, you will discover the reasons why you should willingly sacrifice all you hold dear in the world, and life itself, rather than submit to its dissolution or slightest depression.

For your sakes I have become a member of your Consolidated Union, and while it shall be directed with the same wisdom and justice that it has been from its commencement, and its proceedings shall be made known to the public as you intend them to be, my resolve is to stand by our order, and support the Union to the utmost of my power. It is this Consolidated Union that alone can save the British empire from greater confusion, anarchy and misery than it has ever yet experienced. It is, it will become daily more and more, the real conservative power of society: for its example will be speedily followed by all nations, and through its beneficial example the greatest revolution ever effected in the history of the human race will be commenced, rapidly carried on and completed all over the world, without bloodshed, violence or evil of any kind, merely by an overwhelming moral influence, which influence individuals and nations will speedily perceive the folly and uselessness of attempting to resist.

Experience has forced these important truths into my mind, and I now give them to the population of the world as the most valuable legacy that man can give to man.

PIERRE-JOSEPH PROUDHON
Chapter 1,
What Is Property?: An Inquiry into the Principle of Right and of Government
1840

"This fiery individualist who disdained followers yet wielded such a pervasive influence in his time and afterwards, was born in 1809 in the suburbs of Besancon," writes George Woodcock.[1] "The publication of *What Is Property?* brought him a European fame in the radical circles of his time, and during the early 1840s he came into close contact with many of the men who later were to play dominant roles in the socialist movement. Marx, Bakunin, and Alexander Herzen were all at this time exiles in Paris, living in poor furtive rooms of the Latin Quarter, which Proudhon also inhabited, and he became friendly with all of them, spending days and often nights discussing tactics of the revolution and the philosophy of Hegel . . ." Though volubly denounced by Marx for what Marx believed was philosophic naivete, Proudhon continued to write with infectious enthusiasm for the rights of the impoverished, including a book entitled *La guerre et la paix;* he inspired many champions of social justice, not the least of whom was the greatest novelist of the age, Leo Tolstoy. Proudhon died in 1865.

SOURCE: Pierre-Joseph Proudhon, *What Is Property?: An Inquiry into the Principle of Right and of Government.* Trans. Benjamin R. Tucker. Introduction by George Woodcock (New York: Dover Publications, Inc., 1970), 11–41.

---

1. Pierre-Joseph Proudhon, *What Is Property?: An Inquiry into the Principle of Right and of Government.* Trans. Benjamin R. Tucker. Introduction by George Woodcock (New York: Dover Publications, Inc., 1970), vi.

First Memoir

Adversus hostem œterna auctoritas esto.
Against the enemy, revendication is eternal.
LAW OF THE TWELVE TABLES.

Chapter I.

If I were asked to answer the following question: *What is slavery?* and I should answer in one word, *It is murder,* my meaning would be understood at once. No extended argument would be required to show that the power to take from a man his thought, his will, his personality, is a power of life and death; and that to enslave a man is to kill him. Why, then, to this other question: *What is property?* may I not likewise answer, *It is robbery,* without the certainty of being misunderstood; the second proposition being no other than a transformation of the first?

I undertake to discuss the vital principle of our government and our institutions, property: I am in my right. I may be mistaken in the conclusion which shall result from my investigations: I am in my right. I think best to place the last thought of my book first: still am I in my right.

Such an author teaches that property is a civil right, born of occupation and sanctioned by law; another maintains that it is a natural right, originating in labor,—and both of these doctrines, totally opposed as they may seem, are encouraged and applauded. I contend that neither labor, nor occupation, nor law, can create property; that it is an effect without a cause: am I censurable?

But murmurs arise!

Property is robbery! That is the war-cry of '93! That is the signal of revolutions!

Reader, calm yourself: I am no agent of discord, no firebrand of sedition. I anticipate history by a few days; I disclose a truth whose development we may try in vain to arrest; I write the preamble of our future constitution. This proposition which seems to you blasphemous— *property is robbery*—would, if our prejudices allowed us to consider it, be recognized as the lightning-rod to shield us from the coming thunderbolt; but too many interests stand in the way! . . . Alas! philosophy will not change the course of events: destiny will fulfill itself regardless of prophecy. Besides, must not justice be done and our education be finished?

Property is robbery! . . . What a revolution in human ideas! *Proprietor* and *robber* have been at all times expressions as contradictory as the beings whom they designate are hostile; all languages have perpetuated this opposition. On what authority, then, do you venture to attack universal consent, and give the lie to the human race? Who are you, that you should question the judgment of the nations and the ages?

Of what consequence to you, reader, is my obscure individuality? I live, like you, in a century in which reason submits only to fact and to evidence. My name, like yours, is TRUTHSEEKER.* My mission is written in these words of the law: *Speak without hatred and without fear; tell that which thou knowest!* The work of our race is to build the temple of science, and this science includes man and Nature. Now, truth reveals itself to all; to-day to Newton and Pascal, to-morrow to the herdsman in the valley and the journeyman in the shop. Each one contributes his stone to the edifice; and, his task accomplished, disappears. Eternity precedes us, eternity follows us: between two infinites, of what account is one poor mortal that the century should inquire about him?

Disregard then, reader, my title and my character, and attend only to my arguments. It is in accordance with universal consent that I undertake to correct universal error; from the *opinion* of the human race I appeal to its *faith*. Have the courage to follow me; and, if your will is untrammelled, if your conscience is free, if your mind can unite two propositions and deduce a third therefrom, my ideas will inevitably become yours. In beginning by giving you my last word, it was my purpose to warn you, not to defy you; for I am certain that, if you read me, you will be compelled to assent. The things of which I am to speak are so simple and clear that you will be astonished at not having perceived them before, and you will say: "I have neglected to think." Others offer you the spectacle of genius wresting Nature's secrets from her, and unfolding before you her sublime messages; you will find here only a series of experiments upon *justice* and *right*, a sort of verification of the weights and measures of your conscience. The operations shall be conducted under your very eyes; and you shall weigh the result.

Nevertheless, I build no system. I ask an end to privilege, the abolition of slavery, equality of rights, and the reign of law. Justice, nothing else; that is the alpha and omega of my argument: to others I leave the business of governing the world.

One day I asked myself: Why is there so much sorrow and misery in society? Must man always be wretched? And not satisfied with the explanations given by the reformers, — these attributing the general distress to governmental cowardice and incapacity, those to conspirators and *émeutes*, still others to ignorance and general corruption, — and weary of the interminable quarrels of the tribune and the press, I sought to fathom the matter myself. I have consulted the masters of science; I

---

*In Greek, σκεπτικος, examiner; a philosopher whose business is to seek the truth. (*Note by Proudhon*.)

have read a hundred volumes of philosophy, law, political economy, and history: would to God that I had lived in a century in which so much reading had been useless! I have made every effort to obtain exact information, comparing doctrines, replying to objections, continually constructing equations and reductions from arguments, and weighing thousands of syllogisms in the scales of the most rigorous logic. In this laborious work, I have collected many interesting facts which I shall share with my friends and the public as soon as I have leisure. But I must say that I recognized at once that we had never understood the meaning of these words, so common and yet so sacred: *Justice, equity, liberty;* that concerning each of these principles our ideas have been utterly obscure; and, in fact, that this ignorance was the sole cause, both of the poverty that devours us, and of all the calamities that have ever afflicted the human race.

My mind was frightened by this strange result: I doubted my reason. What! said I, that which eye has not seen, nor ear heard, nor insight penetrated, you have discovered! Wretch, mistake not the visions of your diseased brain for the truths of science! Do you not know (great philosophers have said so) that in points of practical morality universal error is a contradiction?

I resolved then to test my arguments; and in entering upon this new labor I sought an answer to the following questions: Is it possible that humanity can have been so long and so universally mistaken in the application of moral principles? How and why could it be mistaken? How can its error, being universal, be capable of correction?

These questions, on the solution of which depended the certainty of my conclusions, offered no lengthy resistance to analysis. It will be seen, in chapter V. of this work, that in morals, as in all other branches of knowledge, the gravest errors are the dogmas of science; that, even in works of justice, to be mistaken is a privilege which ennobles man; and that whatever philosophical merit may attach to me is infinitely small. To name a thing is easy: the difficulty is to discern it before its appearance. In giving expression to the last stage of an idea, — an idea which permeates all minds, which to-morrow will be proclaimed by another if I fail to announce it to-day, — I can claim no merit save that of priority of utterance. Do we eulogize the man who first perceives the dawn?

Yes: all men believe and repeat that equality of conditions is identical with equality of rights; that *property* and *robbery* are synonymous terms; that every social advantage accorded, or rather usurped, in the name of superior talent or service, is iniquity and extortion. All men in their hearts, I say, bear witness to these truths; they need only to be made to understand it.

Before entering directly upon the question before me, I must say a word of the road that I shall traverse. When Pascal approached a geometrical problem, he invented a method of solution; to solve a problem in philosophy a method is equally necessary. Well, by how much do the problems of which philosophy treats surpass in the gravity of their results those discussed by geometry! How much more imperatively, then, do they demand for their solution a profound and rigorous analysis!

It is a fact placed for ever beyond doubt, say the modern psychologists, that every perception received by the mind is determined by certain general laws which govern the mind; is moulded, so to speak, in certain types pre-existing in our understanding, and which constitutes its original condition. Hence, say they, if the mind has no innate *ideas*, it has at least innate *forms*. Thus, for example, every phenomenon is of necessity conceived by us as happening in *time* and *space*, —that compels us to infer a *cause* of its occurrence; every thing which exists implies the ideas of *substance, mode, relation, number, etc.*; in a word, we form no idea which is not related to some one of the general principles of reason, independent of which nothing exists.

These axioms of the understanding, add the psychologists, these fundamental types, by which all our judgments and ideas are inevitably shaped, and which our sensations serve only to illuminate, are known in the schools as *categories*. Their primordial existence in the mind is to-day demonstrated; they need only to be systematized and catalogued. Aristotle recognized ten; Kant increased the number to fifteen; M. Cousin has reduced it to three, to two, to one; and the indisputable glory of this professor will be due to the fact that, if he has not discovered the true theory of categories, he has, at least, seen more clearly than any one else the vast importance of this question, —the greatest and perhaps the only one with which metaphysics has to deal.

I confess that I disbelieve in the innateness, not only of *ideas*, but also of *forms* or *laws* of our understanding; and I hold the metaphysics of Reid and Kant to be still farther removed from the truth than that of Aristotle. However, as I do not wish to enter here into a discussion of the mind, a task which would demand much labor and be of no interest to the public, I shall admit the hypothesis that our most general and most necessary ideas—such as time, space, substance, and cause—exist originally in the mind; or, at least, are derived immediately from its constitution.

But it is a psychological fact none the less true, and one to which the philosophers have paid too little attention, that habit, like a second nature, has the power of fixing in the mind new categorical forms derived from the appearances which impress us, and by them usually stripped of objective reality, but whose influence over our judgments is no less predetermining than that of the original categories. Hence we reason by the *eternal* and *absolute* laws of our mind, and at the same time by the secondary rules, ordinarily faulty, which are suggested to us by imperfect observation. This is the most fecund source of false prejudices, and the permanent and often invincible cause of a multitude of errors. The bias resulting from these prejudices is so strong that often, even when we are fighting against a principle which our mind thinks false, which is repugnant to our reason, and which our conscience disapproves, we defend it without knowing it, we reason in accordance with it, and we obey it while attacking it. Enclosed within a circle, our mind revolves about itself, until a new observation, creating within us new ideas, brings to view an external principle which delivers us from the phantom by which our imagination is possessed.

Thus, we know to-day that, by the laws of a universal magnetism whose cause is still unknown, two bodies (no obstacle intervening) tend to unite by an accelerated impelling force which we call *gravitation*. It is gravitation which causes unsupported bodies to fall to the ground, which gives them weight, and which fastens us to the earth on which we live. Ignorance of this cause was the sole obstacle which prevented the ancients from believing in the antipodes. "Can you not see," said St. Augustine after Lactantius, "that, if there were men under our feet, their heads would point downward, and that they would fall into the sky?" The bishop of Hippo, who thought the earth flat because it appeared so to the eye, supposed in consequence that, if we should connect by straight lines the zenith with the nadir in different places, these lines would be parallel with each other; and in the direction of these lines he traced every movement from above to below. Thence he naturally concluded that the stars were rolling torches set in the vault of the sky; that, if left to themselves, they would fall to the earth in a shower of fire; that the earth was one vast plain, forming the lower portion of the world, etc. If he had been asked by what the world itself was sustained, he would have answered that he did not know, but that to God nothing is impossible. Such were the ideas of St. Augustine in regard to space and movement, ideas fixed within him by a prejudice derived from an appearance, and which had become with him a general and categorical rule of judgment. Of the reason why bodies fall his mind knew nothing; he could only say that a body falls because it falls.

With us the idea of a fall is more complex: to the general ideas of space and movement which it implies, we add that of attraction or direction towards a centre, which gives us the higher idea of cause. But if physics has fully corrected our judgment in this respect, we still make use of the prejudice of St. Augustine; and when we say that a thing has *fallen*, we do not mean simply and in general that there has been an effect of gravitation, but specially and in particular that it is towards the earth, and *from above to below*, that this movement has taken place. Our mind is enlightened in vain; the imagination prevails, and our language remains forever incorrigible. To *descend from heaven* is as incorrect an expression as to *mount to heaven*; and yet this expression will live as long as men use language.

All these phrases—*from above to below; to descend from heaven; to fall from the clouds, etc.*—are henceforth harmless, because we know how to rectify them in practice; but let us deign to consider for a moment how much they have retarded the progress of science. If, indeed, it be a matter of little importance to statistics, mechanics, hydrodynamics, and ballistics, that the true cause of the fall of bodies should be known, and that our ideas of the general movements in space should be exact, it is quite otherwise when we undertake to explain the system of the universe, the cause of tides, the shape of the earth, and its position in the heavens: to understand these things we must leave the circle of appearances. In all ages there have been ingenious mechanicians, excellent architects, skilful artillerymen: any error, into which it was possible for them to fall in regard to the rotundity of the earth and gravitation, in no wise retarded the development of their art; the solidity of their buildings and accuracy of their aim was not affected by it. But sooner or later they were forced to grapple with phenomena, which the supposed parallelism of all perpendiculars erected from the earth's surface rendered inexplicable: then also commenced a struggle between the prejudices, which for centuries had sufficed in daily practice, and the unprecedented opinions which the testimony of the eyes seemed to contradict.

Thus, on the one hand, the falsest judgments, whether based on isolated facts or only on appearances, always embrace some truths whose sphere, whether large or small, affords room for a certain number of inferences, beyond which we fall into absurdity. The ideas of St. Augustine, for example, contained the following truths: that bodies fall towards the earth, that they fall in a straight line, that either the sun or the earth moves, that either the sky or the earth turns, etc. These general facts always have been true; our science has added nothing to them. But, on the other hand, it being necessary to account for every thing, we are obliged to seek for principles more and more comprehensive: that is why we have had to abandon successively, first the opinion that the world was flat, then the theory which regards it as the stationary centre of the universe, etc.

If we pass now from physical nature to the moral world, we still find ourselves subject to the same deceptions of appearance, to the same influences of spontaneity and habit. But the distinguishing feature of this second division of our knowledge is, on the one hand, the good or the evil which we derive from our opinions; and, on the other, the obstinacy with which we defend the prejudice which is tormenting and killing us.

Whatever theory we embrace in regard to the shape of the earth and the cause of its weight, the physics of the globe does not suffer; and, as for us, our social economy can derive therefrom neither profit nor damage. But it is in us and through us that the laws of our moral nature work; now, these laws cannot be executed without our deliberate aid, and, consequently, unless we know them. If, then, our science of moral laws is false, it is evident that, while desiring our own good, we are accomplishing our own evil; if it is only incomplete, it may suffice for a time for our social progress, but in the long run it will lead us into a wrong road, and will finally precipitate us into an abyss of calamities.

Then it is that we need to exercise our highest judgments; and, be it said to our glory, they are never found wanting: but then also commences a furious struggle between old prejudices and new ideas. Days of conflagration and anguish! We are told of the time when, with the same beliefs, with the same institutions, all the world seemed happy: why complain of these beliefs; why banish these institutions? We are slow to admit that that happy age served the precise purpose of developing the principle of evil which lay dormant in society; we accuse men and gods, the powers of earth and the forces of Nature. Instead of seeking the cause of the evil in his mind and heart, man blames his masters, his rivals, his neighbors, and himself; nations arm themselves, and slay and exterminate each other, until equilibrium is restored by the vast depopulation, and peace again arises from the ashes of the combatants. So loath is humanity to touch the customs of its ancestors, and to change the laws framed by the founders of communities, and confirmed by the faithful observance of the ages.

Nihil motum ex antiquo probabile est: Distrust all innovations, wrote Titus Livius. Undoubtedly it would be better were man not compelled to change: but what! because he is born ignorant, because he exists only on condition of gradual self-instruction, must he abjure the light, abdicate his reason, and abandon himself to fortune? Perfect health is better than convalescence: should the sick man, therefore, refuse to be cured? Reform, reform! cried, ages since, John the Baptist and Jesus Christ. Reform, reform! cried our fathers, fifty years ago; and for a long time to come we shall shout, Reform, reform!

Seeing the misery of my age, I said to myself: Among the principles that support society, there is one which it does not understand, which its ignorance has vitiated, and which causes all the evil that exists. This principle is the most ancient of all; for it is a characteristic of revolutions to tear down the most modern principles, and to respect those of long-standing. Now the evil by which we suffer is anterior to all revolutions. This principle, impaired by our ignorance, is honored and cherished; for if it were not cherished it would harm nobody, it would be without influence.

But this principle, right in its purpose, but misunderstood: this principle, as old as humanity, what is it? Can it be religion?

All men believe in God: this dogma belongs at once to their conscience and their mind. To humanity God is a fact as primitive, an idea as inevitable, a principle as necessary as are the categorical ideas of cause, substance, time, and space to our understanding. God is proven to us by the conscience prior to any inference of the mind; just as the sun is proven to us by the testimony of the senses prior to all the arguments of physics. We discover phenomena and laws by observation and experience; only this deeper sense reveals to us existence. Humanity believes that God is; but, in believing in God, what does it believe? In a word, what is God?

The nature of this notion of Divinity,—this primitive, universal notion, born in the race,—the human mind has not yet fathomed. At each step that we take in our investigation of Nature and of causes, the idea of God is extended and exalted; the farther science advances, the more God seems to grow and broaden. Anthropomorphism and idolatry constituted of necessity the faith of the mind in its youth, the theology of infancy and poesy. A harmless error, if they had not endeavored to make it a rule of conduct, and if they had been wise enough to respect the liberty of thought. But having made God in his own image, man wished to appropriate him still farther; not satisfied with disfiguring the Almighty, he treated him as his patrimony, his goods, his possessions. God, pictured in monstrous forms, became throughout the world the property of man and of the State. Such was the origin of the corruption of morals by religion, and the source of pious feuds and holy wars. Thank Heaven! we have learned to allow every one his own beliefs; we seek for moral laws outside the pale of religion. Instead of legislating as to the nature and attributes of God, the dogmas of theology, and the destiny of our souls, we wisely wait for science to tell us what to reject and what to accept. God, soul, religion,—eternal objects of our unwearied thought and our most fatal aberrations, terrible problems whose solution, for ever attempted, for ever remains unaccomplished,—concerning all these questions we may still be mistaken, but at least our error is harmless. With liberty in religion, and the separation of the spiritual from the temporal power, the influence of religious ideas upon the progress of society is purely negative; no law, no political or civil institution being founded on religion. Neglect of duties imposed by religion may increase the general corruption, but it is not the primary cause; it is only an auxiliary or result. It is universally admitted, and especially in the matter which now engages our attention, that the cause of the inequality of conditions among men—of pauperism, of universal misery, and of governmental embarrassments—can no longer be traced to religion: we must go farther back, and dig still deeper.

But what is there in man older and deeper than the religious sentiment?

There is man himself; that is, volition and conscience, free-will and law, eternally antagonistic. Man is at war with himself: why?

"Man," say the theologians, "transgressed in the beginning; our race is guilty of an ancient offence. For this transgression humanity has fallen; error and ignorance have become its sustenance. Read history, you will find universal proof of this necessity for evil in the permanent misery of nations. Man suffers and always will suffer; his disease is hereditary and constitutional. Use palliatives, employ emollients; there is no remedy."

Nor is this argument peculiar to the theologians; we find it expressed in equivalent language in the philosophical writings of the materialists, believers in infinite perfectibility. Destutt de Tracy teaches formally that poverty, crime, and war are the inevitable conditions of our social state; necessary evils, against which it would be folly to revolt. So, call it *necessity of evil* or *original depravity*, it is at bottom the same philosophy.

"The first man transgressed." If the votaries of the Bible interpreted it faithfully, they would say: *man originally transgressed*, that is, made a mistake; for *to transgress, to fail, to make a mistake*, all mean the same thing.

"The consequences of Adam's transgression are inherited by the race; the first is ignorance." Truly, the race, like the individual, is born ignorant; but, in regard to a multitude of questions, even in the moral and political spheres, this ignorance of the race has been dispelled: who says that it will not depart altogether? Mankind makes continual progress toward truth, and light ever triumphs over darkness. Our disease is not, then, absolutely incurable, and the theory of the theologians is worse than inadequate; it is ridiculous, since it is reducible to this tautology: "Man errs, because he errs." While the true statement is this: "Man errs, because he learns." Now, if man arrives at a knowledge of all that he needs to know, it is reasonable to believe that, ceasing to err, he will cease to suffer.

But if we question the doctors as to this law, said to be engraved upon the heart of man, we shall immediately see that they dispute about a matter of which they know nothing; that, concerning the most important questions, there are almost as many opinions as authors; that we find no two agreeing as to the best form of government, the principle of authority, and the nature of right; that all sail hap-hazard upon a shoreless and bottomless sea, abandoned to the guidance of their private opinions which they modestly take to be right reason. And, in view of this medley of contradictory opinions, we say: "The object of our investigations is the law, the determination of the social principle. Now, the politicians, that is, the social scientists, do not understand each other; then the error lies in themselves; and, as every error has a reality for its object, we must look in their books to find the truth which they have unconsciously deposited there."

Now, of what do the lawyers and the publicists treat? Of *justice, equity, liberty, natural law, civil laws*, etc. But what is justice? What is its principle, its character, its formula? To this question our doctors evidently have no reply; for otherwise their science, starting with a principle clear and well defined, would quit the region of probabilities, and all disputes would end.

What is justice? The theologians answer: "All justice comes from God." That is true; but we know no more than before.

The philosophers ought to be better informed: they have argued so much about justice and injustice! Unhappily, an examination proves that their knowledge amounts to nothing, and that with them—as with the savages whose every prayer to the sun is simply *O! O!*—it is a cry of admiration, love, and enthusiasm; but who does not know that the sun attaches little meaning to the interjection *O!* That is exactly our position toward the philosophers in regard to justice. Justice, they say, is a *daughter of Heaven; a light which illumines every man that comes into the world; the most beautiful prerogative of our nature; that which distinguishes us from the beasts, and likens us to God,*—and a thousand other similar things. What, I ask, does this pious litany amount to? To the prayer of the savages: *O!*

All the most reasonable teachings of human wisdom concerning justice are summed up in that famous adage: *Do unto others that which you would that others should do unto you; Do not unto others that which you would not that others should do unto you.* But this rule of moral practice is unscientific: what have I a right to wish that others should do or not do to me? It is of no use to tell me that my duty is equal to my right, unless I am told at the same time what my right is.

Let us try to arrive at something more precise and positive.

Justice is the central star which governs societies, the pole around which the political world revolves, the principle and the regulator of all transactions. Nothing takes place between men save in the name of *right*; nothing without the invocation of justice. Justice is not the work of the law: on the contrary, the law is only a declaration and application of *justice* in all circumstances where men are liable to come in contact. If, then, the idea that we form of justice and right were ill-defined, if it were imperfect or even false, it is clear that all our legislative applications would be wrong, our institutions vicious, our politics erroneous: consequently there would be disorder and social chaos.

This hypothesis of the perversion of justice in our minds, and, as a necessary result, in our acts, becomes a demonstrated fact when it is shown that the opinions of men have not borne a constant relation to the notion of justice and its applications; that at different periods they have undergone modifications: in a word, that there has been progress in ideas. Now, that is what history proves by the most overwhelming testimony.

Eighteen hundred years ago, the world, under the rule of the Cæsars, exhausted itself in slavery, superstition, and voluptuousness. The people—intoxicated and, as it were, stupefied by their long-continued orgies—had lost the very notion of right and duty: war and dissipation by turns swept them away; usury and the labor of machines (that is of slaves), by depriving them of the means of subsistence, hindered them from continuing the species. Barbarism sprang up again, in a hideous form, from this mass of corruption, and spread like a devouring leprosy over the depopulated provinces. The wise foresaw the downfall of the empire, but could devise no remedy. What could they think indeed? To save this old society it would have been necessary to change the objects of public esteem and veneration, and to abolish the rights affirmed by a justice purely secular; they said: "Rome has conquered through her politics and her gods; any change in theology and public opinion would be folly and sacrilege. Rome, merciful toward conquered nations, though binding them in chains, spared their lives; slaves are the most fertile source of her wealth; freedom of the nations would be the negation of her rights and the ruin of her finances. Rome, in fact, enveloped in the pleasures and gorged with the spoils of the universe, is kept alive by victory and government; her luxury and her pleasures are the price of her conquests: she can neither abdicate nor dispossess herself." Thus Rome had the facts and the law on her side. Her pretensions were justified by universal custom and the law of nations. Her institutions were based upon idolatry in religion, slavery in the State, and epicurism in private life; to touch those was to shake society to its foundations, and to use our modern expression, to open the abyss of revolutions. So the idea occurred to no one; and yet humanity was dying in blood and luxury.

All at once a man appeared, calling himself *The Word of God.* It is not known to this day who he was, whence he came, nor what suggested to him his ideas. He went about proclaiming everywhere that the end of the existing society was at hand, that the world was about to experience a new birth; that the priests were vipers, the lawyers ignoramuses, and the philosophers hypocrites and liars; that master and slave were equals, that usury and every thing akin to it was robbery, that proprietors and idlers would one day burn, while the poor and pure in heart would find a haven of peace.

This man—*The Word of God*—was denounced and arrested as a public enemy by the priests and the lawyers, who well understood how to induce the people to demand his death. But this judicial murder, though it put the finishing stroke to their crimes, did not destroy the doctrinal seeds which *The Word of God* had sown. After his death, his original disciples travelled about in all directions, preaching what they called the *good news,* creating in their turn millions of missionaries; and, when their task seemed to be accomplished, dying by the sword of Roman justice. This persistent agitation, the war of the executioners and martyrs, lasted nearly three centuries, ending in the conversion of the world. Idolatry was destroyed, slavery abolished, dissolution made room for a more austere morality, and the contempt for wealth was sometimes pushed almost to privation. Society was saved by the negation of its own principles, by a revolution in its religion, and by violation of its most sacred rights. In this revolution, the idea of justice spread to an extent that had not before been dreamed of, never to return to its original limits. Heretofore justice had existed only for the masters;* it then commenced to exist for the slaves.

Nevertheless, the new religion at that time had borne by no means all its fruits. There was a perceptible improvement of the public morals, and a partial release from oppression; but, other than that, the *seeds sown by the Son of Man,* having fallen into idolatrous hearts, had produced nothing save innumerable discords and a quasi-poetical mythology. Instead of developing into their practical consequences the principles of morality and government taught by *The Word of God,* his followers busied themselves in speculations as to his birth, his origin, his person, and his actions; they discussed his parables, and from the conflict of the most extravagant opinions upon unanswerable questions

---

*Religion, laws, marriage, were the privileges of freemen, and, in the beginning, of nobles only. *Dii majorum gentium*—gods of the patrician families; *jus gentium*—right of nations; that is, of families or nobles. The slave and the plebeian had no families; their children were treated as the offspring of animals. *Beasts* they were born, *beasts* they must live. (*Note by Proudhon.*)

and texts which no one understood, was born *theology*, —which may be defined as the *science of the infinitely absurd*.

The truth of *Christianity* did not survive the age of the apostles; the *Gospel*, commented upon and symbolized by the Greeks and Latins, loaded with pagan fables, became literally a mass of contradictions; and to this day the reign of the *infallible Church* has been a long era of darkness. It is said that the *gates of hell* will not always prevail, that *The Word of God* will return, and that one day men will know truth and justice; but that will be the death of Greek and Roman Catholicism, just as in the light of science disappeared the caprices of opinion.

The monsters which the successors of the apostles were bent on destroying, frightened for a moment, reappeared gradually, thanks to the crazy fanaticism, and sometimes the deliberate connivance, of priests and theologians. The history of the enfranchisement of the French communes offers constantly the spectacle of the ideas of justice and liberty spreading among the people, in spite of the combined efforts of kings, nobles, and clergy. In the year 1789 of the Christian era, the French nation, divided by caste, poor and oppressed, struggled in the triple net of royal absolutism, the tyranny of nobles and parliaments, and priestly intolerance. There was the right of the king and the right of the priest, the right of the patrician and the right of the plebeian; there were the privileges of birth, province, communes, corporations, and trades; and, at the bottom of all, violence, immorality, and misery. For some time they talked of reformation; those who apparently desired it most favoring it only for their own profit, and the people who were to be the gainers expecting little and saying nothing. For a long time these poor people, either from distrust, incredulity, or despair, hesitated to ask for their rights: it is said that the habit of serving had taken the courage away from those old communes, which in the middle ages were so bold.

Finally a book appeared, summing up the whole matter in these two propositions: *What is the third estate?—Nothing. What ought it to be?—Every thing.* Some one added by way of comment: *What is the king?—The servant of the people.*

This was a sudden revelation: the veil was torn aside, a thick bandage fell from all eyes. The people commenced to reason thus:—

If the king is our servant, he ought to report to us;

If he ought to report to us, he is subject to control;

If he can be controlled, he is responsible;

If he is responsible, he is punishable;

If he is punishable, he ought to be punished according to his merits;

If he ought to be punished according to his merits, he can be punished with death.

Five years after the publication of the *brochure* of Sieyès, the third estate was every thing; the king, the nobility, the clergy, were no more. In 1793, the nation, without stopping at the constitutional fiction of the inviolability of the sovereign, conducted Louis XVI. to the scaffold; in 1830, it accompanied Charles X. to Cherbourg. In each case, it may have erred, in fact, in its judgment of the offence; but, in right, the logic which led to its action was irreproachable. The people, in punishing their sovereign, did precisely that which the government of July was so severely censured for failing to do when it refused to execute Louis Bonaparte after the affair of Strasburg: they struck the true culprit. It was an application of the common law, a solemn decree of justice enforcing the penal laws.*

The spirit which gave rise to the movement of '89 was a spirit of negation; that, of itself, proves that the order of things which was substituted for the old system was not methodical or well-considered; that, born of anger and hatred, it could not have the effect of a science based on observation and study; that its foundations, in a word, were not derived from a profound knowledge of the laws of Nature and society. Thus the people found that the republic, among the so-called new institutions, was acting on the very principles against which they had fought, and was swayed by all the prejudices which they had intended to destroy. We congratulate ourselves, with inconsiderate enthusiasm, on the glorious French Revolution, the regeneration of 1789, the great changes that have been effected, and the reversion of institutions: a delusion, a delusion!

When our ideas on any subject, material, intellectual, or social, undergo a thorough change in consequence of new observations, I call that movement of the mind *revolution*. If the ideas are simply extended or modified, there is only *progress*. Thus the system of Ptolemy was a step in astronomical progress, that of Copernicus was a revolution. So, in 1789, there was struggle and progress; revolution there was none. An examination of the reforms which were attempted proves this.

The nation, so long a victim of monarchical selfishness, thought to deliver itself for ever by declaring that it alone was sovereign. But what was monarchy? The sovereignty of one man. What is democracy? The sovereignty of the nation, or, rather, of the national majority. But it is, in both cases, the sovereignty of man instead of the sovereignty of the law, the sovereignty of the will instead of the sovereignty of the reason;

---

*If the chief of the executive power is responsible, so must the deputies be also. It is astonishing that this idea has never occurred to any one; it might be made the subject of an interesting essay. But I declare that I would not, for all the world, maintain it; the people are yet much too logical for me to furnish them with arguments. (*Note by Proudhon.*)

in one word, the passions instead of justice. Undoubtedly, when a nation passes from the monarchical to the democratic state, there is progress, because in multiplying the sovereigns we increase the opportunities of the reason to substitute itself for the will; but in reality there is no revolution in the government, since the principle remains the same. Now, we have the proof to-day that, with the most perfect democracy, we cannot be free.*

Nor is that all. The nation-king cannot exercise its sovereignty itself; it is obliged to delegate it to agents: this is constantly reiterated by those who seek to win its favor. Be these agents five, ten, one hundred, or a thousand, of what consequence is the number; and what matters the name? It is always the government of man, the rule of will and caprice. I ask what this pretended revolution has revolutionized?

We know, too, how this sovereignty was exercised; first by the Convention, then by the Directory, afterwards confiscated by the Consul. As for the Emperor, the strong man so much adored and mourned by the nation, he never wanted to be dependent on it; but, as if intending to set its sovereignty at defiance, he dared to demand its suffrage: that is, its abdication, the abdication of this inalienable sovereignty; and he obtained it.

But what is sovereignty? It is, they say, the *power to make laws.*** Another absurdity, a relic of despotism. The nation had long seen kings issuing their commands in this form: *for such is our pleasure;* it wished to taste in its turn the pleasure of making laws. For fifty years it has brought them forth by myriads; always, be it understood, through the agency of representatives. The play is far from ended.

The definition of sovereignty was derived from the definition of the law. The law, they said, is *the expression of the will of the sovereign:* then, under a monarchy, the law is the expression of the will of the king; in a republic, the law is the expression of the will of the people. Aside from the difference in the number of wills, the two systems are exactly identical: both share the same error, namely, that the law is the expression of a will; it ought to be the expression of a fact. Moreover they followed good leaders: they took the citizen of Geneva for their prophet, and the *contrat social* for their Koran.

Bias and prejudice are apparent in all the phrases of the new legisla-

---

*See De Tocqueville, "Democracy in the United States;" and Michel Chevalier, "Letters on North America." Plutarch tells us, "Life of Pericles," that in Athens honest people were obliged to conceal themselves while studying, fearing they would be regarded as aspirants for office. (*Note by Proudhon.*)

**"Sovereignty," according to Toullier, "is human omnipotence." A materialistic definition: if sovereignty is any thing, it is a *right,* not a *force* or a *faculty.* And what is human omnipotence? (*Note by Proudhon.*)

tors. The nation had suffered from a multitude of exclusions and privileges; its representatives issued the following declaration: *All men are equal by nature and before the law*; an ambiguous and redundant declaration. *Men are equal by nature*: does that mean that they are equal in size, beauty, talents, and virtue? No; they meant, then, political and civil equality. Then it would have been sufficient to have said: *All men are equal before the law.*

But what is equality before the law? Neither the constitution of 1790, nor that of '93, nor the granted charter, nor the accepted charter, have defined it accurately. All imply an inequality in fortune and station incompatible with even a shadow of equality in rights. In this respect it may be said that all our constitutions have been faithful expressions of the popular will: I am going to prove it.

Formerly the people were excluded from civil and military offices; it was considered a wonder when the following high-sounding article was inserted in the Declaration of Rights: "All citizens are equally eligible to office; free nations know no qualifications in their choice of officers save virtues and talents."

They certainly ought to have admired so beautiful an idea: they admired a piece of nonsense. Why! the sovereign people, legislators, and reformers, see in public offices, to speak plainly, only opportunities for pecuniary advancement. And, because it regards them as a source of profit, it decrees the eligibility of citizens. For of what use would this precaution be, if there were nothing to gain by it? No one would think of ordaining that none but astronomers and geographers should be pilots, nor of prohibiting stutterers from acting at the theatre and the opera. The nation was still aping the kings: like them it wished to award the lucrative positions to its friends and flatterers. Unfortunately, and this last feature completes the resemblance, the nation did not control the list of livings; that was in the hands of its agents and representatives. They, on the other hand, took care not to thwart the will of their gracious sovereign.

This edifying article of the Declaration of Rights, retained in the charters of 1814 and 1830, implies several kinds of civil inequality; that is, of inequality before the law: inequality of station, since the public functions are sought only for the consideration and emoluments which they bring; inequality of wealth, since, if it had been desired to equalize fortunes, public service would have been regarded as a duty, not as a reward; inequality of privilege, the law not stating what it means by *talents* and *virtues*. Under the empire, virtue and talent consisted simply in military bravery and devotion to the emperor; that was shown when Napoleon created his nobility, and attempted to connect it with the ancients. To-day, the man who pays taxes to the amount of two hundred francs is virtuous; the talented man is the honest pickpocket: such truths as these are accounted trivial.

The people finally legalized property. God forgive them, for they knew not what they did! For fifty years they have suffered for their miserable folly. But how came the people, whose voice, they tell us, is the voice of God, and whose conscience is infallible,—how came the people to err? How happens it that, when seeking liberty and equality, they fell back into privilege and slavery? Always through copying the ancient *régime.*

Formerly, the nobility and the clergy contributed towards the expenses of the State only by voluntary aid and gratuitous gift; their property could not be seized even for debt,—while the plebeian, overwhelmed by taxes and statute-labor, was continually tormented, now by the king's tax-gatherers, now by those of the nobles and clergy. He whose possessions were subject to mortmain could neither bequeath nor inherit property; he was treated like the animals, whose services and offspring belong to their master by right of accession. The people wanted the conditions of *ownership* to be alike for all; they thought that every one should *enjoy and freely dispose of his possessions, his income, and the fruit of his labor and industry.* The people did not invent property; but as they had not the same privileges in regard to it, which the nobles and clergy possessed, they decreed that the right should be exercised by all under the same conditions. The more obnoxious forms of property—statute-labor, mortmain, *maîtrise,* and exclusion from public office—have disappeared; the conditions of its enjoyment have been modified: the principle still remains the same. There has been progress in the regulation of the right; there has been no revolution.

These, then, are the three fundamental principles of modern society, established one after another by the movements of 1789 and 1830: 1. *Sovereignty of the human will*; in short, *despotism.* 2. *Inequality of wealth and rank.* 3. *Property*—above JUSTICE, always invoked as the guardian angel of sovereigns, nobles, and proprietors; JUSTICE, the general, primitive, categorical law of all society.

We must ascertain whether the ideas of *despotism, civil inequality,* and *property,* are in harmony with the primitive notion of *justice,* and necessarily follow from it,—assuming various forms according to the condition, position, and relation of persons; or whether they are not rather the illegitimate result of a confusion of different things, a fatal association of ideas. And since justice deals especially with the questions of government, the condition of persons, and the possession of things, we must ascertain under what conditions, judging by universal opinion and the progress of the human mind, government is just, the condition of citizens is just, and the possession of things is just; then, striking out every thing which fails to meet these conditions, the result will at once tell us what legitimate government is, what the legitimate condition of citizens is, and what the legitimate possession of things is; and finally, as the last result of the analysis, what *justice* is.

Is the authority of man over man just?

Everybody answers, "No; the authority of man is only the authority of the law, which ought to be justice and truth." The private will counts for nothing in government, which consists, first, in discovering truth and justice in order to make the law; and, second, in superintending the execution of this law. I do not now inquire whether our constitutional form of government satisfies these conditions; whether, for example, the will of the ministry never influences the declaration and interpretation of the law; or whether our deputies, in their debates, are more intent on conquering by argument than by force of numbers: it is enough for me that my definition of a good government is allowed to be correct. This idea is exact. Yet we see that nothing seems more just to the Oriental nations than the despotism of their sovereigns; that, with the ancients and in the opinion of the philosophers themselves, slavery was just; that in the middle ages the nobles, the priests, and the bishops felt justified in holding slaves; that Louis XIV. thought that he was right when he said, "The State! I am the State;" and that Napoleon deemed it a crime for the State to oppose his will. The idea of justice, then, applied to sovereignty and government, has not always been what it is to-day; it has gone on developing and shaping itself by degrees, until it has arrived at its present state. But has it reached its last phase? I think not: only, as the last obstacle to be overcome arises from the institution of property which we have kept intact, in order to finish the reform in government and consummate the revolution, this very institution we must attack.

Is political and civil inequality just?

Some say yes; others no. To the first I would reply that, when the people abolished all privileges of birth and caste, they did it, in all probability, because it was for their advantage; why then do they favor the privileges of fortune more than those of rank and race? Because, say they, political inequality is a result of property; and without property society is impossible: thus the question just raised becomes a question of property. To the second I content myself with this remark: If you wish to enjoy political equality, abolish property; otherwise, why do you complain?

Is property just?

Everybody answers without hesitation, "Yes, property is just." I say everybody, for up to the present time no one who thoroughly understood the meaning of his words has answered no. For it is no easy thing to reply understandingly to such a question; only time and experience can furnish an answer. Now, this answer is given; it is for us to understand it. I undertake to prove it.

We are to proceed with the demonstration in the following order:—

I. We dispute not at all, we refute nobody, we deny nothing; we accept as sound all the arguments alleged in favor of property, and confine ourselves to a search for its principle, in order that we may then ascertain whether this principle is faithfully expressed by property. In fact, property being defensible on no ground save that of justice, the idea, or at least the intention, of justice must of necessity underlie all the arguments that have been made in defence of property; and, as on the other hand the right of property is only exercised over those things which can be appreciated by the senses, justice, secretly objectifying itself, so to speak, must take the shape of an algebraic formula. By this method of investigation, we soon see that every argument which has been invented in behalf of property, *whatever it may be*, always and of necessity leads to equality; that is, to the negation of property.

The first part covers two chapters: one treating of occupation, the foundation of our right; the other, of labor and talent, considered as causes of property and social inequality.

The first of these chapters will prove that the right of occupation *obstructs* property; the second that the right of labor *destroys* it.

II. Property, then, being of necessity conceived as existing only in connection with equality, it remains to find out why, in spite of this necessity of logic, equality does not exist. This new investigation also covers two chapters: in the first, considering the fact of property in itself, we inquire whether this fact is real, whether it exists, whether it is possible; for it would imply a contradiction, were these two opposite forms of society, equality and inequality, both possible. Then we discover, singularly enough, that property may indeed manifest itself accidentally; but that, as an institution and principle, it is mathematically impossible. So that the axiom of the school—*ab actu ad posse valet consecutio:* from the actual to the possible the inference is good—is given the lie as far as property is concerned.

Finally, in the last chapter, calling psychology to our aid, and probing man's nature to the bottom, we shall disclose the principle of *justice*—its formula and character; we shall state with precision the organic law of society; we shall explain the origin of property, the causes of its establishment, its long life, and its approaching death; we shall definitively establish its identity with robbery. And, after having shown that these three prejudices—*the sovereignty of man, the inequality of conditions, and property*—are one and the same; that they may be taken for each other, and are reciprocally convertible,—we shall have no trouble in inferring therefrom, by the principle of contradiction, the basis of government and right. There our investigations will end, reserving the right to continue them in future works.

The importance of the subject which engages our attention is recognized by all minds.

"Property," says M. Hennequin, "is the creative and conservative principle of civil society. Property is one of those basic institutions, new theories concerning which cannot be presented too soon; for it must not be forgotten, and the publicist and statesman must know, that on the answer to the question whether property is the principle or the result of social order, whether it is to be considered as a cause or an effect, depends all morality, and, consequently, all the authority of human institutions."

These words are a challenge to all men of hope and faith; but, although the cause of equality is a noble one, no one has yet picked up the gauntlet thrown down by the advocates of property; no one has been courageous enough to enter upon the struggle. The spurious learning of haughty jurisprudence, and the absurd aphorisms of a political economy controlled by property have puzzled the most generous minds; it is a sort of password among the most influential friends of liberty and the interests of the people that *equality is a chimera!* So many false theories and meaningless analogies influence minds otherwise keen, but which are unconsciously controlled by popular prejudice. Equality advances every day—*fit aequalitas.* Soldiers of liberty, shall we desert our flag in the hour of triumph?

A defender of equality, I shall speak without bitterness and without anger; with the independence becoming a philosopher, with the courage and firmness of a free man. May I, in this momentous struggle, carry into all hearts the light with which I am filled; and show, by the success of my argument, that equality failed to conquer by the sword only that it might conquer by the pen!

Karl Marx and Frederick Engels
The Manifesto of the Communist Party
1848

"This pamphlet," wrote the Russian revolutionary Leon Trotsky in 1937, "displaying greater genius than any other in world literature, astounds us even today by its freshness. Its most important sections appear to have been written yesterday. Assuredly, the young authors (Marx was 29, Engels 27) were able to look further into the future than anyone before them, and perhaps than anyone since them."[1]

The historian R. W. Postgate notes that *"The Communist Manifesto* not only changed an incoherent movement—a movement with a program whose inadequacy it uneasily felt—into a movement with a program which was a perfect instrument: not only did it turn Socialism for ever from the paths of secret conspiracy into those of open propaganda; it gave to it its place in history. . . . It showed the bourgeoisie to be, not an aggregation of monsters, but a class produced by historical necessity and doomed in time to make way for the proletariat; it showed capitalism, not as the reign of Anti-Christ, but as the loosening of gigantic forces which would in time lead to Communism."[2] The Communist Federation, an organization that Marx (1818–1883) and Engels (1820–1895) joined in 1847, approved and published the document in early 1848, shortly before various revolutions coincidentally broke out across Europe.

The Introduction by R. W. Postgate was written in 1920 and provides vital historical context.

Source: R. W. Postgate, ed., *Revolution from 1789 to 1906* (London: Grant Richards, 1920), 139–163.

1. Leon Trotsky, "The Communist Manifesto Today." Introduction to Karl Marx and Frederick Engels, *The Communist Manifesto* (New York: Pathfinder Press, 1970), 3.
2. R. W. Postgate, ed., *Revolution from 1789 to 1906* (London: Grant Richards, 1920), 139.

Introduction

R. W. Postgate

It would be an impertinence upon my part to venture to criticise or elucidate the document which follows. Yet, while the argument of the Manifesto may be left to explain itself, it will not be superfluous to explain its historical importance.

Marx was a leader of the greatest weight in the German Communist movement, but in that movement alone. He had only very indirect influence in the Chartist movement and none at all in France. Hence, in the latter country, where Socialism alone came out into the daylight, the influence of this document was small. And since France was the pivot of the whole Revolution, it might be thought that this document was unimportant.

However, with the first conscious proletarian movement it is fitting that there should be classed the first definite formulation of its aims and meaning. Hitherto, Communists had had little grasp of social evolution as applied to their movement. All opposition to Socialism was "wicked" and "sinful," it was the evil principle fighting against the light. Socialism was a thing devoid of preconditions: a universal formula to cure any society, whose application was only delayed by ignorance and wicked men. "We have but to will it," said Maréchal, grandly. It was the old fight between virtue and vice. And if the appeal to reason failed—as it always did—what then? Why, nothing was left but violence: conspiracy, assassination, revolts: continual and incessant attempts at revolution, and, at all costs, no peace and quiet for the oppressor.

The Communist Manifesto not only changed an incoherent movement—a movement with a programme whose inadequacy it uneasily felt—into a movement with a programme which was a perfect instrument: not only did it turn Socialism for ever from the paths of secret conspiracy into those of open propaganda; it gave to it its place in history. It destroyed the old "moral" divisions of parties in favour of a new and truer historical appreciation of them. It showed the bourgeoisie to be, not an aggregation of monsters, but a class produced by historical necessity and doomed in time to make way for the proletariat; it showed capitalism, not as the reign of Anti-Christ, but as the loosening of gigantic forces which would in time lead to Communism. By this it destroyed for ever the occupation of the founders of Utopias and made Socialism a thing of world import and not, as Blanqui puts it, "an egg hatched in an obscure corner of the earth." It also gave Communism a dignity it had not had before and brought it into the open, freed it from the tradition of secret societies, conspiracy and incessant violence. Not, indeed, that Marx opposed a Revolution of force. But now the Communists had their eyes open: they could see the signs of the times, and could afford to wait and pick their time: nor had they any excuse for believing that forty-eight hours of insurrection would at once make the whole world Socialist.

This manifesto was issued by the organisation commonly known as the Federation of the Just. This secret society, German in origin, was a section—in fact, if not in theory, the German section—of Barbès' and Blanqui's Society of the Seasons. This was one of Blanqui's many organisations to undermine the monarchy of Louis Philippe. It perished in a futile attempt at insurrection in Paris in May, 1839. With it was shattered the Federation of the Just. Two groups of refugees only remained, in London and in Switzerland. Both were under the influence of Weitling, but the London group gradually, from 1843 onwards, had its theories shattered by contact with Marx and Engels. Weitling, after vainly attempting to purify his party, went to America and left the Federation to Marx's mercy. Marx and Engels joined it in 1847, and a preliminary congress held in the summer of that year instructed them to produce a programme to supplant Weitling's mixture of Babouvism and Fourierism. The name of the Society was changed to the "Communist Federation," and secrecy was as far as possible abandoned. A second congress met in November and December, 1847, which, after a ten-days' discussion, approved the report, which was published as the Communist Manifesto. Almost immediately the revolution of 1848 broke out.

Manifesto of the Communist Party

A spectre is haunting Europe—the spectre of Communism. All the powers of old Europe have united in a holy alliance to exorcise this spectre. The Pope and the Czar, Metternich, and Guizot, the radicals of France, and the police-spies of Germany.

Where is the opposition party that has not been accused of Communism by its opponents in power? Where is the opposition party that has not, in its turn, hurled back at its adversaries, progressive or reactionary, the branding epithet of Communism?

Two things result from these facts:

Communism is now recognised by all European Powers to be itself a power.

It is high time that Communists should lay before the whole world their point of view, their aims and their tendencies, and set against this fable of the spectre of Communism a Manifesto of the Party itself.

To this end the Communists of different nationalities have assembled in London and formulated the following Manifesto, which will be published in English, French, German, Italian, Flemish, and Danish.

I. BOURGEOIS AND PROLETARIANS.

The history of all hitherto existing society is the history of class struggles.

Freeman and slave, patrician and plebeian, baron and serf, guild-master and journeyman, in one word, oppressor and oppressed, standing constantly in opposition to each other, carried on an uninterrupted warfare, now open, now concealed; a warfare which always ended either in a revolutionary transformation of the whole of society or in the common ruin of the contending classes.

In early historic epochs we find almost everywhere a complete organisation of society into various degrees, a manifold gradation of social rank. In ancient Rome we find patricians, knights, plebeians, slaves; in the Middle Ages, feudal lords, vassals, guildmasters, apprentices, and serfs, and within almost all of these classes again further divisions.

Modern bourgeois society, springing from the wreck of feudal society, had not abolished class antagonisms. It has but substituted new classes, new conditions of oppression, new forms of warfare, for the old.

Our epoch, the epoch of the bourgeoisie, possesses, however, the distinctive characteristic that it has simplified class antagonisms. All society is more and more splitting up into two opposing camps, into two great hostile classes: the bourgeoisie and the proletariat.

From the serfs of the Middle Ages sprang the chartered burghers of the first towns; from these burghers evolved the first elements of the bourgeoisie.

The discovery of America, the rounding of the Cape, opened up a new field of action for the rising bourgeoisie. The East Indian and Chinese markets, the colonisation of America, colonial trade, the increase of the means of exchange and of wealth in general, gave an impulse, unknown before, to commerce, navigation and industry, and therewith a rapid development to the revolutionary element in the decaying feudal society.

The former feudal system of industry could no longer satisfy the growing needs which arose with the opening up of new markets. The manufacturing system took its place. The guildmasters were displaced by the industrial middle class. Division of labour among the different corporate guilds disappeared before division of labour in each single workshop.

But markets ever expanded and the demand ever increased. Even manufacture no longer sufficed. Then steam and machinery revolutionised industrial production. The place of manufacture was taken by gigantic Modern Industry, and the place of the industrial middle class was taken by the industrial millionaires, the leaders of whole armies of industrial workers, the modern bourgeoisie.

Modern Industry has established that world-market for which the discovery of America prepared the way. The world-market has given an immense development to commerce, to navigation, and to communication by land. This development reacted in its turn on the expansion of industry, and in proportion as industry, commerce, navigation, and railways extended, in the same proportion the bourgeoisie developed, multiplied its capital, and thrust into the background all classes transmitted from the Middle Ages.

We see, therefore, how the modern bourgeoisie is itself the product of a long course of development, of a series of revolutions in the methods of production and exchange.

Each step in the evolution of the bourgeoisie was accompanied by a corresponding political progress. An oppressed class under the rule of the feudal lords, an armed and self-governing association in the mediæval commune, here an independent urban republic, there a *Third Estate* taxable by the monarchy, afterwards in the manufacturing period serving either the semifeudal or absolute monarchy as a counterpoise against the nobility, everywhere acting as the corner-stone of the great monarchies—the bourgeoisie, since the establishment of modern industry and the world-market, has at last conquered exclusive political power in the modern representative State. The modern State is but an executive committee for administering the affairs of the whole bourgeois class.

The bourgeoisie has played in history a most revolutionary part.

The bourgeoisie, wherever it has conquered power, has destroyed all feudal, patriarchal, and idyllic relations. It has pitilessly torn asunder all the many-coloured feudal bonds which united men to their "natural superiors," and has left no other tie twixt man and man but naked self-interest and callous cash payment. It has drowned religious ecstasy, chivalrous enthusiasm, and middle class sentimentality in the ice-cold water of egotistical calculation. It has transformed personal worth into mere exchange value, and substituted for countless dearly-bought chartered freedoms the one and only unconscionable freedom of Free Trade. It has, in one word, replaced an exploitation veiled by religious and political illusions by exploitation open, unashamed, direct, and brutal.

The bourgeoisie has stripped of its halo every profession previously venerated and regarded as honourable. It has turned doctor, lawyer, priest, poet, and philosopher into its paid wage-workers.

The bourgeoisie has torn away the veil of sentiment from the family relation, and reduced it to a mere money relation.

The bourgeoisie has shown how the brutal manifestation of force, which the reactionaries admire so much in the Middle Ages, found its fitting complement in the most slothful indolence. It has been the first to show what human activity can accomplish. It has created very different marvels from the Egyptian pyramids, Roman aqueducts, and Gothic cathedrals; it has conducted very different expeditions from the ancient migrations and Crusades.

The bourgeoisie cannot exist without incessantly revolutionising the instruments of production, and thereby the methods of production, and consequently all social relations. The preservation of the old methods of production was, on the contrary, the first condition of existence for all previous industrial classes. This continual revolutionising of the methods of production, constant disturbance of the whole social system, perpetual agitation and uncertainty, distinguish the bourgeois epoch from all others. All fixed and deeply rooted social relations, with their train of established and venerated beliefs and ideas, are dissolved; all that replaces them grows old before it can crystallise. All that was solid and established crumbles away, all that was holy is profaned, and man is at last compelled to look with open eyes upon his conditions of life and true social relations.

The need of a constantly expanding market for its products chases the bourgeoisie over the whole globe: Everywhere it must make its nest, everywhere settle, and everywhere establish its connections.

The bourgeoisie has, by the exploitation of the world-market, given a cosmopolitan character to the production and consumption of all countries. It has, to the despair of reactionaries, cut from under the feet of industry its national basis. Old established national industries have been destroyed, and are daily being destroyed. They are dislodged by new industries; whose introduction becomes a vital question for all civilised nations; by industries which no longer use native raw material, but raw material brought from the furthest zone, and whose products are consumed not only in their own countries, but in every quarter of the globe. Instead of the old wants, satisfied by the products of the country, new wants arise, demanding for their satisfaction the products of the most distant lands and climes. Instead of the old local and national isolation and self-sufficiency, universal trade has developed and the interdependence of nations. And as in material, so also in intellectual production. The intellectual productions of one nation become the common property of all. National narrowness and exclusiveness become daily more and more impossible, and out of the many national and local literatures a world literature arises.

The bourgeoisie, by the rapid improvement of all the instruments of production, and by constantly facilitating communication, draws into civilisation even the most barbarian nations. The cheapness of its commodities is the heavy artillery with which it lays low all Chinese walls, with which it compels the most obstinately hostile barbarians to capitulate. It forces all nations, on pain of extinction, to adopt the bourgeois mode of production; it forces them to adopt so-called civilisation, *i.e.*, to become bourgeois. In one word, it creates a world after its own image.

The bourgeoisie has subjected the country to the rule of the town. It has created enormous cities; it has prodigiously augmented the numbers in the towns as compared with the rural districts, and thus has rescued a great part of the population from the idiocy of country life. Just as it has made the country dependent on the town, so has it made barbaric, or semi-barbaric countries dependent on civilised countries, nations of peasants on bourgeois nations, the Orient on the Occident.

The bourgeoisie ever more and more arrests the dispersion of the means of production, property, and population. It has agglomerated population, centralised the means of production, and concentrated property in the hands of a few. The necessary consequence of this was political centralisation. Independent, or loosely connected provinces having separate interests, laws, governments, and tariffs, were lumped together into a single nation, with one government, one constitution, one national class interest, one customs-tariff.

The bourgeoisie, during its class rule of scarce one hundred years, has created more powerful and colossal productive forces than all past generations together. Subjection of the forces of nature, machinery, application of chemistry to industry and agriculture, steamships, railways, electric telegraphs, clearing of whole continents for cultivation, canalisation of rivers, whole populations conjured out of the ground—what previous century even suspected that such productive forces slumbered in the lap of social labour?

Thus have we seen the means of production and exchange, on whose basis the bourgeoisie built itself up, were generated in feudal society. At a certain stage of the development of these means of production and exchange, the conditions under which feudal society produced and exchanged, feudal organisation of agriculture and manufacture, in one word, feudal property relations, become no longer compatible with the already developed productive forces. They hampered production instead of aiding it. They became so many fetters. They had to be burst asunder; they were burst asunder.

Into their place stepped free competition with its corresponding social and political constitution, with the economic and political rule of the bourgeois class.

Under our own eyes a similar movement is going on. Bourgeois conditions of production and exchange, bourgeois property relations, modern bourgeois society which has conjured up such gigantic means of production and exchange, is like a magician who is no longer able to control the infernal powers he has evoked. For many years the history of industry and commerce has been but the history of the revolt of modern productive forces against modern conditions of production, against the property relations which are the conditions of life for the bourgeoisie and its rule. It is enough to mention the commercial crises which, in their periodical recurrence, bring into question, each time more threateningly, the existence of the whole of bourgeois society. In these crises a great part, not only of existing products, but also of previously created productive forces, are periodically destroyed. In these crises a social epidemic breaks out, which would have seemed an absurdity in all previous epochs—the epidemic of over-production. Society finds itself suddenly thrown back into a state of momentary barbarism; a famine, a universal war of devastation, seems to have cut off the supply of all means of life. Industry and commerce seem to be destroyed—and why? Because there is too much civilisation, too much of the means of life, too much industry, too much commerce. The productive forces at the disposal of society are no longer favourable to the development of bourgeois property conditions; on the contrary, they have become too powerful for these conditions, by which they are fettered; and so soon as they free themselves from these fetters they bring disorder into the whole of bourgeois society, they endanger the existence of bourgeois property. The bourgeois system has become too narrow to contain the wealth which it creates. How does the bourgeoisie overcome these crises? On the one hand, by compelling the destruction of a mass of productive forces; on the other hand, by the conquest of new markets and the more thorough exploitation of the old markets. And with what result? With the result that they pave the way for more widespread and more destructive crises, and at the same time diminish the means whereby those crises can be avoided.

The weapons with which the bourgeoisie conquered feudalism are now turned against the bourgeoisie itself.

But the bourgeoisie has not only forged the weapons that bring death to itself; it has also produced the men who will wield these weapons—the modern workers, the PROLETARIANS.

In proportion as the bourgeoisie, *i.e.*, capital, is developed, in the same proportion is developed the Proletariat, the class of modern workers, who live only so long as they find work, and who only find work so long as their work increases capital. These workers, forced to sell themselves piecemeal, are a commodity like every other article of commerce, and are consequently exposed to all the vicissitudes of competition, and all the fluctuations of the market.

The work of the Proletariat has been deprived of its individual character by the extended use of machinery and the division of labour, and therewith all its attraction for the worker has been lost. He becomes a mere appendage of the machine, of whom only the simplest, most monotonous and easily learned operations are required. The cost of production of the worker is in consequence reduced almost entirely to the means of subsistence that he requires for his maintenance and for the propagation of his race. Now the price of a commodity, and therefore of labour, is equal to the cost of its production. In proportion therefore as the repulsiveness of the labour increases the wage decreases. Furthermore, in proportion as the use of machinery and division of labour increase, in the same proportion does the burden of labour increase, either by prolongation of the working hours, by increase of the work exacted in a given time, or by the increased speed of the machine, etc.

Modern industry has converted the little workshop of the patriarchal master into the great factory of the industrial capitalist. Masses of workers, crowded together in the factories, are organised like soldiers. Like soldiers of industry, they are placed under the command of a perfect hierarchy of subalterns and officers. They are not only the slaves of the bourgeois class, the bourgeois State, they are daily and hourly enslaved by the individual bourgeois manufacturer himself. The more openly this despotism proclaims gain to be its object, the more petty, hateful, and galling it becomes.

The less dexterity and strength are required in manual labour, i.e., the more modern industry develops, the more is the labour of men displaced by that of women. The differences of age and sex have no longer any social importance for the working class. All are now mere instruments of labour, whose price varies according to age and sex.

No sooner is the exploitation of the worker by the employer so far at an end that he receives his bare money-wage, then he is set upon by other sections of the bourgeoisie, the landlord, the shopkeeper, the pawnbroker, etc.

The little middle class, the small shopkeepers, trades-people, peasant proprietors, handicraftsmen and peasants, all these classes sink into the proletariat, partly because their small capital is not sufficient for modern industry and is crushed out in the competition with the large capitalists, and partly because their specialised skill is depreciated by the new methods of production. Thus is the proletariat recruited from all classes of the population.

The proletariat goes through various evolutionary stages. Its struggle against the bourgeoisie begins with its birth.

At first it is a struggle of individual workers; then of the workers in one factory; then of the workers of the same trade in one locality against the capitalist who directly exploits them. They do not direct their attacks against the bourgeois mode of production, they direct them against the instruments of production themselves; they destroy foreign competing wares, they break the machines, set fire to factories; they seek to restore by force the lost position of the worker of the Middle Ages.

At this stage the workers form an incoherent mass scattered over the whole country and disunited by competition. When they unite to form more compact bodies it is not as yet the result of their own union, but of the union of the bourgeoisie, which to gain its own political ends must set in motion the entire proletariat, and is yet, for a time, able to do so. At this stage the proletariat does not fight its own enemies, but the enemies of its enemies, the remnants of the absolute monarchy, the landowners, the non-industrial and petty-bourgeoisie. The whole historical movement is thus concentrated in the hands of the bourgeoisie, every victory so obtained is a victory for the bourgeoisie.

But with the development of industry the proletariat not only increases in number; it is concentrated in larger masses, its strength grows and it feels that strength more. The interests, the life conditions within the proletariat, become always more equalised as machinery more and more obliterates all distinctions of labour and reduces wages almost everywhere to the same low level. With the growing competition among capitalists, and the consequent commercial crises, the workers' wages fluctuate more and more. The unceasing improvement of machinery, ever more rapidly developing, makes their whole livelihood increasingly insecure; the collisions between the individual workers and the individual bourgeois take more and more the character of collisions between two classes. The workers begin thereupon to form combinations against the bourgeoisie; they combine together to keep up the rate of wages. They form themselves into permanent associations to provide beforehand for the occasional struggles. Here and there the struggle breaks out into revolt.

From time to time the workers are victorious, but only for a time. The real fruit of their struggle lies not in the immediate result, but in the always growing unity of the workers. This is aided by the improved means of communication which are created by modern industry, and which bring the workers of different localities into contact with one another. This was just the contact required to centralise the numerous local struggles, all of the same character, into a national, into a class struggle. Now every class struggle is a political struggle. And the union, which it took centuries for the burghers of the Middle Ages with their wretched highways, to establish, the modern proletariat achieves by means of railways in a few years.

This organisation of the proletarians into a class, and, consequently, into a political party, is continually hampered by the competition among the workers themselves. But it always arises again, stronger, firmer, mightier. It compels legislative recognition of particular working class interests by profiting by the divisions within the bourgeoisie itself. For instance, the Ten Hours' Bill in England.

The collisions between the classes of the old society further in many ways the development of the proletariat. The bourgeoisie finds itself in a perpetual state of warfare: at first with the aristocracy; later with those sections of the bourgeoisie itself whose interests have become antagonistic to the progress of industry; at all times with the bourgeoisie of foreign countries. In all these battles it finds itself compelled to appeal to the proletariat, to call for its aid, and thus to draw it into the political arena. It thus provides the proletariat with the elements of social education, *i.e.*, with the weapons to be used against the bourgeoisie itself.

Furthermore, as we have seen, by the advance of industry whole sections of the ruling class are precipitated into the ranks of the proletariat, or their livelihood is at least threatened. They also supply the proletariat with numerous elements of progress.

Finally, at the moment when the class struggle approaches the decisive hour, the process of dissolution within the ruling class, within the whole of society in fact, takes a character so violent and glaring, that a small part of the ruling class cuts itself off and joins the revolutionary class, the class which holds the future in its hands. Just as formerly, a portion of the nobility went over to the bourgeoisie, so now a portion of the bourgeoisie goes over to the proletariat, and particularly that portion of the bourgeois ideologists who have reached a theoretical understanding of the whole historical movement.

Of all the classes which stand at present in opposition to the bourgeoisie the proletariat alone is a truly revolutionary class. The other classes decay and go under before modern industry; the proletariat is its special and direct product.

The lower middle class, the small manufacturer, the small shopkeeper, the peasant proprietor, all struggle against the bourgeoisie to save from extinction their position as sections of the middle class. They are therefore not revolutionary, but conservative. And what is more, they are reactionary, because they try to turn back the wheel of history. Should they ever be revolutionary, they are so from fear of being forced down into the ranks of the proletariat, thus defending not their present but their future interests, and thus abandoning their own standpoint to adopt that of the proletariat.

The slum population, that passively putrifying scum of the lowest layers of past society, is sometimes set in movement by a proletarian revolution, but its whole conditions of life prepare it rather to sell itself to the reactionary forces.

The social conditions of past society are already swamped in the social conditions of the proletariat. The proletarian is propertiless; his relations to wife and children have nothing now in common with bourgeois family relations; modern industrial labour, modern enslavement by capital, the same in England as in France, in America as in Germany, has despoiled him of all national character. Law, morality, religion, are for him merely so many bourgeois prejudices, behind which as many bourgeois interests are concealed.

All previous classes that have conquered power tried to consolidate their acquired position by subjecting the whole of society to their own mode of appropriation. The proletarians cannot become masters of the productive forces of society without abolishing their own previous mode of appropriation, and with it every other previous mode of production. The proletarians have nothing of their own to secure. They must destroy all previous securities for, and insurances of, individual property.

All previous historical movements were movements of minorities, or in the interest of minorities. The proletarian movement is the conscious movement of the immense majority in the interest of the immense majority. The proletariat, the lowest stratum of existing society cannot stir, cannot raise itself up without the whole of the higher strata forming official society being sprung into the air.

Though not the substance, yet the form of the struggle of the proletariat against the bourgeoisie, is national at first. The proletariat of each country naturally must first settle accounts with its own bourgeoisie.

In sketching the most general phases of the development of the proletariat, we have depicted the more or less concealed civil war within existing society up to the point where it breaks out into open revolution, and where the violent overthrow of the bourgeoisie lays the foundation of the rule of the proletariat.

All previous forms of society were based, as we have seen, on the antagonism of the oppressing and oppressed classes. But in order to be able to oppress a class it is at least necessary to guarantee to it the conditions for continuing its slavish existence. The serf in feudal times raised himself to membership in the commune, just as the petty-bourgeois attained the position of a bourgeois under the yoke of feudal absolutism. The modern worker, on the contrary, instead of rising with the progress of industry, sinks ever deeper beneath the social conditions of his own class. The labourer becomes the pauper, and pauperism increases even more rapidly than population and wealth. It is thus clear that the bourgeoisie is unfit any longer to remain the ruling class in society, and to impose on society as a supreme law the social system of its class. It is unfit to rule because it is unable to assure existence in slavery to its slave, because it is forced to let him sink into a state in which it must feed him, instead of being fed by him. Society can exist under its rule no longer, *i.e.*, its existence is no longer compatible with that of society.

The essential condition for the existence and rule of the bourgeois class is the accumulation of wealth in private hands, the formation and increase of capital; the essential condition of capital is wage-labour. Wage-labour rests entirely on the competition among the workers. The progress of industry, of which the bourgeoisie is the involuntary and irresistible agent, replaces the isolation of the workers, due to competition, by their revolutionary union through association. With the development of modern industry, therefore, the very ground whereby it has established its system of production and appropriation is cut from under the feet of the bourgeoisie. It produces, above all, its own gravediggers. Its downfall and the victory of the proletariat are equally inevitable.

II. Proletarians and Communists.

In what relation do the Communists stand to the proletarians as a whole?

The Communists are no separate party distinct from other working-class parties.

They have no interests separate from the interests of the proletariat in general.

They set up no sectarian principles on which they wish to model the proletarian movement.

The Communists are only distinguished from other proletarian parties by this; that in the different national struggles of the proletarians they point out and bring to the fore the common interests of the proletariat independent of nationality; and, again, that in the different evolutionary stages which the struggle between the proletariat and the bourgeoisie must pass through, they represent always the interests of the movement as a whole.

Thus the Communists are, practically, the most progressive and resolute section of the working class of all countries; they have, theoretically, the advantage over the great mass of the proletariat of understanding the conditions and general results of the proletarian movement.

The immediate aim of the Communists is the same as that of all other proletarian parties: organisation of the proletariat on a class basis; overthrow of the supremacy of the bourgeois; conquest of political power by the proletariat.

The theoretical propositions of the Communists in no way rest upon ideas or principles invented or discovered by this or that universal reformer.

They are but the general expression of actual conditions of an existing class struggle, of a historical movement going on under our own eyes. The abolition of hitherto existing property relations is not a distinctive feature of Communism.

All property relations have undergone continual historic change corresponding to the change in historic social conditions.

The French Revolution, for example, abolished feudal property in favour of bourgeois property.

Thus the distinctive feature of Communism is not the abolition of property in general, but the abolition of bourgeois property.

But modern bourgeois private property is the final and most perfect expression of the system of producing and appropriating products based on class antagonism, on the exploitation of one by another.

In this sense the Communists can condense their theory into one sentence: abolition of private property.

We Communists have been reproached with wishing to abolish personal property acquired by labour; property which is alleged to be the foundation of all personal freedom, activity and independence.

Hard-won, self-earned, self-acquired property! Do you mean the property of the small tradesman and peasant, which preceded the bourgeois form of property? We have no need to abolish that; the development of industry has abolished, and is abolishing it daily.

Or do you mean modern bourgeois private property?

Does wage-labour, the labour of the proletarian, create any property for him? Not at all. It creates capital, *i.e.*, the property which exploits wage-labour, and which can increase only by producing a new supply of wage-labour for further exploitation. Property, in its present form, is based on the antagonism of capital and wage-labour. Let us examine both sides of that antagonism.

To be a capitalist is to have not only a merely personal, but a social position in production. Capital is a collective product, and can only be set in motion by the united action of many members of society, and even, in the last resort, by the united action of all its members.

Thus capital is not a personal, but a social power.

When, therefore, capital is converted into common property, belonging to all members of society, personal property is not thereby converted into social property. It is only the social character of the property that is changed. It loses its class character.

We come now to wage-labour.

The average price of wage-labour is the minimum wage, *i.e.*, the sum of the necessaries of life absolutely needful to keep the worker in life as a worker. Thus what the wage-earner appropriates by his labour is just so much as is necessary to assure to him a bare existence. We by no means wish to abolish this personal appropriation of the product of labour, an appropriation indispensable to the maintenance and reproduction of human life, an appropriation leaving no surplus which could give power over the labour of others. We wish only to suppress the miserable character of this appropriation, by which the worker only lives in order to increase capital, and only lives so long as the interests of the ruling class demand it.

In bourgeois society living labour is but a means of increasing accumulated labour. In communist society accumulated labour is but a means of enlarging, enriching, and promoting the existence of the labourer.

Thus in bourgeois society the past dominates the present; in communist society the present dominates the past. In bourgeois society capital is independent and personal, whilst the living individual is dependent and deprived of personality.

And the bourgeoisie calls the abolition of this state of things the abolition of individuality and freedom! And with reason. It certainly means the abolition of bourgeois individuality, independence, and freedom.

By freedom, under the present bourgeois conditions of production, is meant free trade, free buying and selling.

But if trade disappears, free trade disappears also. All the talk of free trade, like all the rest of the freedom-bravado of our bourgeoisie, has meaning only by contrast with restricted trade, by contrast with the fettered burghers of the Middle Ages, but none when contrasted with the communistic abolition of trade, bourgeois conditions of production, and the bourgeoisie itself.

You are horrified because we would abolish private property. But in your existing society private property is already abolished for nine-tenths of the population; the essential for its existence is that it shall not exist for these nine-tenths. Thus you reproach us with desiring to abolish a form of property the necessary condition of whose existence is that the great majority of society shall be entirely propertyless.

In one word, you reproach us because we would abolish your property. Precisely so; that is our intention.

From the moment when labour can no longer be converted into capital, money, rent—briefly, into a social power capable of being monopolised, *i.e.*, from the moment when individual property can no longer be converted into bourgeois property, into capital, from that moment you declare the individual is suppressed.

You confess, therefore, that by "individual" you merely mean bourgeois, the bourgeois owner of property. And this individual must certainly be abolished.

Communism deprives none of the power to appropriate his social product, it only deprives him of the power to subjugate the labour of others by this appropriation.

It has been objected that upon the abolition of private property all activity will cease and society be plunged in universal laziness.

If that were so, bourgeois society would have been ruined long since by idleness; for those who work therein gain nothing, and those who gain do not work. The whole objection merely expresses the tautology that there can be no more wage-labour so soon as there is no more capital.

All objections urged against the communistic mode of production and appropriation of the material product have equally been urged against its mode of producing and appropriating intellectual products. Just as, for the bourgeoisie, the disappearance of class-property is the disappearance of production itself, so, for him, the disappearance of class culture means the disappearance of culture altogether.

That culture, whose loss he deplores, is for the enormous majority merely a culture towards functioning as a machine.

But do not dispute with us so long as you apply to the abolition of bourgeois property the standard of your bourgeois ideas of freedom, culture, justice, etc. Your very ideas themselves are but products of bourgeois conditions of production and property, as your justice is but the will of your class uplifted into law; a will whose character is determined by the material conditions of existence of your class.

You share with every previous ruling class the interested conception which causes you to transform into eternal laws of nature and reason the social relations which result from your historically changing relations of production and property. What you perceive in the case of ancient property, what you perceive in the case of feudal property, you dare not admit in the case of bourgeois property.

Abolition of the family! Even the most radical are enraged by this scandalous proposal of the Communists.

On what is the present family, the bourgeois family, based? On capital, on private gain. In its fully developed form it exists only for the bourgeoisie; but it finds its complement in the destruction of family life for the proletariat, and in public prostitution.

The bourgeois family vanishes naturally when its complement vanishes, and both disappear with the disappearance of capital.

Do you reproach us with wishing to stop the exploitation of children by their parents? We confess to this crime.

But, you say, we would destroy the most sacred of relations by replacing home education by social.

And is not your education conditioned by society? By the social conditions under which you educate, by direct or indirect social intervention, by means of schools, etc.? The Communists have not invented this interference of society in education; they would merely alter its character, and rescue education from the influence of the ruling class.

The bourgeois declamations about the family and education, about the sacred relations of parents and children, become all the more disgusting as the development of Modern Industry tears asunder all family ties for the proletarians and transforms their children into mere commodities and instruments of labour.

But you Communists would introduce community of women, shrieks the whole bourgeoisie in chorus.

The bourgeois sees in his wife a mere instrument of production. He hears that the instruments of production are to become common property, and naturally can only think that the lot of becoming common property will likewise fall to women.

He never suspects that the real point aimed at is to do away with the position of women as mere instruments of production.

For the rest, nothing is more ridiculous than the virtuous horror of our bourgeois at the community of women which he pretends will be officially established by the Communists. The Communists have no need to introduce community of women; it has nearly always existed.

The members of our bourgeoisie, not content with having the wives and daughters of their proletarians at their disposal, not to speak of official prostitution, take special delight in mutually seducing each other's wives.

Bourgeois marriage is in reality community of wives. The Communists could at most be accused of wishing to replace a hypocritical and concealed community of women by an official and open community of women. For the rest, it is evident that with the abolition of the present system of production will disappear also the community of women resulting from it, *i.e.*, public prostitution.

The Communists are further accused of wishing to abolish countries and national spirit.

The workers have no country. What they have not got cannot be taken from them. Since the proletariat must first conquer political power, must rise to be the dominant class of the nation, must constitute itself as the nation, it is so far national itself, though not at all in the bourgeois sense.

National differences and antagonisms are to-day vanishing ever more and more with the development of the bourgeoisie, free trade, the world market, the uniformity of industrial production and the conditions of life corresponding thereto.

With the victory of the proletariat they will vanish still faster. United action, of civilised countries at least, is one of the first conditions of the emancipation of the workers.

In the same measure as the exploitation of one individual by another is ended, the exploitation of one nation by another will be ended also.

With the disappearance of classes within the nation the state of enmity between nations will come to an end.

The accusations which are made against Communism from a religious, philosophical, and generally idealogical standpoint, deserve no very serious examination.

Does it require deep insight to understand that with changes in man's material conditions of life, social relations and social system, his ideas, views, and conceptions, in one word his consciousness, also changes?

What does the history of ideas prove but that intellectual production changes with material production? The ruling ideas of any particular age have ever been only the ideas of its ruling class.

When people speak of ideas that revolutionise society, the fact is merely expressed that within the old society the elements of the new are formed, that the dissolution of the old ideas keeps pace with the dissolution of the old social relations.

When the ancient world was in its decline the ancient religions were overcome by the Christian religion. When, in the eighteenth century, Christian ideas gave place to rationalist ideas, feudal society fought its death battle with the then revolutionary bourgeoisie. The ideas of religious liberty, and liberty of conscience, merely expressed the rule of free competition within the domain of knowledge.

"Undoubtedly," it will be said, "religious, moral, philosophical, political, and juridical ideas have been modified in the course of historical development. But amid these changes religion, morals, philosophy, politics, and law remained.

"There are, moreover, eternal truths, such as freedom, justice, etc., which are common to all social systems. But Communism abolishes these eternal truths; it abolishes religion and morality instead of constituting them on a new basis, which is contrary to all past historical development."

What does this accusation amount to? The history of all past society is the history of class antagonisms, which took different forms in different epochs.

But whatever form they may have taken, the exploitation of one section of society by another is a fact common to all previous centuries. No wonder then that the social consciousness of all centuries, despite multiplicity and diversity, always moved in certain common forms, in lines of thought which can only completely vanish with the entire disappearance of class antagonism.

The Communist revolution is the most radical rupture with traditional property relations; no wonder that in the course of its development it breaks most radically with traditional ideas.

But let us leave bourgeois objections to Communism.

We have already seen that the first step in the working class revolution is the raising of the proletariat to the position of ruling class, the victory of Democracy.

The proletariat will use its political power to wrest by degrees all capital from the bourgeoisie, to centralise all instruments of production in the hands of the State, *i.e.*, of the proletariat organised as the ruling class, and to increase as rapidly as possible the total mass of productive forces.

This, naturally, cannot be accomplished at first except by despotic inroads on the rights of property and on the bourgeois conditions of production; by measures, therefore, which appear economically insufficient and untenable, but which in the course of the movement outstrip themselves, and are indispensable as means of revolutionising the whole mode of production.

These measures will naturally be different, in different countries.

Nevertheless, for the most advanced countries, the following will be pretty generally applicable: —

1. Abolition of property in land and confiscation of ground rents to the State.

2. A heavily progressive income tax.

3. Abolition of inheritance.

4. Confiscation of the property of emigrants and rebels.

5. Centralisation of credit in the hands of the State, by means of a national bank with State capital and an exclusive monopoly.

6. Centralisation of the means of transport in the hands of the State.

7. Extension of national factories and instruments of production, cultivation and improvement of waste lands in accordance with a general social plan.

8. Obligation of all to labour; organisation of industrial armies, especially for agriculture.

9. Combination of agricultural and industrial labour, in order to remove the distinction between town and country.

10. Free public education for all children. Abolition of factory labour for children in its present form. Combination of education with material production, etc.

When in the course of development class distinctions have disappeared, and all production is concentrated in the hands of associated individuals, the public power will lose its political character. Political power, properly speaking, is the organised power of one class for the purpose of oppressing another. If the proletariat, forced in its struggle against the bourgeoisie to organise as a class, makes itself by a revolution the ruling class, and as the ruling class destroys by force the old conditions of production, it destroys along with these conditions of production the conditions of existence of class antagonism, classes in general, and, therewith, its own domination as a class.

In the place of the old bourgeois society, with its classes and class antagonisms, an association appears in which the free development of each is the condition for the free development of all.

III. Socialist and Communist Literature.

1. REACTIONARY SOCIALISM

(a) *Feudal Socialism.* — The French and English aristocracy were led by their historical position to write pamphlets against modern bourgeois society. In the French revolution of 1830, and in the English reform movement, they succumbed again to the hated upstart. A serious political contest was thenceforth out of the question. A literary battle alone remained possible. But even in the domain of literature the old cries of the restoration period had become impossible. To arouse sympathy the aristocracy must appear to lose sight of its own interests, and to formulate its indictment against the bourgeoisie in the interests of the exploited working class alone. It prepared for vengeance by singing lampoons on its new master, and by whispering in his ear sinister prophecies of impending ruin.

In this manner arose feudal socialism, a mixture of lamentation, pasquinades, echoes of the past and menaces of the future — by its witty and lacerating criticism striking the bourgeoisie to the very heart, but yet remaining ridiculous through its total incapacity to understand the march of modern history.

As their banner the aristocrats waved aloft the alms-bags of the proletariat in order to rally the people around them. But as often as the working class joined them it caught sight on their hindquarters of the old feudal escutcheon and dispersed with loud and irreverent laughter.

One section of the French Legitimists and "Young England" presented this spectacle at its best.

When the feudalists point out that their method of exploitation was different from bourgeois exploitation they only forget that they exploited under circumstances and conditions that were quite different, and are now superannuated. When they point out that the modern proletariat did not exist under their rule, they only forget that the modern bourgeoisie was a necessary offspring of their own social system.

For the rest, they conceal so little the reactionary character of their criticism that their chief accusation against the bourgeoisie is precisely that under its *régime* is developed a class which will shatter to pieces the old social system.

They upbraid the bourgeoisie, not so much for having created a proletariat, as for having created a revolutionary proletariat.

In political practice, therefore, they join in all coercive measures against the working class, and in ordinary life they stoop, in spite of all their vapoury phrases, to pick up the golden apples dropped from the tree of industry, and to barter truth, love, and honour for traffic in wool, beetroot-sugar, and spirits.

As the parson has ever gone hand in hand with the landlord, so has clerical socialism gone hand in hand with feudal socialism.

Nothing is easier than to give Christian asceticism a socialist veneer. Has not Christianity also declaimed against private property, against marriage, against the State? In their place has it not preached charity, celibacy, mortification of the flesh, monasticism, and the church? Christian Socialism is but the Holy Water with which the priest consecrates the envy of the aristocrat.

(b) *Middle Class Socialism.*—The feudal aristocracy is not the only class that has been ruined by the bourgeoisie, and whose conditions of life starved and perished in modern bourgeois society. The medieval burghers and the peasant proprietors were the precursors of the modern bourgeoisie. In the countries in which industry and commerce are but little developed this class still vegetates alongside the rising bourgeoisie.

In countries where modern civilisation is developed, a new middle class has arisen, fluctuating between the proletariat and the bourgeoisie and ever renewing itself as a supplementary section of bourgeois society; but its individual members are constantly hurled down by competition into the proletariat, and, moreover, with the development of modern industry they see the hour approach when they will completely disappear as an independent section of modern society, and be replaced in commerce, manufacture, and agriculture by overseers and stewards.

In countries like France, where the peasants form much more than half the population, it was natural that writers who sided with the proletariat against the bourgeoisie should take, in their criticism of the bourgeois *régime*, the standard of the little middle class and peasant proprietors, and champion the working class from the standpoint of the petty-bourgeoisie. Thus middle class socialism arose. Sismondi was the head of this school, not only in France, but in England also.

This socialism analysed with great acuteness the contradictions inherent in modern conditions of production. It laid bare the hypocritical apologies of the economists. It proved incontrovertibly the disastrous effects of machinery and the division of labour, the concentration of capital and property in land, over-production, crises, the inevitable ruin of the lower middle class and peasantry, the misery of the proletariat, the anarchy in production, the crying disproportion in the distribution of wealth, the industrial war of extermination between nations, the dissolution of old customs, of the old family relations, of the old nationalities.

The positive aim, however, of this kind of socialism is to re-establish the old means of production and exchange, and with them the old property relations and the old form of society; or else it aims at cramping the modern means of production and exchange within the framework of the old property relations, which have been shattered by those means as they were bound to be. In either case it is both reactionary and utopian.

Corporate gilds for manufacture, patriarchal relations in agriculture—that is its last word.

In its further development it succumbed to a miserable fit of melancholia.

(c) *German or "True" Socialism.*—The Socialist and Communist literature in France, which originated under the pressure of a ruling bourgeoisie and was the literary expression of the battle against that rule, was introduced into Germany at a time when the bourgeoisie there had just begun its struggle against feudal absolutism.

German philosophers, quasi-philosophers, and "fine writers" eagerly seized on this literature, only forgetting that with the importation of these writings from France, French social conditions had not likewise been imported. In contact with German social conditions the French literature lost all its immediate practical significance and took on a purely literary character. It appeared merely as an idle speculation on the perfectibility of human nature. Thus to the German philosophers of the eighteenth century the demands of the first French Revolution were nothing more than the demands of "Practical Reason" in general, and the manifestation of the will of the revolutionary French bourgeoisie signified in their eyes the laws of pure will, of necessary will, of true human will.

The work of the German *literati* consisted exclusively in bringing the new French ideas into harmony with their philosophical conscience, or rather in appropriating the French ideas and accommodating them to their own philosophical point of view.

This appropriation took place in the same way in which a foreign language is appropriated—by translation.

It is well known how the monks wrote *over* the classical works of pagan authors the absurd tales of catholic saints. The German *literati* reversed this process with the profane French literature. They wrote their philosophical rubbish *beneath* the French original. For instance, beneath the French criticism of the functions of money they wrote "Alienation of the Human Entity"; beneath the French criticism of the bourgeois State they wrote "Elimination of the Supremacy of the Abstract Universal," etc.

The introduction of this philosophical phraseology under the French historical criticisms they christened "Philosophy of Action," "True Socialism," "German Science of Socialism," "Philosophical Basis of Socialism," etc.

The French socialist-communistic literature was thus completely emasculated. And because it ceased in the hands of the Germans to express the struggle of one class against another, the Germans thought they had overcome "French one-sidedness," and that they had defended, instead of true needs "the needs of Truth," and instead of the interests of the proletarians the interests of Human Nature, of Mankind in general—Man, who has no class, and no reality, except in the shadowy realms of philosophical phantasy.

This German socialism, which took its schoolboy task so seriously and solemnly and extolled it in such charlatan fashion, nevertheless lost little by little its pedantic innocence.

The struggle of the German, especially of the Prussian, bourgeoisie against feudalism and absolute monarchy, in one word, the liberal movement, became more earnest. By this "True" socialism was offered the much desired opportunity of confronting the political movement with the socialist demands, of hurling the traditional anathemas against liberalism, against representative government, against bourgeois competition, bourgeois freedom of the press, bourgeois law, bourgeois liberty and equality, and of preaching to the masses that they had nothing to gain, but, on the contrary, everything to lose by this bourgeois movement. German socialism forgot, very conveniently, that the French criticism, whose foolish echo it was, presupposed modern bourgeois society with its corresponding conditions of existence and the political constitution adapted thereto—precisely the things whose attainment had yet to be fought for in Germany.

It served the absolute governments, with their following of priests, pedagogues, country squires and officials, as a welcome scarecrow against the threatening advance of the bourgeoisie.

It was a sweet complement to the bitter floggings and bullets which these same governments administered to the rebellious working class of Germany.

While "True" socialism served as a weapon in the hand of the government against the German bourgeoisie, it also directly represented a reactionary interest—the interest of the German middle class. In Germany the little middle class, transmitted from the sixteenth century, and since then constantly reappearing under various forms, is the real social basis of the existing state of things.

Its preservation implies the preservation of the existing state of things in Germany. The industrial and political supremacy of the bourgeoisie threatens it with certain destruction, on the one hand, from the concentration of capital, on the other hand, from the rise of a revolutionary proletariat. "True" socialism appeared to kill both birds with one stone. It spread like an epidemic.

The garment, woven of speculative cobwebs, embroidered with flowers of rhetoric and saturated with the dews of sickly sentiment, this transcendental garment in which the German socialists enveloped their pitifully emaciated "eternal truths," only served to increase the sale of their goods to the public.

On its side German socialism recognised more and more its own vocation as the pompous representative of the petty-bourgeoisie.

It proclaimed the German nation to be the model nation, and the German petty-bourgeoisie to be the Normal Man. It gave to each baseness of the latter an occult, superior, socialistic meaning, the exact contrary of its true character. It went to the extreme length of directly opposing the "brutally destructive" tendency of Communism, and of declaring its impartial and lofty superiority to all class struggles. With very few exceptions all that is circulated as socialist and communist writing in Germany belongs to this foul and enervating literature.

2. CONSERVATIVE OR BOURGEOIS SOCIALISM

One section of the bourgeoisie desires to redress social grievances in order to secure the continuance of bourgeois society.

To this section belong: economists, philanthropists, humanitarians, reformers of working class conditions, charity organisers, temperance fanatics, and all the motley variety of reformers of every description. And this bourgeois socialism has been elaborated into complete systems.

We may cite as an example Proudhon's *Philosophie de la Misère*.

The bourgeois socialists want to have the conditions of life of modern society without the necessarily resulting struggles and dangers. They want the existing state of society with the elimination of its revolutionary and disintegrating elements. They want the bourgeoisie without the proletariat. The bourgeoisie naturally regards the world in which it rules as the best world. Bourgeois socialism elaborates this comforting conception into systems more or less complete. When it summons the proletariat to realise its system and to enter the New Jerusalem, it only requires in reality that the proletariat should remain in existing social conditions, but should cast away its hateful ideas about those conditions.

A second, more practical, but less systematic form of this socialism, sought to disgust the working class with every revolutionary movement by showing that not this or that political reform, but only a change in the material conditions of existence, in economic relations, could be of any benefit. By a change in the material conditions of life this form of socialism by no means refers to a change in bourgeois relations of production, for which a revolution is necessary, but to administrative reforms carried out on the basis of these relations of production, thus leaving unaltered the relations of capital and wage-labour, and, at best, merely lessening the cost of government for the bourgeoisie and simplifying its administrative work.

Bourgeois socialism only attains adequate expression when it becomes a mere figure of rhetoric.

Free trade—in the interest of the working class! Protection—in the interest of the working class! Prison reform—in the interest of the working class! That is the last and only serious word of bourgeois socialism.

The socialism of the bourgeoisie is summed up in the phrase: the bourgeois is a bourgeois—in the interest of the working class.

3. CRITICAL-UTOPIAN SOCIALISM AND COMMUNISM

We do not here refer to that literature which, in all great modern revolutions, has expressed the demands of the proletariat (the writings of Baboeuf, etc.).

The first direct efforts of the proletariat to attain its own ends, made in times of general agitation in the period of the overthrow of feudal society, necessarily failed, owing as much to the undeveloped state of the proletariat itself as to the absence of the economic conditions for its emancipation, which conditions could only be the product of the bourgeois epoch. The revolutionary literature which accompanied these first movements of the proletariat was necessarily reactionary in character. It preached universal asceticism and a crude levelling process.

The genuine Socialist and Communist systems, the systems of St. Simon, Fourier, Owen, etc., sprang up during the early undeveloped period of the struggle between the proletariat and the bourgeoisie which we have described above. (See *Bourgeoisie and Proletariat.*)

The founders of these systems perceive indeed the class antagonism as well as the action of the decomposing elements in the prevailing form of society. But on the side of the proletariat they can find no historical initiative and no independent political movement.

Since the development of class antagonism keeps pace with the development of industry, they find none of the material conditions for the emancipation of the proletariat, and therefore search after a social science, social laws, in order to create these conditions.

Social activity is to be replaced by their personal inventive activity; historical conditions of emancipation to be replaced by fantastical conditions; the gradual and spontaneous organisation of the proletariat as a class is to be replaced by an organisation of society specially invented by themselves. The future history of the world becomes for them, the propaganda and practical application of their social plans.

In the formation of their plans they are conscious, above all, of defending the interests of the working class as being the most suffering class. Only under this aspect of being the most suffering class does the proletariat exist for them.

The undeveloped state of the class struggle, as well as their own social position, cause them to fancy themselves far superior to all class antagonisms. They want to improve the conditions of all members of society, even the most favoured.

Hence they appeal continually to the whole of society without distinction, and even by preference to the ruling class. For how can anyone who understands their system fail to recognise in it the best possible plan of the best possible society?

They therefore reject all political, and especially all revolutionary action; they wish to attain their ends by peaceful means, and endeavour by small experiments, necessarily foredoomed to failure, and by the force of example, to prepare the way for the new social gospel.

This fantastic picture of future society, painted at a time when the proletariat was still but little developed and had but a fantastical conception of its own position, corresponds to the first instinctive aspirations of the workers towards a complete transformation of society.

But these socialist and communist writings also contain a critical element. They attacked society at its very basis. Thus they provided the most valuable materials for the enlightenment of the working class. Their positive propositions as to future society, *e.g.*, the abolition of the distinction between town and country, the family, private gain, wage-labour, the proclamation of social harmony, the conversion of the State into a mere machine for the administration of production—all these propositions merely indicate the disappearance of that class antagonism that had then only just begun to develop, and which they only knew as yet in its first indistinct and undefined forms. These proposals are, therefore, of a purely utopian character.

The significance of Critical Utopian Socialism and Communism is in inverse proportion to historical development. In proportion as the class struggle develops and takes shape, this fantastic disdain of the struggle, these fantastic attacks upon it, lose all practical value and all theoretical justification. Therefore, while the founders of this system were revolutionary in many respects, their disciples form mere reactionary sects. They hold fast by the old views of their masters in opposition to the historical evolution of the proletariat. Thus they consistently endeavour to suppress the class struggle and to reconcile antagonisms. They ever dream of the experimental realisation of their social utopia, of establishing isolated "Phalanstères," of founding home colonies, of setting up little "Icarias,"[1] duodecimo editions of the New Jerusalem—and to realise all these castles in the air they are forced to appeal to the philanthropy of the bourgeois hearts and purses. By degrees they fall into the category of the reactionary or conservative socialists, described above, and are only distinguished from these by their more systematic pedantry and by their fanatical and superstitious belief in the miraculous power of their social science.

They therefore bitterly oppose all political action of the working class, which could only result from a blind unbelief in their new gospel.

The Owenites in England and the Fourierists in France respectively oppose the Chartists and the "Reformists."

IV. Position of the Communists in Relation to the Various Opposition Parties.

The relation of the Communists to the existing working class parties is explained in Section II., which includes their relations to the Chartists in England and the Agrarian Reformers in America.

They fight for the attainment of the immediate and momentary aims and interests of the working class, but in the movement of the present they also defend the future of that movement. In France the Communists ally

---

1. Owen called his communistic model societies "Home-Colonies." *Phalanstères* was the name given by Fourier to his plan of social palaces. The utopian fantasy by which Cabet described his communistic institutions, was called *Icaria*.

themselves with the Social Democratic Party[1] against the conservative and radical bourgeoisie, reserving however the right to criticise the phrases and illusions handed down by the revolutionary tradition.

In Switzerland they support the radicals, without forgetting that this party consists of contradictory elements, half being democratic socialists in the French sense, and half radical bourgeois.

In Poland the Communists support the party that sees in an agrarian revolution the means to national freedom, that party which caused the insurrection of Cracow in 1846.

In Germany the Communist Party fights with the bourgeoisie whenever it acts in a revolutionary manner against the absolute monarchy, the feudal landlords, and the little middle class.

But the Communists never cease for one moment to instil into the workers the clearest possible recognition of the antagonism between bourgeoisie and proletariat, in order that the German workers may use the social and political conditions necessarily created by the bourgeois rule as weapons against the bourgeoisie, and in order that after the fall of the reactionary classes in Germany the fight against the bourgeoisie itself may begin immediately.

The Communists turn their attention chiefly to Germany, because Germany is on the eve of a bourgeois revolution, and because this revolution will be carried out under the most advanced conditions of European civilisation and with a much more developed proletariat than that of England in the seventeenth and France in the eighteenth centuries; the German bourgeois revolution, consequently, can only be the immediate prelude to a proletarian revolution.

In short, the Communists everywhere support every revolutionary movement against the existing social and political order of things.

In all these movements they bring the property question to the front as the fundamental question of the movement, no matter what its particular degree of development may be.

Finally, the Communists work everywhere for the union and agreement of the democratic parties of all countries.

The Communists disdain to conceal their views and aims. They openly declare that their ends can only be attained by the forcible overthrow of existing social conditions. Let the ruling classes tremble at a Communistic revolution. The proletarians have nothing to lose but their chains. They have a world to win.

WORKERS OF ALL LANDS, UNITE!

---

1. Of Ledru-Rollin.

KARL MARX AND FREDERICK ENGELS
Address of the Central Committee to the Communist League
MARCH 1850

Delivered to the committee members in writing, the Address promotes the idea that "it is our interest and our task to make the revolution permanent, until all more or less possessing classes have been forced out of their position of dominance . . ."

SOURCE: Karl Marx and Frederick Engels, *Selected Works* (Moscow: Foreign Languages Publishing House, 1962), 106–117.

The Central Committee to the League

Brothers! In the two revolutionary years 1848–49 the League proved itself in double fashion: first, in that its members energetically took part in the movement in all places, that in the press, on the barricades and on the battlefields, they stood in the front ranks of the only decidedly revolutionary class, the proletariat. The League further proved itself in that its conception of the movement as laid down in the circulars of the congresses and of the Central Committee of 1847 as well as in the *Communist Manifesto* turned out to be the only correct one, that the expectations expressed in those documents were completely fulfilled and the conception of present-day social conditions, previously propagated only in secret by the League, is now on everyone's lips and is openly preached in the market places. At the same time the former firm organisation of the League was considerably slackened. A large part of the members who directly participated in the revolutionary movement believed the time for secret societies to have gone by and public activities alone sufficient. The individual circles and communities allowed their connections with the Central Committee to become loose and gradually dormant. Consequently, while the democratic party, the party of the petty bourgeoisie, organised itself more and more in Germany, the workers' party lost its only firm foothold, remained organised at the most in separate localities for local purposes and in the general movement thus came completely under the domination and leadership of the petty-bourgeois democrats. An end must be put to this state of affairs, the independence of the workers must be restored. The Central Committee realised this necessity and therefore already in the winter of 1848–49 it sent an emissary, Josef Moll, to Germany for the reorganisation of the League. Moll's mission, however, was without lasting effect, partly because the German workers at that time had not acquired sufficient experience and partly because it was interrupted by the insurrection of the previous May. Moll himself took up the musket, entered the Baden-Palatinate army and fell on July 19 in the encounter at the Murg. The League lost in him one of its oldest, most active and most trustworthy members, one who had been active in all the congresses and Central Committees and even prior to this had carried out a series of missions with great success. After the defeat of the revolutionary parties of Germany and France in July 1849, almost all the members of the Central Committee came together again in London, replenished their numbers with new revolutionary forces and set about the reorganisation of the League with renewed zeal.

Reorganisation can only be carried out by an emissary, and the Central Committee considers it extremely important that the emissary should leave precisely at this moment when a new revolution is impending, when the workers' party, therefore, must act in the most organised, most unanimous and most independent fashion possible if it is not to be exploited and taken in tow again by the bourgeoisie as in 1848.

Brothers! We told you as early as 1848 that the German liberal bourgeois would soon come to power and would immediately turn their newly acquired power against the workers. You have seen how this has been fulfilled. In fact it was the bourgeois who, immediately after the March movement of 1848, took possession of the state power and used this power to force back at once the workers, their allies in the struggle, into their former oppressed position. Though the bourgeoisie was not able to accomplish this without uniting with the feudal party, which had been disposed of in March, without finally even surrendering power once again to this feudal absolutist party, still it has secured conditions for itself which, in the long run, owing to the financial embarrassment of the government, would place power in its hands and would safeguard all its interests, if it were possible for the revolutionary movement to assume already now a so-called peaceful development. The bourgeoisie, in order to safeguard its rule, would not even need to make itself obnoxious by violent measures against the people, since all such violent steps have already been taken by the feudal counter-revolution. Developments, however, will not take this peaceful course. On the contrary, the revolution, which will accelerate this development, is near at hand, whether it will be called forth by an independent uprising of the French proletariat or by an invasion of the Holy Alliance against the revolutionary Babylon.

And the role, this so treacherous role which the German liberal bourgeois played in 1848 against the people, will in the impending revolution be taken over by the democratic petty bourgeois, who at present occupy the same position in the opposition as the liberal bourgeois before 1848. This party, the democratic party, which is far more dangerous to the workers than the previous liberal one, consists of three elements:

I. Of the most advanced sections of the big bourgeoisie, which pursue the aim of the immediate complete overthrow of feudalism and absolutism. This faction is represented by the one-time Berlin compromisers, by the tax resisters.

II. Of the democratic-constitutional petty bourgeois, whose main aim during the previous movement was the establishment of a more or less democratic federal state as striven for by their representatives, the Lefts in the Frankfort Assembly, and later by the Stuttgart parliament, and by themselves in the campaign for the Reich Constitution.

III. Of the republican petty bourgeois, whose ideal is a German federative republic after the manner of Switzerland, and who now call themselves Red and social-democratic because they cherish the pious wish of abolishing the pressure of big capital on small capital, of the big bourgeois on the small bourgeois. The representatives of this faction were the members of the democratic congresses and committees, the leaders of the democratic associations, the editors of the democratic newspapers.

Now, after their defeat, all these factions call themselves Republicans or Reds, just as the republican petty bourgeois in France now call themselves Socialists. Where, as in Württemberg, Bavaria, etc., they still find opportunity to pursue their aims constitutionally, they seize the occasion to retain their old phrases and to prove by deeds that they have not changed in the least. It is evident, moreover, that the altered name of this party does not make the slightest difference in its attitude to the workers, but merely proves that they are now obliged to turn against the bourgeoisie, which is united with absolutism, and to seek support in the proletariat.

The petty-bourgeois democratic party in Germany is very powerful; it comprises not only the great majority of the bourgeois inhabitants of the towns, the small people in industry and trade and the guild masters; it numbers among its followers also the peasants and the rural proletariat, in so far as the latter has not yet found a support in the independent urban proletariat.

The relation of the revolutionary workers' party to the petty-bourgeois democrats is this: it marches together with them against the faction which it aims at overthrowing, it opposes them in everything whereby they seek to consolidate their position in their own interests.

Far from desiring to revolutionise all society for the revolutionary proletarians, the democratic petty bourgeois strive for a change in social conditions by means of which existing society will be made as tolerable and comfortable as possible for them. Hence they demand above all diminution of state expenditure by a curtailment of the bureaucracy and shifting the chief taxes on to the big landowners and bourgeois. Further, they demand the abolition of the pressure of big capital on small, through public credit institutions and laws against usury, by which means it will be possible for them and the peasants to obtain advances, on favourable conditions, from the state instead of from the capitalists; they also demand the establishment of bourgeois property relations in the countryside by the complete abolition of feudalism. To accomplish all this they need a democratic state structure, either constitutional or republican, that will give them and their allies, the peasants, a majority; also a democratic communal structure that will give them direct control over communal property and over a series of functions now performed by the bureaucrats.

The domination and speedy increase of capital is further to be counteracted partly by restricting the right of inheritance and partly by transferring as many jobs of work as possible to the state. As far as the workers are concerned, it remains certain above all that they are to remain wage-workers as before; the democratic petty bourgeois only desire better wages and a more secure existence for the workers and hope to achieve this through partial employment by the state and through charity measures; in short, they hope to bribe the workers by more or less concealed alms and to break their revolutionary potency by making their position tolerable for the moment. The demands of the petty-bourgeois democracy here summarised are not put forward by all of its factions at the same time and only a very few members of them consider that these demands constitute definite aims in their entirety. The further separate individuals or factions among them go, the more of these demands will they make their own, and those few who see their own programme in what has been outlined above might believe that thereby they have put forward the utmost that can be demanded from the revolution. But these demands can in nowise suffice for the party of the proletariat. While the democratic petty bourgeois wish to bring the revolution to a conclusion as quickly as possible, and with the achievement, at most, of the above demands, it is our interest and our task to make the revolution permanent, until all more or less possessing classes have been forced out of their position of dominance, until the proletariat has conquered state power, and the association of proletarians, not only in one country but in all the dominant countries of the world, has advanced so far that competition among the proletarians of these countries has ceased and that at least the decisive productive forces are concentrated in the hands of the proletarians. For us the issue cannot be the alteration of private property but only its annihilation, not the smoothing over of class antagonisms but the abolition of classes, not the improvement of existing society but the foundation of a new one. That, during the further development of the revolution, the petty-bourgeois democracy will for a moment obtain predominating influence in Germany is not open to doubt. The question, therefore, arises as to what the attitude of the proletariat and in particular of the League will be in relation to it:

1. During the continuance of the present conditions where the petty-bourgeois democrats are likewise oppressed;

2. In the next revolutionary struggle, which will give them the upper hand;

3. After this struggle, during the period of preponderance over the overthrown classes and the proletariat.

1. At the present moment, when the democratic petty bourgeois are everywhere oppressed, they preach in general unity and reconciliation to the proletariat, they offer it their hand and strive for the establishment of a large opposition party which will embrace all shades of opinion in the democratic party, that is, they strive to entangle the workers in a party organisation in which general social-democratic phrases predominate, behind which their special interests are concealed and in which the particular demands of the proletariat may not be brought forward for the sake of beloved peace. Such a union would turn out solely to their advantage and altogether to the disadvantage of the proletariat. The proletariat would lose its whole independent, laboriously achieved position and once more sink down to being an appendage of official bourgeois democracy. This union must, therefore, be most decisively rejected. Instead of once again stooping to serve as the applauding chorus of the bourgeois democrats, the workers, and above all the League, must exert themselves to establish an independent, secret and public organisation of the workers' party alongside of the official democrats and make each section the central point and nucleus of workers' societies in which the attitude and interests of the proletariat

will be discussed independently of bourgeois influences. How far the bourgeois democrats are from seriously considering an alliance in which the proletarians would stand side by side with them with equal power and equal rights is shown, for example, by the Breslau democrats who, in their organ, the *Neue Oder-Zeitung*, most furiously attack the independently organised workers, whom they style Socialists. In the case of a struggle against a common adversary no special union is required. As soon as such an adversary has to be fought directly, the interests of both parties, for the moment, coincide, and, as previously, so also in the future, this connection, calculated to last only for the moment, will arise of itself. It is self-evident that in the impending bloody conflicts, as in all earlier ones, it is the workers who, in the main, will have to win the victory by their courage, determination and self-sacrifice. As previously, so also in this struggle, the mass of the petty bourgeois will as long as possible remain hesitant, undecided and inactive, and then, as soon as the issue has been decided, will seize the victory for themselves, will call upon the workers to maintain tranquillity and return to their work, will guard against so-called excesses and bar the proletariat from the fruits of victory. It is not in the power of the workers to prevent the petty-bourgeois democrats from doing this, but it is in their power to make it difficult for them to gain the upper hand as against the armed proletariat, and to dictate such conditions to them that the rule of the bourgeois democrats will from the outset bear within it the seeds of their downfall, and that their subsequent extrusion by the rule of the proletariat will be considerably facilitated. Above all things, the workers must counteract, as much as is at all possible, during the conflict and immediately after the struggle, the bourgeois endeavours to allay the storm, and must compel the democrats to carry out their present terrorist phrases. Their actions must be so aimed as to prevent the direct revolutionary excitement from being suppressed again immediately after the victory. On the contrary, they must keep it alive as long as possible. Far from opposing so-called excesses, instances of popular revenge against hated individuals or public buildings that are associated only with hateful recollections, such instances must not only be tolerated but the leadership of them taken in hand. During the struggle and after the struggle, the workers must, at every opportunity, put forward their own demands alongside of the demands of the bourgeois democrats. They must demand guarantees for the workers as soon as the democratic bourgeois set about taking over the government. If necessary they must obtain these guarantees by force and in general they must see to it that the new rulers pledge themselves to all possible concessions and promises—the surest way to compromise them. In general, they must in every way restrain as far as possible the intoxication of victory and the enthusiasm for the new state of things, which make their appearance after every victorious street battle, by a calm and dispassionate estimate of the situation and by unconcealed mistrust in the new government. Alongside of the new official governments they must establish simultaneously their own revolutionary workers' governments, whether in the form of municipal committees and municipal councils or in the form of workers' clubs or workers' committees, so that the bourgeois-democratic governments not only immediately lose the support of the workers but from the outset see themselves supervised and threatened by authorities which are backed by the whole mass of the workers. In a word, from the first moment of victory, mistrust must be directed no longer against the conquered reactionary party, but against the workers' previous allies, against the party that wishes to exploit the common victory for itself alone.

2. But in order to be able energetically and threateningly to oppose this party, whose treachery to the workers will begin from the first hour of victory, the workers must be armed and organised. The arming of the whole proletariat with rifles, muskets, cannon and munitions must be put through at once, the revival of the old Citizens' Guard directed against the workers must be resisted. However, where the latter is not feasible the workers must attempt to organise themselves independently as a proletarian guard with commanders elected by themselves and with a general staff of their own choosing, and to put themselves at the command not of the state authority but of the revolutionary community councils which the workers will have managed to get adopted. Where workers are employed at the expense of the state they must see that they are armed and organised in a separate corps with commanders of their own choosing or as part of the proletarian guard. Arms and ammunition must not be surrendered on any pretext; any attempt at disarming must be frustrated, if necessary by force. Destruction of the influence of the bourgeois democrats upon the workers, immediate independent and armed organisation of the workers and the enforcement of conditions as difficult and compromising as possible upon the inevitable momentary rule of the bourgeois democracy—these are the main points which the proletariat and hence the League must keep in view during and after the impending insurrection.

3. As soon as the new governments have consolidated their positions to some extent, their struggle against the workers will begin. Here, in order to be able to offer energetic opposition to the democratic petty bourgeois, it is above all necessary that the workers shall be independently organised and centralised in clubs. After the overthrow of the existing governments, the Central Committee will, as soon as it is at all possible, betake itself to Germany, immediately convene a congress

and put before the latter the necessary proposals for the centralisation of the workers' clubs under a leadership established in the chief seat of the movement. The speedy organisation of at least a provincial interlinking of the workers' clubs is one of the most important points for the strengthening and development of the workers' party; the immediate consequence of the overthrow of the existing governments will be the election of a national representative assembly. Here the proletariat must see to it:

I. That no groups of workers are barred on any pretext or by any kind of trickery on the part of local authorities or government commissioners.

II. That everywhere workers' candidates are put up alongside of the bourgeois-democratic candidates, that they should consist as far as possible of members of the League, and that their election is promoted by all possible means. Even where there is no prospect whatsoever of their being elected, the workers must put up their own candidates in order to preserve their independence, to count their forces and to bring before the public their revolutionary attitude and party standpoint. In this connection they must not allow themselves to be seduced by such arguments of the democrats as, for example, that by so doing they are splitting the democratic party and making it possible for the reactionaries to win. The ultimate intention of all such phrases is to dupe the proletariat. The advance which the proletarian party is bound to make by such independent action is infinitely more important than the disadvantage that might be incurred by the presence of a few reactionaries in the representative body. If the democracy from the outset comes out resolutely and terroristically against the reaction, the influence of the latter in the elections will be destroyed in advance.

The first point on which the bourgeois democrats will come into conflict with the workers will be the abolition of feudalism. As in the first French Revolution, the petty bourgeois will give the feudal lands to the peasants as free property, that is to say, try to leave the rural proletariat in existence and form a petty-bourgeois peasant class which will go through the same cycle of impoverishment and indebtedness which the French peasant is now still going through.

The workers must oppose this plan in the interest of the rural proletariat and in their own interest. They must demand that the confiscated feudal property remain state property and be converted into workers' colonies cultivated by the associated rural proletariat with all the advantages of large-scale agriculture, through which the principle of common property immediately obtains a firm basis in the midst of the tottering bourgeois property relations. Just as the democrats combine with the peasants so must the workers combine with the rural proletariat. Further, the democrats will work either directly for a federative republic or, if they cannot avoid a single and indivisible republic, they will at least attempt to cripple the central government by the utmost possible autonomy and independence for the communities and provinces. The workers, in opposition to this plan, must not only strive for a single and indivisible German republic, but also within this republic for the most determined centralisation of power in the hands of the state authority. They must not allow themselves to be misguided by the democratic talk of freedom for the communities, of self-government, etc. In a country like Germany where there are still so many relics of the Middle Ages to be abolished, where there is so much local and provincial obstinacy to be broken, it must under no circumstances be permitted that every village, every town and every province should put a new obstacle in the path of revolutionary activity, which can proceed with full force only from the centre. It is not to be tolerated that the present state of affairs should be renewed, that Germans must fight separately in every town and in every province for one and the same advance. Least of all is it to be tolerated that a form of property, namely, communal property, which still lags behind modern private property and which everywhere is necessarily passing into the latter, together with the quarrels resulting from it between poor and rich communities, as well as communal civil law, with its trickery against the workers, that exists alongside of state civil law, should be perpetuated by a so-called free communal constitution. As in France in 1793 so today in Germany it is the task of the really revolutionary party to carry through the strictest centralisation.*

---

*It must be recalled today that this passage is based on a misunderstanding. At that time—thanks to the Bonapartist and liberal falsifiers of history—it was considered as established that the French centralised machine of administration had been introduced by the Great Revolution and in particular that it had been operated by the Convention as an indispensable and decisive weapon for defeating the royalist and federalist reaction and the external enemy. It is now, however, a well-known fact that throughout the whole revolution up to the eighteenth Brumaire the whole administration of the departments, arrondissements and communes consisted of authorities elected by the respective constituents themselves, and that these authorities acted with complete freedom within the general state laws; that precisely this provincial and local self-government, similar to the American, became the most powerful lever of the revolution and indeed to such an extent that Napoleon, immediately after his *coup d'état* of the eighteenth Brumaire, hastened to replace it by an administration by prefects, which still exists and which, therefore, was a pure instrument of reaction from the beginning. But just as little as local and provincial self-government is in contradiction to political, national centralisation, so is it to an equally small extent necessarily bound up with that narrow-minded, cantonal or communal self-seeking which strikes us as so repulsive in Switzerland, and which all the South German federal republicans wanted to make the rule in Germany in 1849. [*Note by Engels to the 1885 edition.*]

We have seen how the democrats will come to power with the next movement, how they will be compelled to propose more or less socialistic measures. It will be asked what measures the workers ought to propose in reply. At the beginning of the movement, of course, the workers cannot yet propose any directly communistic measures. But they can:

1. Compel the democrats to interfere in as many spheres as possible of the hitherto existing social order, to disturb its regular course and to compromise themselves as well as to concentrate the utmost possible productive forces, means of transport, factories, railways, etc., in the hands of the state:

2. They must drive the proposals of the democrats, who in any case will not act in a revolutionary but in a merely reformist manner, to the extreme and transform them into direct attacks upon private property; thus, for example, if the petty bourgeois propose purchase of the railways and factories, the workers must demand that these railways and factories shall be simply confiscated by the state without compensation as being the property of reactionaries. If the democrats propose proportional taxes, the workers must demand progressive taxes; if the democrats themselves put forward a moderately progressive tax, the workers must insist on a tax with rates that rise so steeply that big capital will be ruined by it; if the democrats demand the regulation of state debts, the workers must demand state bankruptcy. Thus, the demands of the workers must everywhere be governed by the concessions and measures of the democrats.

If the German workers are not able to attain power and achieve their own class interests without completely going through a lengthy revolutionary development, they at least know for a certainty this time that the first act of this approaching revolutionary drama will coincide with the direct victory of their own class in France and will be very much accelerated by it.

But they themselves must do the utmost for their final victory by clarifying their minds as to what their class interests are, by taking up their position as an independent party as soon as possible and by not allowing themselves to be seduced for a single moment by the hypocritical phrases of the democratic petty bourgeois into refraining from the independent organisation of the party of the proletariat. Their battle cry must be: The Revolution in Permanence.

FERDINAND LASSALLE
"The Working Man's Programme"
APRIL 12, 1862

In this speech in Berlin, Lassalle, who was deeply influenced by Marx but whom Marx regularly attacked, describes the importance of the *"Fourth Estate,"* the working class. *"Its* interest is in truth the interest of the *whole of humanity,* its freedom is the freedom of humanity itself, and its domination is the domination of *all."* He argues that the object of the State is to allow each person "to reach such a *stage of existence* as they *never* could have reached as individuals; to make them capable of acquiring an amount of *education, power,* and *freedom* which would have been wholly unattainable by them as individuals." Born in 1825, Lassalle was killed in a duel in 1864.

SOURCE: Ferdinand Lassalle, *The Working Man's Programme* (London: The Modern Press, 1881), 43–56.

The Working Man's Programme

On the 24th February 1848, the dawn of a new period of history appeared.

For on that day in France (that country in whose great struggles the victory or the defeat of freedom means victory or defeat for the whole human race) a revolution broke out which called a working man into the provisional Government, declared that the object of the State was the improvement of the lot of the working classes, and proclaimed the universal and direct right to the suffrage, by which every citizen who had attained his twenty-first year, without any reference to the amount of his property, received an equal share in the government of the State in the direction of its will and the determination of its aims.

You see, gentlemen, that if the Revolution of 1789 was the

Revolution of the *Tiers état*, the *Third* class, it is now the *Fourth* class, which in 1789 was still enfolded within the third class and appeared to be identical with it, which will now raise its principle to be the dominating principle of the community, and cause all its arrangements to be permeated by it.

But here, in the domination of the fourth class comes to light this immense difference, that the fourth class is the last and the outside of all, the disinterested class of the community, which sets up and can set up *no* further exclusive condition, either legal or actual, neither nobility nor landed possessions nor the possession of capital, which it could make into a new *privilege* and force upon the arrangements of society.

We are *all* working men in so far as we have even the *will* to make ourselves useful in any way to the community.

This *Fourth* class in whose heart therefore *no* germ of a new privilege is contained, is for this very reason synonomous with the *whole human race*. *Its* interest is in truth the interest of the *whole of humanity*, its freedom is the freedom of humanity itself, and its domination is the domination of *all*.

Whoever therefore invokes the idea of the working class as the ruling principle of society, in the sense in which I have explained it to you, does not put forth a cry that divides and separates the classes of society. On the contrary, he utters a cry of *reconciliation*, a cry which embraces the whole of the community, a cry for doing away with all the contradictions in every circle of society; a cry of *union* in which all should join who do not wish for privileges, and the oppression of the people by privileged classes; a cry of *love* which having once gone up from the heart of the people, will *for ever remain the true cry of the people*, and whose meaning will make it still a *cry of love*, even when it sounds the war cry of the people.

We will now consider the principle of the working class as the ruling principle of the community only in three of its relations: —

(1) In relation to the formal means of its realisation.

(2) In relation to its moral significance.

(3) In relation to the political conception of the object of the State, which is inherent in that principle.

We cannot on this occasion enter upon its other aspects, and even those to which we have referred can be only very cursorily examined in the short time that remains to us.

The formal means of carrying out this principle is the universal and direct suffrage which we have already discussed. I say universal and *direct* suffrage, gentlemen, not that mere universal suffrage which we had in the year 1848. The introduction of two degrees in the electoral act, namely, original electors and electors simply, is nothing but an ingenious method purposely introduced with the object of falsifying as far as possible the will of the people by means of the electoral act.

It is true that even universal and direct suffrage is no magic wand, gentlemen, which is able to protect you from temporary mistakes.

We have seen in France two bad elections following one another, in 1848 and 1849. But universal and direct suffrage is the *only* means which in the long run of itself corrects the mistakes to which its momentary wrong use may lead. It is that spear which heals the wounds itself has made. It is impossible in the long run with universal and direct suffrage that the elected body should be any other than the exact and true likeness of the people which has elected it.

The people must therefore at all times regard universal and direct suffrage as its indispensable political weapon, as the most fundamental and important of its demands.

I will now glance at the *moral* significance of the principle of society which we are considering.

It is possible that the idea of converting the principle of the *lower classes* of society into the ruling principle of the State and the community may appear to be extremely dangerous and immoral, and to threaten the destruction of morality and education by a "modern barbarism."

And it is no wonder that this idea should be so regarded at the present day since even public opinion, gentlemen—I have already indicated by what means, namely, the newspapers—receives its impressions from the mind of *capital*, and from the hands of the privileged wealthy Bourgeoisie.

Nevertheless this fear is only a prejudice, and it can be proved on the contrary, that the idea would exhibit the greatest advance and triumph of morality that the history of the world has ever recorded.

That view is a prejudice I repeat, and it is simply the prejudice of *the present time* which is dominated by privilege.

At another time, namely, that of the first French Republic of the year 1793 (of which I have already told you that I cannot enter into further particulars on this occasion, but that it was destined to perish by its own want of definite aims) the *opposite* prejudice prevailed. It was then a current dogma that all the upper classes were immoral and corrupt, and that only the lower classes were good and moral. In the new declaration of the rights of man issued by the French convention, that powerful constituent assembly of France, this was actually laid down by a special article, namely, article nineteen, which runs as follows, "Toute institution qui ne suppose le peuple bon, et le magistrat corruptible, est vicieuse." "Every institution which does not assume that the people are good and the magistracy contemptible is vicious." You see that this is exactly the opposite to the happy faith now required, according to which there is no greater sin than to doubt of the goodwill and the virtue of the Government, while it is taken for granted that *the people* are a sort of tiger and a sink of curruption.

At the time of which we are speaking the opposite dogma had advanced so far, that almost every one who had a whole coat on his back was thought to be a bad man, or at least an object of suspicion; and virtue, purity, and patriotic morality were thought to be possessed only by those who had no decent clothes. It was the period of sansculottism.

This view, gentlemen, is in fact founded on a *truth*, but it presents itself in an *untrue* and *perverted* form. Now there is nothing more dangerous than a truth which presents itself in an untrue perverted form. For in whatever way we deal with it, we are certain to go wrong. If we adopt such a truth in its untrue perverted form, it will lead at certain times to most pernicious destruction, as was the case with sansculottism. But if we regard the whole statement as untrue on account of its untrue perverted form, then we are much worse. For we have rejected a *truth*, and, in the case before us, a truth without the recognition of which not a single sound step in our political life can be taken.

The only course that remains open to us, therefore, is to set aside the untrue and perverted form of the statement, and to bring its true essence into distinct relief.

The public opinion of the present day is inclined, as I have said, to declare the whole statement to be utterly untrue, and mere declamation on the part of Rousseau and the French Revolution. But even if it were possible to adopt the course of rejection in the case of Rousseau and the French Revolution, it is quite impossible to do so in the case of one of the greatest of German philosophers, the centenary of whose birth-day will be celebrated in this town next month: I allude to the philosopher Fichte, one of the greatest thinkers of all nations and times.

Even Fichte declares expressly in so many words, that the higher the rank the greater the moral deterioration, that—these are his very words—"Wickedness increases in proportion to the elevation of rank."

But Fichte did not develop the ultimate ground of this statement. He adduces, as the ground of this corruption, the selfishness and egoism of the upper classes. But then the question must immediately arise, whether selfishness does not also prevail in the lower classes, or why it should prevail less in these. Nay, it must at first sight appear to be an extraordinary paradox to assert that less selfishness should prevail in the lower classes than in the higher who have a considerable advantage over them in education and training which are recognised as moralising elements.

The following is the true ground of what as I said appears at first sight to be extraordinary paradox.

In a long period in the past, as we have seen, the development of the people, which is the life-breath of history, proceeds by an ever advancing abolition of the privileges which guarantee to the higher classes their position as higher and ruling classes. The desire to maintain this, in other words their personal interest, brings therefore every member of the higher classes who has not once for all by a high range of vision elevated himself above his purely personal existence—and you will understand, gentlemen, that this can never be more than a very small number of exceptional characters—into a position thoroughly *hostile* in principle to the development of the people, to the progress of education and science, to the advance of culture, to all the life-breath and victory of historic life.

It is this opposition of the personal interest of the higher classes to the development of the nation in culture which evokes the great and necessary immorality of the higher classes. It is a life, whose daily conditions you need only represent to yourselves, in order to perceive the deep inward deterioration to which it must lead. To be compelled daily to *oppose* all that is great and good, to be obliged to *grieve* at its successes, to rejoice at its failures, to restrain its further progress, to be obliged to undo or to execrate the advantages it has already attained. It is to lead their life as in the country of an *enemy*—and this enemy is the moral community of their *own people*, amongst whom they live, and *for* whom to strive constitutes all true morality. It is to lead their lives, I say, as in the country of an *enemy*; this enemy is their own people, and the fact that it is regarded and treated as their enemy must generally at all events be cunningly concealed, and this hostility must more or less artfully be covered with a veil.

And to this we must add that either they must do all this *against* the voice of their own conscience and intelligence, or they must have stifled the voice by habit so as not to be oppressed by it, or lastly they must have never known this voice, never known anything different and better than the religion of their own advantage!

This life, gentlemen, leads therefore necessarily to a thorough depreciation and contempt of all striving to realize an ideal, to a compassionate smile at the bare mention of the great name of the Idea, to a deeply seated want of sympathy and even antipathy to all that is beautiful and great, to a complete swallowing up of every moral element in us, by the one passion of selfish seeking for our own advantage, and of immoderate desire for pleasure.

It is this *opposition*, gentlemen, between personal interest and the development of the nation in culture, which the lower classes, happily for them, are *without*.

It is unfortunately true that there is always enough of selfishness in the lower classes, much more than there should be, but this selfishness of theirs, wherever it is found, is the fault of single persons, of *individuals*, and not the inevitable fault of the *class*.

A very reasonable instinct warns the members of the lower classes, that so long as each of them relates himself only to himself, and each one thinks only of himself, he can hope for no important improvement in his position.

But the more earnestly and deeply the lower classes of society strive after the improvement of their condition as a class, the improvement of the *lot of their class*, the more does this personal interest, instead of opposing the movement of history and thereby being condemned to that immorality of which we have spoken, assume a *direction* which thoroughly accords with the development of the whole *people*, with the victory of the *idea*, with the advance of *culture*, with the living principle of history itself, which is no other than the development of *freedom*. Or in other words, as we have already seen, *its* interest is the interest of the entire human race.

You are therefore in this happy position, gentlemen, that instead of its being possible for you to be dead to the idea, you are on the contrary urged to the deepest sympathy for it by your own *personal interests*. You are in the happy position that the idea which constitutes your true personal interest, is one with the throbbing pulse of history, and with the living principle of moral development. You are able therefore to devote yourselves with *personal passion* to this historical development, and to be certain that the more strongly this *passion* grows and burns within you in the true sense in which I have explained it to you, the higher is the moral position you have attained.

These are the reasons, gentlemen, why the dominion of the fourth class in the State must produce such an efflorescence of morality, culture, and science, as has not yet been witnessed in history.

But there is yet another reason for this, one which is most intimately connected with all the views I have explained to you, and forms their keystone.

The fourth estate not only has a different formal political principle from that of the Bourgeoisie, namely, the universal direct franchise, instead of the census of the Bourgeoisie, and not only has through its position in life a different relation to moral forces than the higher classes, but has also—and partly in consequence of these—quite another and a different conception of the moral *object of the State* from that of the Bourgeoisie.

According to the Bourgeoisie, the moral idea of the State is exclusively this, that the unhindered exercise by himself of his own faculties should be guaranteed to each individual.

If we were all equally strong, equally clever, equally educated, and equally rich, this might be regarded as a sufficient and a moral idea.

But since we neither *are* nor *can be* thus equal, this idea is not satisfactory, and therefore necessarily leads in its consequences to deep immorality, for it leads to this, that the stronger, the cleverer, and the richer fleece the weaker and pick their pockets.

The moral idea of the State according to the working class on the contrary is this, that the unhindered and free activity of individual powers exercised by the individual is not *sufficient*, but that something *must be added* to this in a morally ordered community—namely, *solidarity* of interests, community and reciprocity in development.

In accordance with this difference, the Bourgeoisie conceive the moral object of the State to consist solely and exclusively in the protection of the personal freedom and the property of the individual.

This is a policeman's idea, gentlemen, a policeman's idea for this reason, because it represents to itself the State from a point of view of a policeman, whose whole function consists in preventing robbery and burglary. Unfortunately this policeman's idea is not only familiar to genuine liberals, but is even to be met with not unfrequently among so-called democrats, owing to their defective imagination. If the Bourgeoisie would express the logical inference from their idea, they must maintain that according to it if there were no such thing as robbers and thieves, the State itself would be entirely superfluous.

Very differently, gentlemen, does the fourth estate regard the object of the State, for it apprehends it in its true nature.

History, gentlemen, is a struggle with nature; with the misery, the ignorance, the poverty, the weakness, and consequent slavery in which we were involved when the human race came upon the scene in the beginning of history. The progressive *victory* over this weakness—this is the development of freedom which history displays to us.

In this struggle we should never have made one step forward, nor shall we ever advance one step more by acting on the principle of *each one for himself, each one alone.*

It is *the State* whose function it is to carry on *this development of freedom*, this development of the human race until its freedom is attained.

The State is this unity of individuals into a moral whole, a unity which increases a million-fold the strength of *all* the individuals who are comprehended in it, and multiplies a million times the power which would be at the disposal of them *all* as individuals.

The object of the State, therefore, is not only to *protect* the personal freedom and property of the individual with which he is supposed according to the idea of the Bourgeoisie to have entered the State. On the contrary, the object of the State is precisely this, to place the individuals *through this* union in a position to attain to *such objects*, and reach such a *stage of existence* as they *never* could have reached as individuals; to make them capable of acquiring an amount of *education*, *power*, and *freedom* which would have been wholly unattainable by them as individuals.

Accordingly the object of the State is to bring man to positive expansion, and progressive development, in other words; to bring the destiny of man—that is the culture of which the human race *is capable*—into *actual existence*; it is the *training and development* of the human race to freedom.

This is the true moral nature of the State, gentlemen, its true and high mission. So much is this the case, that from the beginning of time through the very *force* of events it has more or less been carried out by the State without the exercise of will, and unconsciously even against the will of its leaders.

But the working class, gentlemen, the lower classes of the community in general, through the helpless condition in which its members find themselves placed as individuals, have always acquired the deep instinct, that this is and must be the duty of the State, to help the individual by means of the union of all to such a development as he would be *incapable* of attaining as an individual.

A State therefore which was ruled by the idea of the working class, would no longer be driven, as all States have hitherto been, unconsciously and against their will by the nature of things, and the force of circumstances, but it would make this moral nature of the State its mission, with perfect clearness of vision and complete consciousness. It would complete with *unchecked desire* and perfect *consistency*, that which hitherto has only been wrung in scanty and imperfect fragments from wills that were opposed to it, and *for this very reason*—though time does not permit me to explain in any detail this necessary connection of cause and effect—it would produce a soaring flight of the human spirit, a development of an amount of happiness, culture, wellbeing, and freedom without example in the history of the world, and in comparison with which, the most favourable conditions that have existed in former times would appear but dim shadows of the reality.

This it is, gentlemen, which must be called the working man's idea of the State, his conception of the object of the State, which, as you see is just as different from the bourgeois conception of the object of the State, as the principle of the working class, of the claim of *all* to direct the will of the State, or universal suffrage, is different from the principle held by the Bourgeoisie, the census.

PETER KROPOTKIN
"An Appeal to the Young"

1880

The Russian revolutionary and anarchist Kropotkin was born a prince, in the line of the Ruriks, in 1842. As a young man he served at court, became disillusioned with the ethics and practices of the Czar and his governors, and traveled in Siberia, where he wrote about geography and became a revolutionary. He and Michael Bakunin are the most famous of Russian anarchists. After being jailed in 1874 for revolutionary activities, he escaped and lived in France (where in the mid-1880s he was jailed for three years), Switzerland and, for the most part, in England until he returned to Russia in 1917. While publicly admired by Lenin, he was critical of Lenin's and the Bolsheviks' ruthless principles (see p. 243, "The Russian Revolution and the Soviet Government"). Kropotkin died of pneumonia in 1921.

"This plea to young men and women of the upper class to join the workers' revolutionary cause is one of the best known and most widely read of Kropotkin's 'editorials,'" notes Roger N. Baldwin. "Its impulse must have been drawn largely from Kropotkin's own experience in Russia, and in the 'to the people' movement of the students and professional men and women who championed the revolutionary cause."[1]

SOURCE: Peter Kropotkin, *Anarchism: A Collection of Revolutionary Writings.* Ed. Roger N. Baldwin (Mineola, N.Y.: Dover Publications, Inc., 2002), 261–282.

An Appeal to the Young

It is to the young that I wish to address myself. Let the old—I mean of course the old in heart and mind—lay this down without tiring their eyes in reading what will tell them nothing.

---

1. Peter Kropotkin, *Anarchism: A Collection of Revolutionary Writings.* Ed. Roger N. Baldwin (Mineola, N.Y.: Dover Publications, Inc., 2002), 260.

I assume that you are about eighteen or twenty years of age, that you have finished your apprenticeship or your studies, that you are just entering on life. I take it for granted that you have a mind free from the superstition which your teachers have sought to force upon you; that you do not fear the devil, and that you do not go to hear parsons and ministers rant. More, that you are not one of the fops, sad products of a society in decay, who display their well-cut trousers and their monkey faces in the park, and who even at their early age have only an insatiable longing for pleasure at any price . . . I assume on the contrary that you have a warm heart and for this reason I talk to you.

A first question, I know, occurs to you. You have often asked yourself—"What am I going to be?" In fact when a man is young he understands that after having studied a trade or a science for several years—at the cost of society, mark—he has not done this in order that he should make use of his acquirements as instruments of plunder for his own gain, and he must be depraved indeed and utterly cankered by vice, who has not dreamed that one day he would apply his intelligence, his abilities, his knowledge to help on the enfranchisement of those who today grovel in misery and in ignorance.

You are one of those who has had such a vision, are you not? Very well, let us see what you must do to make your dream a reality.

I do not know in what rank you were born. Perhaps, favored by fortune, you have turned your attention to the study of science; you are to be a doctor, a lawyer, a man of letters, or a scientific man. A wide field opens up before you. You enter upon life with extensive knowledge, with a trained intelligence. Or on the other hand, you are perhaps only an artisan whose knowledge of science is limited by the little you learned at school. But you have had the advantage of learning at first hand what a life of exhausting toil is the lot of the worker of our time.

TO THE "INTELLECTUALS"

To Doctors

I stop at the first supposition, to return afterwards to the second; I assume then that you have received a scientific education. Let us suppose you intend to be a doctor.

Tomorrow a man attired in rough clothes will come to fetch you to see a sick woman. He will lead you into one of those alleys where the neighbors opposite can almost shake hands over the heads of the passers-by. You ascend into a foul atmosphere by the flickering light of a little ill-trimmed lamp. You climb two, three, four, five flights of filthy stairs, and in a dark, cold room you find the sick woman lying on a pallet covered with dirty rags. Pale, livid children, shivering under their scanty garments, gaze with their big eyes wide open. The husband has worked all his life twelve or thirteen hours a day at no matter what. Now he has been out of work for three months. To be out of employment is not rare in his trade; it happens every year, periodically. But formerly when he was out of work his wife went out as a charwoman—perhaps to wash your shirts; now she has been bedridden for two months, and misery glares upon the family in all its squalid hideousness.

What will you prescribe for the sick woman, doctor? You have seen at a glance that the cause of her illness is a general anaemia, want of good food, lack of fresh air. Say a good beefsteak every day? A little exercise in the country? A dry and well-ventilated bedroom? What irony! If she could have afforded it this would have been done long since without waiting for your advice.

If you have a good heart, a frank address, an honest face, the family will tell you many things. They will tell you that the woman on the other side of the partition, who coughs a cough which tears your heart, is a poor ironer; that a flight of stairs lower down all the children have the fever; that the washwoman who occupies the ground floor will not live to see the spring; and that in the house next door things are worse.

What will you say to all these sick people? Recommend them generous diet, change of air, less exhausting toil. . . . You only wish you could, but you daren't and you go out heartbroken with a curse on your lips.

The next day, as you still brood over the fate of the dwellers in this dog house, your partner tells you that yesterday a footman came to fetch him, this time in a carriage. It was for the owner of a fine house, for a lady worn out with sleepless nights, who devotes all her life to dressing, visits, balls and squabbles with a stupid husband. Your friend has prescribed for her a less preposterous habit of life, a less heating diet, walks in the fresh air, an even temperament, and, in order to make up in some measure for the want of useful work, a little gymnastic exercise in her bedroom.

The one is dying because she has never had enough food nor enough rest in her whole life. The other pines because she has never known what work is since she was born.

If you are one of those characterless natures who adapt themselves to anything, who at the sight of the most revolting spectacles console themselves with a gentle sigh, then you will gradually become used to these contrasts, and the nature of the beast favoring your endeavors, your sole idea will be to maintain yourself in the ranks of pleasure-seekers, so that you may never find yourself among the wretched. But if you are a *Man*, if every sentiment is translated in your case into an action of the will, if in you the beast has not crushed the intelligent being, then you will return home one day saying to yourself: "No, it is unjust: this must not go on any longer. It is not enough to cure diseases; we must prevent them. A little good living and intellectual development would score off our lists half the patients and half the diseases. Throw physic to the dogs! Air, good diet, less crushing toil—that is how we must begin. Without this, the whole profession of a doctor is nothing but trickery and humbug."

That very day you will understand socialism. You will wish to know it thoroughly, and if altruism is not a word devoid of significance for you, if you apply to the study of the social question the rigid induction of the natural philosopher, you will end by finding yourself in our ranks, and you will work, as we work, to bring about the social revolution.

To Scientists

But perhaps you will say, "Mere practical business may go to the devil! As an astronomer, a physiologist, a chemist, I will devote myself to science. Such work as that always bears fruit, if only for future generations."

Let us first try to understand what you seek in devoting yourself to science. Is it only the pleasure—doubtless immense—which we derive from the study of nature and the exercise of our mental faculties? In that case I ask you in what respect does the philosopher, who pursues science in order that he may pass life pleasantly to himself, differ from that drunkard there, who only seeks the immediate gratification that gin affords him? The philosopher has, past all question, chosen his enjoyment more wisely, since it affords him a pleasure far deeper and more lasting than that of the toper. But that is all! Both one and the other have the same selfish end in view, personal gratification.

But no, you have no wish to lead this selfish life. By working at science you mean to work for humanity, and this is the idea which will guide you in your investigations. A charming illusion! Which of us has not hugged it for a moment when giving himself up for the first time to science?

But then, if you are really thinking about humanity, if it is the good of mankind at which you aim, a formidable question arises before you; for, however little you may have of critical spirit, you must at once note that in our society of today science is only an appendage to luxury, rendering life pleasanter for the few, but remaining absolutely inaccessible to the bulk of mankind.

More than a century has passed since science laid down sound propositions as to the origin of the universe, but how many have mastered them or possess the really scientific spirit of criticism? A few thousands at the outside, who are lost in the midst of hundreds of millions still steeped in prejudices and superstitions worthy of savages, who are consequently ever ready to serve as puppets for religious impostors.

Or, to go a step further, let us glance at what science has done to establish rational foundations for physical and moral health. Science tells us how we ought to live in order to preserve the health of our own bodies, how to maintain in good condition the crowded masses of our population. But does not all the vast amount of work done in these two directions remain a dead letter in our books? We know it does. And why? Because science today exists only for a handful of privileged persons, because social inequality, which divides society into two classes — the wage-slaves and the grabbers of capital — renders all its teachings as to the conditions of a rational existence only the bitterest irony to nine-tenths of mankind.

At the present moment we no longer need to accumulate scientific truths and discoveries. The most important thing is to spread the truths already acquired, to practice them in daily life, to make of them a common inheritance. We have to order things in such wise that all humanity may be capable of assimilating and applying them, so that science ceasing to be a luxury becomes the basis of everyday life. Justice requires this.

Furthermore, the very interests of science require it. Science only makes real progress when its truths find environments ready prepared for their reception. The theory of the mechanical origin of heat remained for eighty years buried in academic records until such knowledge of physics and spread widely enough to create a public capable of accepting it. Three generations had to go before the ideas of Erasmus Darwin on the variation of species could be favorably received from his grandson and admitted by academic philosophers, and even then not without pressure from public opinion. The philosopher like the poet or artist is always the product of the society in which he moves and teaches.

But if you are imbued with these ideas, you will understand that it is important above all to bring about a radical change in this state of affairs which today condemns the philosopher to be crammed with scientific truths, and almost the whole of the rest of human beings to remain what they were five or ten centuries ago, — that is to say, in the state of slaves and machines, incapable of mastering established truths. And the day when you are imbued with wide, deep, humane, and profoundly scientific truth, that day will you lose your taste for pure science. You will set to work to find out the means to effect this transformation, and if you bring to your investigations the impartiality which has guided you in your scientific researches you will of necessity adopt the cause of socialism; you will make an end of sophisms and you will come among us. Weary of working to procure pleasures for this small group, which already has a large share of them, you will place your information and devotion at the service of the oppressed.

And be sure that the feeling of duty accomplished and of a real accord established between your sentiments and your actions, you will then find powers in yourself of whose existence you never even dreamed. When, too, one day—it is not far distant in any case, saving the presence of our professors—when one day, I say, the change for which you are working shall have been brought about, then, deriving new forces from collective scientific work, and from the powerful help of armies of laborers who will come to place their energies at its service, science will take a new bound forward, in comparison with which the slow progress of today will appear the simple exercise of tyros. Then you will enjoy science; that pleasure will be a pleasure for all.

To Lawyers

If you have finished reading law and are about to be called to the bar, perhaps you, too, have some illusions as to your future activity—I assume that you are one of the nobler spirits, that you know what altruism means. Perhaps you think, "To devote my life to an unceasing and vigorous struggle against all injustice; to apply my whole faculties to bringing about the triumph of law, the public expression of supreme justice—can any career be nobler!" You begin the real work of life confident in yourself and the profession you have chosen.

Very well; let us turn to any page of the law reports and see what actual life will tell you.

Here we have a rich landowner. He demands the eviction of a farmer tenant who has not paid his rent. From a legal point of view the case is beyond dispute. Since the poor farmer can't pay, out he must go. But if we look into the facts we shall learn something like this. The landlord has squandered his rents persistently in rollicking pleasure; the tenant has worked hard all day and every day. The landlord has done nothing to improve his estate. Nevertheless its value has trebled in fifty years owing to the rise in price of land due to the construction of a railway, to the making of new highroads, to the draining of a marsh, to the enclosure and cultivation of waste lands. But the tenant who has contributed largely towards this increase has ruined himself. He fell into the hands of usurers, and head over ears in debt, he can no longer pay the landlord. The law, always on the side of property, is quite clear; the landlord is in the right. But you, whose feeling of justice has not yet been stifled by legal fictions, what will you do? Will you contend that the farmer ought to be turned out upon the highroad—for that is what the law ordains—or will you urge that the landlord should pay back to the farmer the whole of the increase of value in his property which is due to the farmer's labor—this is what equity decrees? Which side will you take? For the law and against justice, or for justice and against the law?

Or when workmen have gone out on strike against a master, without notice, which side will you take then? The side of the law, that is to say the part of the master, who, taking advantage of a period of crisis, has made outrageous profits, or against the law but on the side of the workers who received during the whole time only miserable wages, and saw their wives and children fade away before their eyes? Will you stand up for that piece of chicanery which consists in affirming "freedom of contract"? Or will you uphold equity, according to which a contract entered into between a man who has dined well and a man who sells his labor for a bare subsistence, between the strong and the weak, is not a contract at all?

Take another case. Here in London a man was loitering near a butcher's shop. He stole a beefsteak and ran off with it. Arrested and questioned, it turns out that he is an artisan out of work, and that he and his family have had nothing to eat for four days. The butcher is asked to let the man off but he is all for the triumph of justice! He prosecutes and the man is sentenced to six months' imprisonment. Does not your conscience revolt against society when you hear similar judgments pronounced every day?

Or again, will you call for the enforcement of the law against this man, who badly brought up and ill-used from his childhood, has arrived at man's estate without having heard one sympathetic word, and completes his career by murdering his neighbor in order to rob him? Will you demand his execution, or, worse still, that he should be imprisoned for twenty years, when you know very well that he is rather a madman than a criminal, and, in any case, that his crime is the fault of our entire society?

Will you claim that these weavers should be thrown into prison who in a moment of desperation have set fire to a mill; that this man who shot at a crowned murderer should be imprisoned for life; that these insurgents should be shot down who plant the flag of the future on the barricades? No, a thousand times no!

If you *reason* instead of repeat what is taught you; if you analyze the law and strip off those cloudy fictions with which it has been draped in order to conceal its real origin, which is the right of the stronger, and its substance, which has ever been the consecration of all the tyrannies handed down to mankind through its long and bloody history; when you have comprehended this your contempt for the law will be profound indeed. You will understand that to remain the servant of the written law is to place yourself every day in opposition to the law of conscience, and to make a bargain on the wrong side, and since this struggle cannot go on for ever, you will either silence your conscience and become a scoundrel, or you will break with tradition, and you will work with us for the utter destruction of all this injustice, economic, social and political. But then you will be a *socialist, you will be a revolutionist!*

To Engineers

And you, young engineer, who dream of bettering the lot of the workers by applying the inventions of science to industry, what a sad disenchantment, what deceptions await you. You devote the youthful energy of your intellect to working out the plan of some railway which, winding round by the edges of precipices, and piercing the heart of huge mountains, will unite two countries separated by nature. But when once the work is on foot you see whole regiments of workers decimated by privations and sickness in this gloomy tunnel, you see others returning home taking with them only a little money and the seeds of consumption, you will see each yard of the line marked off by human corpses, the result of grovelling greed, and finally, when the line is at last opened, you see it used as the highway for the artillery of an invading army.

You have devoted your youth to make a discovery destined to simplify production, and after many efforts, many sleepless nights, you have at last this valuable invention. You put it into practice and the result surpasses your expectations. Ten, twenty thousand beings are thrown out of work; those who remain, mostly children, are reduced to the condition of mere machines! Three, four, or maybe ten capitalists will make a fortune and drink champagne by the bottleful. Was that your dream?

Finally, you study recent industrial advances, and you see that the seamstress has gained nothing, absolutely nothing, by the invention of the sewing machine; that the laborer in the St. Gothard tunnel dies of ankylostomiasis, notwithstanding diamond drills; that the mason and the day laborer are out of work just as before. If you discuss social problems with the same independence of spirit which has guided you in your mechanical investigations, you necessarily come to the conclusion that under the domination of private property and wage-slavery, every new invention, far from increasing the well-being of the worker, only makes his slavery heavier, his labor more degrading, the periods of slack work more frequent, the crisis sharper, and that the man who already has every conceivable pleasure for himself is the only one who profits by it.

What will you do when you have once come to this conclusion? Either you will begin by silencing your conscience by sophisms; then one fine day you will bid farewell to the honest dreams of your youth and you will try to obtain, for yourself, what commands pleasure and enjoyment—you will then go over to the camp of the exploiters. Or, if you have a tender heart, you will say to yourself:—"No, this is not the time for inventions. Let us work first to transform the domain of production. When private property is put to an end, then each new advance in industry will be made for the benefit of all mankind, and this mass of workers, mere machines as they are to-day, will then become thinking beings who apply to industry their intelligence, strengthened by study and skilled in manual labor, and thus mechanical progress will take a bound forward which will carry out in fifty years what now-a-days we cannot even dream of."

To Teachers

And what shall I say to the schoolmaster—not to the man who looks upon his profession as a wearisome business, but to him who, when surrounded by a joyous band of youngsters, feels exhilarated by their cheery looks and in the midst of their happy laughter; to him who tries to plant in their little heads those ideas of humanity which he cherished himself when he was young.

Often I see that you are sad, and I know what it is that makes you knit your brows. This very day, your favorite pupil, who is not very well up in Latin, it is true, but who has none the less an excellent heart, recited the story of William Tell with so much vigor! His eyes sparkled; he seemed to wish to stab all tyrants there and then; he gave with such fire the passionate lines of Schiller:—

> Before the slave when he breaks his chain,
> Before the free man tremble not.

But when he returned home, his mother, his father, his uncle, sharply rebuked him for want of respect to the minister or the rural policeman. They held forth to him by the hour on "prudence, respect for authority, submission to his betters," till he put Schiller aside in order to read *Self-Help*.

And then only yesterday you were told that your best pupils have all turned out badly. One does nothing but dream of becoming an officer; another in league with his master robs the workers of their slender wages; and you, who had such hopes of these young people, you now brood over the sad contrast between your ideal and life as it is.

You still brood over it. Then I foresee that in two years at the outside, after having suffered disappointment after disappointment, you will lay your favorite authors on the shelf, and you will end by saying that Tell was no doubt a very honest fellow, but after all a trifle cracked; that poetry is a first-rate thing for the fireside, especially when a man has been teaching the rule-of-three all day long, but still poets are always in the clouds and their views have nothing to do with the life of today, nor with the next visit of the inspector of schools. . . .

Or, on the other hand, the dreams of your youth will become the firm convictions of your mature age. You will wish to have wide, human education for all, in school and out of school. And seeing that this is impossible in existing conditions, you will attack the very foundations of bourgeois society. Then discharged as you will be by the board of education, you will leave your school and come among us and be of us. You will tell men of riper years but of smaller attainments than yourself how enticing knowledge is, what mankind ought to be, nay, what we could be. You will come and work with socialists for the complete transformation of the existing system, will strive side by side with us to attain true equality, true fraternity, never-ending liberty for the world.

To Artists

Lastly, you, young artist, sculptor, painter, poet, musician, do you not observe that the sacred fire which inspired your predecessors is wanting in the men of today; that art is commonplace and mediocrity reigns supreme?

Could it be otherwise? The delight at having rediscovered the ancient world, of having bathed afresh in the springs of nature which created the masterpieces of the Renaissance no longer exists for the art of our time. The revolutionary ideal has left it cold until now, and failing an ideal, our art fancies that it has found one in realism when it painfully photographs in colors the dewdrop on the leaf of a plant, imitates the muscles in the leg of a cow, or describes minutely in prose and in verse the suffocating filth of a sewer, the boudoir of a whore of high degree.

"But if this is so, what is to be done?" you say. If, I reply, the sacred fire that you say you possess is nothing better than a smouldering wick, then you will go on doing as you have done, and your art will speedily degenerate into the trade of decorator of tradesmen's shops, of a purveyor of libretti to third-rate operettas and tales for Christmas books — most of you are already running down that grade with a fine head of steam on. . . .

But, if your heart really beats in unison with that of humanity, if like a true poet you have an ear of Life, then, gazing out upon this sea of sorrow whose tide sweeps up around you, face to face with these people dying of hunger, in the presence of these corpses piled up in these mines, and these mutilated bodies lying in heaps on the barricades, in full view of this desperate battle which is being fought, amid the cries of pain from the conquered and the orgies of the victors, of heroism in conflict with cowardice, of noble determination face to face with contemptible cunning—you cannot remain neutral. You will come and take the side of the oppressed because you know that the beautiful, the sublime, the spirit of life itself are on the side of those who fight for light, for humanity, for justice!

WHAT YOU CAN DO

You stop me at last! "What the devil!" you say. "But if abstract science is a luxury and practice of medicine mere chicane; if law spells injustice, and mechanical invention is but a means of robbery; if the school, at variance with the wisdom of the 'practical man,' is sure to be overcome, and art without the revolutionary idea can only degenerate, what remains for me to do?"

A vast and most enthralling task, a work in which your actions will be in complete harmony with your conscience, an undertaking capable of rousing the noblest and most vigorous natures.

What work? I will now tell you.

Two courses are open to you. You can either tamper for ever with your conscience and finish one day by saying "Humanity can go to the devil as long as I am enjoying every pleasure to the full and so long as the people are foolish enough to let me do so." Or else you will join the ranks of the socialists and work with them for the complete transformation of society. Such is the necessary result of the analysis we have made. Such is the logical conclusion at which every intelligent being must arrive provided he judge impartially the things he sees around him, and disregard the sophisms suggested to him by his middle-class education and the interested views of his friends.

Having once reached this conclusion, the question which arises is "what is to be done?" The answer is easy. Quit the environment in which you are placed and in which it is customary to speak of the workers as a lot of brutes; go among the people, and the question will solve itself.

You will find that everywhere in England as in Germany, in Italy as in the United States, wherever there are privileged classes and oppressed, a tremendous movement is on foot among the working-classes, the aim of which is to destroy once and for ever the slavery imposed by capitalists, and to lay the foundations of a new society based on the principles of justice and equality. It no longer suffices for the people to voice their misery in those songs whose melody breaks one's heart, and which the serfs of the eighteenth century sang. He works today fully conscious of what he has done, in spite of every obstacle to his enfranchisement. His thoughts are continually occupied in considering what to do so that life instead of being a mere curse to three-fourths of the human race may be a blessing to all. He attacks the most difficult problems of sociology, and strives to solve them with his sound common sense, his observation, and his sad experience. To come to a common understanding with his fellows in misfortune, he tries to form groups and to organize. He forms societies, sustained with difficulty by slender contributions. He tries to make terms with his fellows beyond the frontier. And he does more than all the loud-mouthed philanthropists to hasten the advent of the day when wars between nations will become impossible. To know what his brothers are doing, to improve his acquaintance with them, to elaborate and propagate his ideas, he sustains, at the cost of what efforts, his working-class press. What a ceaseless struggle! What labor, constantly requiring to be recommenced. Sometimes to fill the gaps made by desertion—the result of lassitude, of corruption, of persecutions; sometimes to reorganize the ranks decimated by fusillades and grape shot, sometimes to resume studies suddenly cut short by wholesale massacres.

The papers are conducted by men who have had to snatch from society scraps of knowledge by depriving themselves of food and sleep. The agitation is supported with the pennies of the workers saved from the strict necessaries of life. And all this is done, shadowed by the continual apprehension of seeing their families plunged into destitution as soon as the master perceives that his worker, his slave, is a socialist.

These are the things you will see if you go among the people. And in this ceaseless struggle how often has the worker, sinking under the weight of difficulties, exclaimed in vain: "Where then are those young men who have been educated at our expense, whom we have clothed and fed while they studied? For whom, with backs bowed down under heavy loads, and with empty stomachs, we have built these houses, these academies, these museums? For whom we, with pallid faces, have printed those fine books we cannot so much as read? Where are they, those professors who claim to possess the science of humanity, and yet in whose eyes mankind is not worth a rare species of caterpillar? Where are those men who preach of liberty and who never rise to defend ours, daily trodden under foot? These writers, these poets, these painters, all this band of hypocrites, in short, who speak of the people with tears in their eyes, and who nevertheless never come among us to help us in our work?"

Some complacently enjoy their condition of cowardly indifference, others, the majority, despise the "rabble" and are ever ready to pounce down on it if it dare to attack their privileges.

From time to time, it is true, a young man appears on the scene who dreams of drums and barricades, and who is in search of sensational scenes and situations, but who deserts the cause of the people as soon as he perceives that the road to the barricades is long, that the laurels he counts on winning on the way are mixed with thorns. Generally these men are ambitious adventurers, who after failing in their first attempts, seek to obtain the votes of the people, but who later on will be the first to denounce it, if it dare to try and put into practice the principles they themselves advocated, and who perhaps will even point the cannon at the proletariat if it dare move before they, the leaders, have given the word of command.

Add to this stupid insults, haughty contempt, and cowardly calumny on the part of a great number, and you have all the help that the middle-class youth give the people in their powerful social evolution.

And then you ask, "what shall we do?" when there is everything to be done! When a whole army of young people would find plenty to employ the entire vigor of their youthful energy, the full force of their intelligence and their talents to help the people in the vast enterprise they have undertaken!

What shall we do? Listen.

You lovers of pure science, if you are imbued with the principles of socialism, if you have understood the real meaning of the revolution which is even now knocking at the door, do you not see that all science has to be recast in order to place it in harmony with the new principles? That it is your business to accomplish in this field a revolution far greater than that which was accomplished in every branch of science during the eighteenth century? Do you not understand that history—which today is an old woman's tale about great kings, great statesmen and great parliaments—that history itself has to be written from the point of view of the people in the long evolution of mankind? That social economy—which today is merely the sanctification of capitalist robbery—has to be worked out afresh in its fundamental principles as well as in its innumerable applications? That anthropology, sociology, ethics, must be completely recast, and that the natural sciences themselves, regarded from another point of view, must undergo a profound modification, alike in regard to the conception of natural phenomena and with respect to the method of exposition?

Very well, then, set to work! Place your abilities at the command of the good cause. Especially help us with your clear logic to combat prejudice and to lay by your synthesis the foundation of a better organization. Yet more, teach us to apply in our daily arguments the fearlessness of true scientific investigation, and show us as your predecessors did, how man dare sacrifice even life itself for the triumph of the truth.

You, doctors who have learnt socialism by a bitter experience, never weary of telling us today, tomorrow, in and out of season, that humanity itself hurries onward to decay if man remain in the present conditions of existence and work; that all your medicaments must be powerless against disease while the majority of mankind vegetate in conditions absolutely contrary to those which science tells us are healthful. Convince the people that it is the causes of disease which must be uprooted, and show us all what is necessary to remove them.

Come with your scalpel and dissect for us with unerring hand this society of ours fast hastening to putrefaction. Tell us what a rational existence should and might be. Insist, as true surgeons, that a gangrenous limb must be amputated when it may poison the whole body.

You who have worked at the application of science to industry, come and tell us frankly what has been the outcome of your discoveries. Convince those who dare not march boldly towards the future what new inventions the knowledge we have already acquired carries in its womb, what industry could do under better conditions, what man might easily produce if he produced always with a view to enhance his own productions.

You poets, painters, sculptors, musicians, if you understand your true mission and the very interests of art itself, come with us. Place your pen, your pencil, your chisel, your ideas at the service of the revolution. Figure forth to us, in your eloquent style, or your impressive pictures, the heroic struggles of the people against their oppressors, fire the hearts of our youth with that glorious revolutionary enthusiasm which inflamed the souls of our ancestors. Tell women what a noble career is that of a husband who devotes his life to the great cause of social emancipation! Show the people how hideous is their actual life, and place your hands on the causes of its ugliness. Tell us what a rational life would be, if it did not encounter at every step the follies and the ignominies of our present social order.

Lastly, all of you who possess knowledge, talent, capacity, industry, if you have a spark of sympathy in your nature, come you, and your companions, come and place your services at the disposal of those who most need them. And remember, if you do come, that you come not as masters, but as comrades in the struggle; that you come not to govern but to gain strength for yourselves in a new life which sweeps upwards to the conquest of the future: that you come less to teach than to grasp the aspiration of the many; to divine them, to give them shape, and then to work, without rest and without haste, with all the fire of youth and all the judgment of age, to realize them in actual life. Then and then only, will you lead a complete, a noble, a rational existence. Then you will see that your every effort on this path bears with it fruit in abundance, and this sublime harmony once established between your actions and the dictates of your conscience will give you powers you never dreamt lay dormant in yourselves, the never-ceasing struggle for truth, justice, and equality among the people, whose gratitude you will earn—what nobler career can the youth of all nations desire than this?

It has taken me long to show you of the well-to-do classes that in view of the dilemma which life presents to you, you will be forced, if courageous and sincere, to come and work side by side with the socialists, and champion in their ranks, the cause of the social revolution.

And yet how simple this truth is after all! But when one is speaking to those who have suffered from the effects of bourgeois surroundings, how many sophisms must be combated, how many prejudices overcome, how many interested objections put aside!

TO WORKING CLASS YOUTHS

It is easy to be brief today in addressing you, the youth of the people. The very pressure of events impels you to become socialists, however little you may have the courage to reason and to act.

To rise from the ranks of the working people, and not devote oneself to bringing about the triumph of socialism, is to misconceive the real interests at stake, to give up the cause, and the true historic mission.

Do you remember the time, when still a mere lad, you went down one winter's day to play in your dark court? The cold nipped your shoulders through your thin clothes, and the mud worked into your worn-out shoes. Even then when you saw chubby children richly clad pass in the distance, looking at you with an air of contempt, you knew right well that these imps were not the equals of yourself and your comrades, either in intelligence, common sense or energy. But later when you were forced to shut yourself up in a filthy factory from seven o'clock in the morning, to remain hours on end close to a whirling machine, and, a machine yourself, you were forced to follow day after day for whole years in succession its movements with relentless throbbing—during all this time they, the others, were going quietly to be taught at fine schools, at academies, at the universities. And now these same children, less intelligent, but better taught than you, have become your masters, are enjoying all the pleasures of life and all the advantages of civilization. And you? What sort of lot awaits you?

You return to little, dark, damp lodgings where five or six human beings pig together within a few square feet. Where your mother, sick of life, aged by care rather than years, offers you dry bread and potatoes

as your only food, washed down by a blackish fluid called in irony "tea."
And to distract your thoughts you have ever the same never-ending
question, "How shall I be able to pay the baker tomorrow, and the landlord the day after?"

What! must you drag on the same weary existence as your father and
mother for thirty and forty years? Must you toil your life long to procure
for others all the pleasures of well-being, of knowledge, of art, and keep
for yourself only the eternal anxiety as to whether you can get a bit of
bread? Will you forever give up all that makes life so beautiful to devote
yourself to providing every luxury for a handful of idlers? Will you wear
yourself out with toil and have in return only trouble, if not misery,
when hard times—the fearful hard times—come upon you? Is this
what you long for in life?

Perhaps you will give up. Seeing no way whatever out of your condition, maybe you say to yourself, "Whole generations have undergone
the same lot, and I, who can alter nothing in the matter, I must submit
also. Let us work on then and endeavor to live as well as we can!"

Very well. In that case life itself will take pains to enlighten you. One
day a crisis comes, one of those crises which are no longer mere passing phenomena, as they were formerly, but a crisis which destroys a
whole industry, which plunges thousands of workers into misery, which
crushes whole families. You struggle against the calamity like the rest.
But you will soon see how your wife, your child, your friend, little by
little succumb to privations, fade away under your very eyes. For sheer
want of food, for lack of care and medical assistance, they end their
days on the pauper's stretcher, whilst the life of the rich flows on joy-
ously midst the sunny streets of the great city, careless of those who
starve and perish. You will then understand how utterly revolting is this
society. You will then reflect upon the causes of this crisis, and your
examinations will scrutinize to the depths that abomination which puts
millions of human beings at the mercy of the brutal greed of a handful
of useless triflers. Then you will understand that socialists are right
when they say that our present society can be, that it must be, reorga-
nized from top to bottom.

To pass from general crises to your particular case. One day when
your master tries by a new reduction of wages to squeeze out of you a
few more dollars in order to increase his fortune still further you will
protest. But he will haughtily answer, "Go and eat grass, if you will not
work at the price I offer." Then you will understand that your master
not only tries to shear you like a sheep, but that he looks upon you as
an inferior kind of animal altogether; that not content with holding you
in his relentless grip by means of the wage system, he is further anxious
to make you a slave in every respect. Then you will, perhaps, bow down

before him, you will give up the feeling of human dignity, and you will end by suffering every possible humiliation. Or the blood will rush to your head, you shudder at the hideous slope on which you are slipping down, you will retort, and, turned out workless on the street, you will understand how right socialists are when they say, "Revolt! rise against this economic slavery!" Then you will come and take your place in the ranks of the socialists, and you will work with them for the complete destruction of all slavery—economic, social and political.

Every one of you then, honest young people, men and women, peasants, laborers, artisans, and soldiers, you will understand what are your rights and you will come along with us. You will come in order to work with your brethren in the preparation of that revolution which is sweeping away every vestige of slavery, tearing the fetters asunder, breaking with the old worn-out traditions and opening to all mankind a new and wider scope of joyous existence, and which shall at length establish true liberty, real equality, ungrudging fraternity throughout human society. Work with all, work for all—the full enjoyment of the fruits of their labor, the complete development of all their faculties, a rational, human and happy life!

Don't let anyone tell us that we—but a small band—are too weak to attain unto the magnificent end at which we aim. Count and see how many there are who suffer this injustice. We peasants who work for others, and who mumble the straw while our master eats the wheat, we by ourselves are millions of men. We workers who weave silks and velvet in order that we may be clothed in rags, we, too, are a great multitude; and when the clang of the factories permits us a moment's repose, we overflow the streets and squares like the sea in a spring tide. We soldiers who are driven along to the word of command, or by blows, we who receive the bullets for which our officers get crosses and pensions, we, too, poor fools who have hitherto known no better than to shoot our brothers, why we have only to make a right about face towards these plumed and decorated personages who are so good as to command us, to see a ghastly pallor overspread their faces.

Ay, all of us together, we who suffer and are insulted daily, we are a multitude whom no man can number, we are the ocean that can embrace and swallow up all else. When we have but the will to do it, that very moment will justice be done: that very instant the tyrants of the earth shall bite the dust.

MIKHAIL BAKUNIN
From *God and the State*
1882

Mikhail Bakunin (1814–1876), having served in the Russian military, left Russia in 1840 for western Europe, where he became acquainted with Proudhon and Marx, and participated in various uprisings in 1848. He was jailed in 1849 for his revolutionary activism, and escaped from exile in Siberia in 1861. He characterized himself, in contrast to Marx, as one who acted rather than theorized. His posthumously published *God and the State* (written in 1871 as a section of the unfinished *The Knouto-Germanic Empire*), has become his most popular work. Bakunin, hardly interested in compromise, hopes to do away with God: "For, if God is, he is necessarily the eternal, supreme, absolute master, and, if such a master exists, man is a slave; now, if he is a slave, neither justice, nor equality, nor fraternity, nor prosperity are possible for him." Paul Avrich notes, "In vivid language and relatively brief compass, [*God and the State*] sets forth the basic elements of Bakunin's anarchist creed."

SOURCE: Michael Bakunin, *God and the State*. Introduction by Paul Avrich (New York: Dover Publications, Inc., 1970), 23–35, 83–86.

God and the State

I have stated the chief practical reason of the power still exercised today over the masses by religious beliefs. These mystical tendencies do not signify in man so much an aberration of mind as a deep discontent at heart. They are the instinctive and passionate protest of the human being against the narrowness, the platitudes, the sorrows, and the shame of a wretched existence. For this malady, I have already said, there is but one remedy — Social Revolution.

In the meantime I have endeavored to show the causes responsible for the birth and historical development of religious hallucinations in the human conscience. Here it is my purpose to treat this question of the existence of a God, or of the divine origin of the world and of man, solely from the standpoint of its moral and social utility, and I shall say only a few words, to better explain my thought, regarding the theoretical grounds of this belief.

All religions, with their gods, their demigods, and their prophets, their messiahs and their saints, were created by the credulous fancy of men who had not attained the full development and full possession of their faculties. Consequently, the religious heaven is nothing but a mirage in which man, exalted by ignorance and faith, discovers his own image, but enlarged and reversed—that is, *divinized*. The history of religions, of the birth, grandeur, and decline of the gods who have succeeded one another in human belief, is nothing, therefore, but the development of the collective intelligence and conscience of mankind. As fast as they discovered, in the course of their historically progressive advance, either in themselves or in external nature, a power, a quality, or even any great defect whatever, they attributed them to their gods, after having exaggerated and enlarged them beyond measure, after the manner of children, by an act of their religious fancy. Thanks to this modesty and pious generosity of believing and credulous men, heaven has grown rich with the spoils of the earth, and, by a necessary consequence, the richer heaven became, the more wretched became humanity and the earth. God once installed, he was naturally proclaimed the cause, reason, arbiter, and absolute disposer of all things: the world thenceforth was nothing, God was all; and man, his real creator, after having unknowingly extracted him from the void, bowed down before him, worshipped him, and avowed himself his creature and his slave.

Christianity is precisely the religion *par excellence*, because it exhibits and manifests, to the fullest extent, the very nature and essence of every religious system, which is *the impoverishment, enslavement, and annihilation of humanity for the benefit of divinity*.

God being everything, the real world and man are nothing. God being truth, justice, goodness, beauty, power, and life, man is falsehood, iniquity, evil, ugliness, impotence, and death. God being master, man is the slave. Incapable of finding justice, truth, and eternal life by his own effort, he can attain them only through a divine revelation. But whoever says revelation says revealers, messiahs, prophets, priests, and legislators inspired by God himself; and these, once recognized as the representatives of divinity on earth, as the holy instructors of humanity, chosen by God himself to direct it in the path of salvation, necessarily exercise absolute power. All men owe them passive and unlimited obedience; for against the divine reason there is no human reason, and against the justice of God no terrestrial justice holds. Slaves of God, men must also be slaves of Church and State, *in so far as the State is consecrated by the Church.* This truth Christianity, better than all other religions that exist or have existed, understood, not excepting even the old Oriental religions, which included only distinct and privileged nations, while Christianity aspires to embrace entire humanity; and this truth Roman Catholicism, alone among all the Christian sects, has proclaimed and realized with rigorous logic. That is why Christianity is the absolute religion, the final religion; why the Apostolic and Roman Church is the only consistent, legitimate, and divine church.

With all due respect, then, to the metaphysicians and religious idealists, philosophers, politicians, or poets: *The idea of God implies the abdication of human reason and justice; it is the most decisive negation of human liberty, and necessarily ends in the enslavement of mankind, both in theory and practice.*

Unless, then, we desire the enslavement and degradation of mankind, as the Jesuits desire it, as the *mômiers*, pietists, or Protestant Methodists desire it, we may not, must not make the slightest concession either to the God of theology or to the God of metaphysics. He who, in this mystical alphabet, begins with A will inevitably end with Z; he who desires to worship God must harbor no childish allusions about the matter, but bravely renounce his liberty and humanity.

If God is, man is a slave; now, man can and must be free; then, God does not exist.

I defy anyone whomsoever to avoid this circle; now, therefore, let all choose.

Is it necessary to point out to what extent and in what manner religions debase and corrupt the people? They destroy their reason, the principal instrument of human emancipation, and reduce them to imbecility, the essential condition of their slavery. They dishonor human labor, and make it a sign and source of servitude. They kill the idea and sentiment of human justice, ever tipping the balance to the side of triumphant knaves, privileged objects of divine indulgence. They kill human pride and dignity, protecting only the cringing and humble. They stifle in the heart of nations every feeling of human fraternity, filling it with divine cruelty instead.

All religions are cruel, all founded on blood; for all rest principally on the idea of sacrifice—that is, on the perpetual immolation of humanity to the insatiable vengeance of divinity. In this bloody mystery man is always the victim, and the priest—a man also, but a man privileged by grace—is the divine executioner. That explains why the priests of all religions, the best, the most humane, the gentlest, almost always have at the bottom of their hearts—and, if not in their hearts, in their imaginations, in their minds (and we know the fearful influence of either on the hearts of men)—something cruel and sanguinary.

None know all this better than our illustrious contemporary idealists. They are learned men, who know history by heart; and, as they are at the same time living men, great souls penetrated with a sincere and profound love for the welfare of humanity, they have cursed and branded all these misdeeds, all these crimes of religion with an eloquence unparalleled. They reject with indignation all solidarity with the God of positive religions and with his representatives, past, present, and on earth.

The God whom they adore, or whom they think they adore, is distinguished from the real gods of history precisely in this—that he is not at all a positive god, defined in any way whatever, theologically or even metaphysically. He is neither the supreme being of Robespierre and J. J. Rousseau, nor the pantheistic god of Spinoza, nor even the at once immanent, transcendental, and very equivocal god of Hegel. They take good care not to give him any positive definition whatever, feeling very strongly that any definition would subject him to the dissolving power of criticism. They will not say whether he is a personal or impersonal god, whether he created or did not create the world; they will not even speak of his divine providence. All that might compromise him. They content themselves with saying "God" and nothing more. But, then, what is their God? Not even an idea; it is an aspiration.

It is the generic name of all that seems grand, good, beautiful, noble, human to them. But why, then, do they not say, "Man." Ah! because King William of Prussia and Napoleon III and all their compeers are likewise men: which bothers them very much. Real humanity presents a mixture of all that is most sublime and beautiful with all that is vilest and most monstrous in the world. How do they get over this? Why, they call one *divine* and the other *bestial*, representing divinity and animality as two poles, between which they place humanity. They either will not or cannot understand that these three terms are really but one, and that to separate them is to destroy them.

They are not strong on logic, and one might say that they despise it. That is what distinguishes them from the pantheistical and deistical metaphysicians, and gives their ideas the character of a practical idealism, drawing its inspiration much less from the severe development of a thought than from the experiences, I might almost say the emotions, historical and collective as well as individual, of life. This gives their propaganda an appearance of wealth and vital power, but an appearance only; for life itself becomes sterile when paralyzed by a logical contradiction.

This contradiction lies here: they wish God, and they wish humanity. They persist in connecting two terms which, once separated, can come together again only to destroy each other. They say in a single breath: "God and the liberty of man," "God and the dignity, justice, equality, fraternity, prosperity of men"—regardless of the fatal logic by virtue of which, if God exists, all these things are condemned to non-existence. For, if God is, he is necessarily the eternal, supreme, absolute master, and, if such a master exists, man is a slave; now, if he is a slave, neither justice, nor equality, nor fraternity, nor prosperity are possible for him. In vain, flying in the face of good sense and all the teachings of history, do they represent their God as animated by the tenderest love of human liberty: a master, whoever he may be and however liberal he may desire to show himself, remains none the less always a master. His existence necessarily implies the slavery of all that is beneath him. Therefore, if God existed, only in one way could he serve human liberty—by ceasing to exist.

A jealous lover of human liberty, and deeming it the absolute condition of all that we admire and respect in humanity, I reverse the phrase of Voltaire, and say that, *if God really existed, it would be necessary to abolish him.*

The severe logic that dictates these words is far too evident to require a development of this argument. And it seems to me impossible that the illustrious men, whose names so celebrated and so justly respected I have cited, should not have been struck by it themselves, and should not have perceived the contradiction in which they involve themselves in speaking of God and human liberty at once. To have disregarded it, they must have considered this inconsistency or logical license *practically* necessary to humanity's well-being.

Perhaps, too, while speaking of *liberty* as something very respectable and very dear in their eyes, they give the term a meaning quite different from the conception entertained by us, materialists and Revolutionary Socialists. Indeed, they never speak of it without immediately adding another word, *authority*—a word and a thing which we detest with all our heart.

What is authority? Is it the inevitable power of the natural laws which manifest themselves in the necessary concatenation and succession of phenomena in the physical and social worlds? Indeed, against these laws revolt is not only forbidden—it is even impossible. We may misunderstand them or not know them at all, but we cannot disobey them; because they constitute the basis and fundamental conditions of our existence; they envelop us, penetrate us, regulate all our movements, thoughts, and acts; even when we believe that we disobey them, we only show their omnipotence.

Yes, we are absolutely the slaves of these laws. But in such slavery there is no humiliation, or, rather, it is not slavery at all. For slavery supposes an external master, a legislator outside of him whom he commands, while these laws are not outside of us; they are inherent in us; they constitute our being, our whole being, physically, intellectually, and morally: we live, we breathe, we act, we think, we wish only through these laws. Without them we are nothing, *we are not*. Whence, then, could we derive the power and the wish to rebel against them?

In his relation to natural laws but one liberty is possible to man—that of recognizing and applying them on an ever-extending scale in conformity with the object of collective and individual emancipation or humanization which he pursues. These laws, once recognized, exercise an authority which is never disputed by the mass of men. One must, for instance, be at bottom either a fool or a theologian or at least a metaphysician, jurist, or bourgeois economist to rebel against the law by which twice two make four. One must have faith to imagine that fire will not burn nor water drown, except, indeed, recourse be had to some subterfuge founded in its turn on some other natural law. But these revolts, or, rather, these attempts at or foolish fancies of an impossible revolt, are decidedly the exception; for, in general, it may be said that the mass of men, in their daily lives, acknowledge the government of common sense—that is, of the sum of the natural laws generally recognized—in an almost absolute fashion.

The great misfortune is that a large number of natural laws, already established as such by science, remain unknown to the masses, thanks to the watchfulness of these tutelary governments that exist, as we know, only for the good of the people. There is another difficulty—namely, that the major portion of the natural laws connected with the development of human society, which are quite as necessary, invariable, fatal, as the laws that govern the physical world, have not been duly established and recognized by science itself.

Once they shall have been recognized by science, and then from science, by means of an extensive system of popular education and instruction, shall have passed into the consciousness of all, the question of liberty will be entirely solved. The most stubborn authorities must admit that then there will be no need either of political organization or direction or legislation, three things which, whether they emanate from the will of the sovereign or from the vote of a parliament elected by universal suffrage, and even should they conform to the system of natural laws—which has never been the case and never will be the case—are always equally fatal and hostile to the liberty of the masses from the very fact that they impose upon them a system of external and therefore despotic laws.

The liberty of man consists solely in this: that he obeys natural laws because he has *himself* recognized them as such, and not because they have been externally imposed upon him by any extrinsic will whatever, divine or human, collective or individual.

Suppose a learned academy, composed of the most illustrious representatives of science; suppose this academy charged with legislation for and the organization of society, and that, inspired only by the purest love of truth, it frames none but laws in absolute harmony with the latest discoveries of science. Well, I maintain, for my part, that such legislation and such organization would be a monstrosity, and that for two reasons: first, that human science is always and necessarily imperfect, and that, comparing what it has discovered with what remains to be discovered, we may say that it is still in its cradle. So that were we to try to force the practical life of men, collective as well as individual, into strict and exclusive conformity with the latest data of science, we should condemn society as well as individuals to suffer martyrdom on a bed of Procrustes, which would soon end by dislocating and stifling them, life ever remaining an infinitely greater thing than science.

The second reason is this: a society which should obey legislation emanating from a scientific academy, not because it understood itself the rational character of this legislation (in which case the existence of the academy would become useless), but because this legislation, emanating from the academy, was imposed in the name of a science which it venerated without comprehending—such a society would be a society, not of men, but of brutes. It would be a second edition of those missions in Paraguay which submitted so long to the government of the Jesuits. It would surely and rapidly descend to the lowest stage of idiocy.

But there is still a third reason which would render such a government impossible—namely that a scientific academy invested with a sovereignty, so to speak, absolute, even if it were composed of the most illustrious men, would infalliby and soon end in its own moral and intellectual corruption. Even to-day, with the few privileges allowed them, such is the history of all academies. The greatest scientific genius, from the moment that he becomes an academician, an officially licensed *savant*, inevitably lapses into sluggishness. He loses his spontaneity, his revolutionary hardihood, and that troublesome and savage energy characteristic of the grandest geniuses, ever called to destroy old tottering worlds and lay the foundations of new. He undoubtedly gains in politeness, in utilitarian and practical wisdom, what he loses in power of thought. In a word, he becomes corrupted.

It is the characteristic of privilege and of every privileged position to kill the mind and heart of men. The privileged man, whether politically or economically, is a man depraved in mind and heart. That is a social law which admits of no exception, and is as applicable to entire nations as to classes, corporations, and individuals. It is the law of equality, the supreme condition of liberty and humanity. The principal object of this treatise is precisely to demonstrate this truth in all the manifestations of human life.

A scientific body to which had been confided the government of society would soon end by devoting itself no longer to science at all, but to quite another affair; and that affair, as in the case of all established powers, would be its own eternal perpetuation by rendering the society confided to its care ever more stupid and consequently more in need of its government and direction.

But that which is true of scientific academies is also true of all constituent and legislative assemblies, even those chosen by universal suffrage. In the latter case they may renew their composition, it is true, but this does not prevent the formation in a few years' time of a body of politicians, privileged in fact though not in law, who, devoting themselves exclusively to the direction of the public affairs of a country, finally form a sort of political aristocracy or oligarchy. Witness the United States of America and Switzerland.

Consequently, no external legislation and no authority—one, for that matter, being inseparable from the other, and both tending to the servitude of society and the degradation of the legislators themselves.

Does it follow that I reject all authority? Far from me such a thought. In the matter of boots, I refer to the authority of the bootmaker; concerning houses, canals, or railroads, I consult that of the architect or engineer. For such or such special knowledge I apply to such or such a *savant*. But I allow neither the bootmaker nor the architect nor the *savant* to impose his authority upon me. I listen to them freely and with all the respect merited by their intelligence, their character, their knowledge, reserving always my incontestable right of criticism and censure. I do not content myself with consulting a single authority in any special branch; I consult several; I compare their opinions, and choose that which seems to me the soundest. But I recognize no infallible authority, even in special questions; consequently, whatever respect I may have for the honesty and the sincerity of such or such an individual, I have no absolute faith in any person. Such a faith would be fatal to my reason, to my liberty, and even to the success of my undertakings; it would immediately transform me into a stupid slave, an instrument of the will and interests of others.

If I bow before the authority of the specialists and avow my readiness to follow, to a certain extent and as long as may seem to me necessary, their indications and even their directions, it is because their authority is imposed upon me by no one, neither by men nor by God. Otherwise I would repel them with horror, and bid the devil take their counsels, their directions, and their services, certain that they would make me pay, by the loss of my liberty and self-respect, for such scraps of truth, wrapped in a multitude of lies, as they might give me.

I bow before the authority of special men because it is imposed upon me by my own reason. I am conscious of my inability to grasp, in all its details and positive developments, any very large portion of human knowledge. The greatest intelligence would not be equal to a comprehension of the whole. Thence results, for science as well as for industry, the necessity of the division and association of labor. I receive and I give—such is human life. Each directs and is directed in his turn. Therefore there is no fixed and constant authority, but a continual exchange of mutual, temporary, and, above all, voluntary authority and subordination.

This same reason forbids me, then, to recognize a fixed, constant, and universal authority, because there is no universal man, no man capable of grasping in that wealth of detail, without which the application of science to life is impossible, all the sciences, all the branches of social life. And if such universality could ever be realized in a single man, and if he wished to take advantage thereof to impose his authority upon us, it would be necessary to drive this man out of society, because his authority would inevitably reduce all the others to slavery and imbecility. I do not think that society ought to maltreat men of genius as it has done hitherto; but neither do I think it should indulge them too far, still less accord them any privileges or exclusive rights whatsoever; and that for three reasons: first, because it would often mistake a charlatan for a man of genius; second, because, through such a system of privileges, it might transform into a charlatan even a real man of genius, demoralize him, and degrade him; and, finally, because it would establish a master over itself.

To sum up. We recognize, then, the absolute authority of science, because the sole object of science is the mental reproduction, as well-considered and systematic as possible, of the natural laws inherent in the material, intellectual, and moral life of both the physical and the social worlds, these two worlds constituting, in fact, but one and the same natural world. Outside of this only legitimate authority, legitimate because rational and in harmony with human liberty, we declare all other authorities false, arbitrary and fatal.

We recognize the absolute authority of science, but we reject the infallibility and universality of the *savant*. In our church—if I may be permitted to use for a moment an expression which I so detest: Church and State are my two *bêtes noires*—in our church, as in the Protestant church, we have a chief, an invisible Christ, science; and, like the Protestants, more logical even than the Protestants, we will suffer neither pope, nor council, nor conclaves of infallible cardinals, nor bishops, nor even priests. Our Christ differs from the Protestant and Christian Christ in this—that the latter is a personal being, ours impersonal; the Christian Christ, already completed in an eternal past, presents himself as a perfect being, while the completion and perfection of our Christ, science, are ever in the future: which is equivalent to saying that they will never be realized. Therefore, in recognizing *absolute science* as the only absolute authority, we in no way compromise our liberty.

I mean by the words "absolute science," the truly universal science which would reproduce ideally, to its fullest extent and in all its infinite detail, the universe, the system or co-ordination of all the natural laws manifested by the incessant development of the world. It is evident that such a science, the sublime object of all the efforts of the human mind, will never be fully and absolutely realized. Our Christ, then, will remain eternally unfinished, which must considerably take down the pride of his licensed representatives among us. Against that God the Son in whose name they assume to impose upon us their insolent and pedantic authority, we appeal to God the Father, who is the real world, real life, of which he (the Son) is only a too imperfect expression, whilst we real beings, living, working, struggling, loving, aspiring, enjoying, and suffering, are its immediate representatives.

But, while rejecting the absolute, universal, and infallible authority of men of science, we willingly bow before the respectable, although relative, quite temporary, and very restricted authority of the representatives of special sciences, asking nothing better than to consult them by turns, and very grateful for such precious information as they may extend to us, on condition of their willingness to receive from us on occasions when, and concerning matters about which, we are more learned than they. In general, we ask nothing better than to see men endowed with great knowledge, great experience, great minds, and, above all, great hearts, exercise over us a natural and legitimate influence, freely accepted, and never imposed in the name of any official authority whatsoever, celestial or terrestrial. We accept all natural authorities and all influences of fact, but none of right; for every authority or every influence of right, officially imposed as such, becoming directly an oppression and a falsehood, would inevitably impose upon us, as I believe I have sufficiently shown, slavery and absurdity.

In a word, we reject all legislation, all authority, and all privileged, licensed, official, and legal influence, even though arising from universal suffrage, convinced that it can turn only to the advantage of a dominant minority of exploiters against the interests of the immense majority in subjection to them.

This is the sense in which we are really Anarchists.

There are only two ways of convincing the masses of the goodness of any social institution whatever. The first, the only real one, but also the most difficult to adopt—because it implies the abolition of the State, or, in other words, the abolition of the organized political exploitation of the majority by any minority whatsoever—would be the direct and complete satisfaction of the needs and aspirations of the people, which would be equivalent to the complete liquidation of the political and economical existence of the bourgeois class, or, again, to the abolition of the State. Beneficial means for the masses, but detrimental to bourgeois interests; hence it is useless to talk about them.

The only way, on the contrary, harmful only to the people, precious in its salvation of bourgeois privileges, is no other than religion. That is the eternal *mirage* which leads away the masses in a search for divine treasures, while, much more reserved, the governing class contents itself with dividing among all its members—very unequally, moreover, and always giving most to him who possesses most—the miserable goods of earth and the plunder taken from the people, including their political and social liberty.

There is not, there cannot be, a State without religion. Take the freest States in the world—the United States of America or the Swiss Confederation, for instance—and see what an important part is played in all official discourses by divine Providence, that supreme sanction of all States.

But whenever a chief of State speaks of God, be he William I., the Knouto-Germanic emperor, or Grant, the president of the great republic, be sure that he is getting ready to shear once more his people-flock.

The French liberal and Voltairean bourgeoisie, driven by temperament to a positivism (not to say a materialism) singularly narrow and brutal, having become the governing class of the State by its triumph of 1830, had to give itself an official religion. It was not an easy thing. The bourgeoisie could not abruptly go back under the yoke of Roman Catholicism. Between it and the Church of Rome was an abyss of blood and hatred, and, however practical and wise one becomes, it is never possible to repress a passion developed by history. Moreover, the French bourgeoisie would have covered itself with ridicule if it had gone back to the Church to take part in the pious ceremonies of its worship, an essential condition of a meritorious and sincere conversion. Several attempted it, it is true, but their heroism was rewarded by no other result than a fruitless scandal. Finally, a return to Catholicism was impossible on account of the insolvable contradiction which separates the invariable politics of Rome from the development of the economical and political interests of the middle class.

In this respect Protestantism is much more advantageous. It is the bourgeois religion *par excellence*. It accords just as much liberty as is necessary to the bourgeois, and finds a way of reconciling celestial aspirations with the respect which terrestrial conditions demand. Consequently it is especially in Protestant countries that commerce and industry have been developed. But it was impossible for the French bourgeoisie to become Protestant. To pass from one religion to another—unless it be done deliberately, as sometimes in the case of the Jews of Russia and Poland, who get baptised three or four times in order to receive each time the remuneration allowed them—to seriously change one's religion, a little faith is necessary. Now, in the exclusive positive heart of the French bourgeois, there is no room for faith. He professes the most profound indifference for all questions which touch neither his pocket first nor his social vanity afterwards. He is as indifferent to Protestantism as to Catholicism. On the other hand, the French bourgeois could not go over to Protestantism without putting himself in conflict with the Catholic routine of the majority of the French people, which would have been great imprudence on the part of a class pretending to govern the nation.

There was still one way left—to return to the humanitarian and revolutionary religion of the eighteenth century. But that would have led too far. So the bourgeoisie was obliged, in order to sanction its new State, to create a new religion which might be boldly proclaimed, without too much ridicule and scandal, by the whole bourgeois class.

Thus was born *doctrinaire* Deism.

Others have told, much better than I could tell it, the story of the birth and development of this school, which had so decisive and—we may well add—so fatal an influence on the political, intellectual, and moral education of the bourgeois youth of France. It dates from Benjamin Constant and Madame de Staël; its real founder was Royer-Collard; its apostles, Guizot, Cousin, Villemain, and many others. Its boldly avowed object was the reconciliation of Revolution with Reaction, or, to use the language of the school, of the principle of liberty with that of authority, and naturally to the advantage of the latter.

This reconciliation signified: in politics, the taking away of popular liberty for the benefit of bourgeois rule, represented by the monarchical and constitutional State; in philosophy, the deliberate submission of free reason to the eternal principles of faith. We have only to deal here with the latter.

We know that this philosophy was specially elaborated by M. Cousin, the father of French eclecticism. A superficial and pedantic talker, incapable of any original conception, of any idea peculiar to himself, but very strong on commonplace, which he confounded with common sense, this illustrious philosopher learnedly prepared, for the use of the studious youth of France, a metaphysical dish of his own making, the use of which, made compulsory in all schools of the State under the University, condemned several generations one after the other to a cerebral indigestion. Imagine a philosophical vinegar sauce of the most opposed systems, a mixture of Fathers of the Church, scholastic philosophers, Descartes and Pascal, Kant and Scotch psychologists, all this a superstructure on the divine and innate ideas of Plato, and covered up with a layer of Hegelian immanence, accompanied, of course, by an ignorance, as contemptuous as it is complete, of natural science, and proving, just as two times two make *five*, the existence of a personal God.

V. I. LENIN
"May Day"

APRIL 15, 1904

Lenin (1870–1924), the most famous revolutionary of the twentieth century, was born Vladimir Ilych Ulyanov in the city of Simbirsk on the Volga River. (He adopted the revolutionary pseudonym "Lenin" in 1901.) When Lenin was seventeen his brother Alexander was executed for conspiring to assassinate the Czar. This led Lenin to become not only a lawyer but a devoted student of Marxism. In 1897–1900 he was exiled to Siberia for revolutionary activities. He then left for western Europe, where he lived for most of the next seventeen years in exile publishing books, essays, and pamphlets, and continually marshaling his ideas and positions. In 1903 he formed the Bolshevik ("Majority," although it was in fact a minority) wing of the outlawed Russian Social Democratic Party. In February 1917 the Revolution overthrew the Czarist government; in April Lenin returned to Russia, triumphantly, to lead the Bolshevik faction in the Provisional Government. After the Bolshevik-led revolution in October 1917 he became the chairman of the Union of Soviet Socialist Republics. With Leon Trotsky, commissar of the Red Army, he steered the country through civil war and invasion by outside powers. Lenin suffered strokes in 1922 and 1923, and died in 1924. Though virtually deified after his death, and quoted ad nauseum by Soviet authors on all subjects, he was less a writer than a brilliantly effective politician. The philosopher Eric Hoffer seems to have had Lenin, among others, in mind when he wrote: "The quality of ideas seems to play a minor role in mass movement leadership. What counts is the arrogant gesture, the complete disregard of the opinion of others, the singlehanded defiance of the world."[1]

Lenin's most volatile and passionate works were short and hastily written. This "May Day" call to action of 1904, when Czarist Russia was at war with Japan, is a rough draft of the less compelling revised version that was later published. "The old Russia is dying," predicts Lenin, a year before the first Russian revolution. "A free Russia is coming to take its place."

SOURCE: Vladimir Ilych Lenin, *On Proletarian Internationalism* (Moscow: Progress Publishers, 1967), 29–32.

---

1. Eric Hoffer, *The True Believer: Thoughts on the Nature of Mass Movements* (New York: Harper and Row, 1951), 116.

May Day

Comrade workers! May Day is coming, the day when the workers of all lands celebrate their awakening to a class-conscious life, their solidarity in the struggle against all coercion and oppression of man by man, the struggle to free the toiling millions from hunger, poverty, and humiliation. Two worlds stand facing each other in this great struggle: the world of capital and the world of labour, the world of exploitation and slavery and the world of brotherhood and freedom.

On one side stand the handful of rich blood-suckers. They have seized the factories and mills, the tools and machinery, have turned millions of acres of land and mountains of money into their private property. They have made the government and the army their servants, faithful watchdogs of the wealth they have amassed.

On the other side stand the millions of the disinherited. They are forced to beg the money-bags for permission to work for them. By their labour they create all wealth; yet all their lives long they have to struggle for a crust of bread, beg for work as for charity, sap their strength and health by back-breaking toil, and starve in hovels in the villages or in the cellars and garrets of the big cities.

But now these disinherited toilers have declared war on the money-bags and exploiters. The workers of all lands are fighting to free labour from wage slavery, from poverty and want. They are fighting for a system of society where the wealth created by the common labour will go to benefit, not a handful of rich men, but all those who work. They want to make the land and the factories, mills, and machines the common property of all toilers. They want to do away with the division into rich and poor, want the fruits of labour to go to the labourers themselves, and all the achievements of the human mind, all improvements in ways of working, to improve the lot of the man who works, and not serve as a means of oppressing him.

The great struggle of labour against capital has cost the workers of all countries immense sacrifices. They have shed rivers of blood in behalf of their right to a better life and real freedom. Those who fight for the workers' cause are subjected by the governments to untold persecution. But in spite of all persecution the solidarity of the workers of the world is growing and gaining in strength. The workers are uniting more and more closely in socialist parties, the supporters of those parties are mounting into millions and are advancing steadily, step by step, towards complete victory over the class of capitalist exploiters.

The Russian proletariat, too, has awakened to a new life. It too has joined this great struggle. Gone are the days when our worker slaved submissively, seeing no escape from his state of bondage, no glimmer of light in his bitter life. Socialism has shown him the way out, and thousands upon thousands of fighters have thronged to the red banner, as to a guiding star. Strikes have shown the workers the power of unity, have taught them to fight back, have shown how formidable to capital organised labour can be. The workers have seen that it is off their labour that the capitalists and the government live and get fat. The workers have been fired with the spirit of united struggle, with the aspiration for freedom and for socialism. The workers have realised what a dark and evil force the tsarist autocracy is. The workers need freedom for their struggle, but the tsarist government binds them hand and foot. The workers need freedom of assembly, freedom to organise, freedom for newspapers and books, but the tsarist government crushes, with knout, prison and bayonet, every striving for freedom. The cry "Down with the autocracy!" has swept through the length and breadth of Russia, it has been sounded more and more often in the streets, at great mass meetings of the workers. Last summer tens of thousands of workers throughout the South of Russia rose up to fight for a better life, for freedom from police tyranny. The bourgeoisie and government trembled at the sight of the formidable army of workers, which at one stroke brought to a standstill the entire industrial life of huge cities. Dozens of fighters for the workers' cause fell beneath the bullets of the troops that tsarism sent against the internal enemy.

But there is no force that can vanquish this internal enemy, for the ruling classes and the government only live by its labour. There is no force on earth that could break the millions of workers, who are growing more and more class-conscious, more and more united and organised. Every defeat the workers sustain brings new fighters into the ranks, it awakens broader masses to new life and makes them prepare for fresh struggles.

And the events Russia is now passing through are such that this awakening of the worker masses is bound to be even more rapid and widespread, and we must strain every nerve to unite the ranks of the proletariat and prepare it for even more determined struggle. The war is making even the most backward sections of the proletariat take an interest in political affairs and problems. The war is showing up ever more clearly and vividly the utter rottenness of the autocratic order, the utter criminality of the police and court gang that is ruling Russia. Our people are perishing from want and starvation at home—yet they have been dragged into a ruinous and senseless war for alien territories lying thousands of miles away and inhabited by foreign races. Our people are ground down in political slavery—yet they have been dragged into a war for the enslavement of other peoples. Our people demand a change of political order at home—but it is sought to divert their attention by the thunder of guns at the other end of the world. But the tsarist government has gone too far in its gamble, in its criminal squandering of the nation's wealth and young manhood, sent to die on the shores of the Pacific. Every war puts a strain on the people, and the difficult war against cultured and free Japan is a frightful strain upon Russia. And this strain comes at a time when the structure of police despotism has already begun to totter under the blows of the awakening proletariat. The war is laying bare all the weak spots of the government, the war is tearing off all false disguises, the war is revealing all the inner rottenness; the war is making the preposterousness of the tsarist autocracy obvious to all and is showing everyone the death-agony of the old Russia, the Russia where the people are disfranchised, ignorant and cowed, the Russia that is still in serf bondage to the police government.

The old Russia is dying. A free Russia is coming to take its place. The dark forces that guarded the tsarist autocracy are going under. But only the class-conscious and organised proletariat can deal them their death-blow. Only the class-conscious and organised proletariat can win real, not sham, freedom for the people. Only the class-conscious and organised proletariat can thwart every attempt to deceive the people, to curtail their rights, to make them a mere tool in the hands of the bourgeoisie.

Comrade workers! Let us then prepare with redoubled energy for the decisive battle that is at hand! Let the ranks of the Social-Democrat proletarians close ever firmer! Let their word spread ever farther afield! Let campaigning for the workers' demands be carried on ever more boldly! Let the celebration of May Day win thousands of new fighters to our cause and swell our forces in the great struggle for the freedom of all the people, for the liberation of all who toil from the yoke of capital!

Long live the eight-hour day!

Long live international revolutionary Social-Democracy!

Down with the criminal and plundering tsarist autocracy!

LEON TROTSKY
"The Proletariat and the Revolution"
JANUARY 9, 1905

Leon Trotsky (1879–1940), who took his revolutionary pseudonym from one of his Siberian jailers, was born Lev Davidovich Bronstein, the son of a Jewish farmer on the Ukrainian steppes. He was not only a great writer and orator, but proved to be a great military leader, as he created and led (and repeatedly rallied) the Red Army to victory in the civil war that followed the revolution of 1917. Though he became Lenin's most valued ally in war and peace, he refused to accept the leadership of the Communist Party that Lenin offered him. After Lenin's death in 1924, Josef Stalin forced Trotsky out of the party and into exile, where in 1940, after years of exposing Stalinist terror, one of Stalin's henchmen murdered him in Mexico.

"His conceptions represent a very definite, a clear-cut and intrinsically consistent trend of revolutionary thought, quite apart from the other leaders," notes the translator Moissaye J. Olgin. "Trotsky's writings, besides their theoretical and political value, represent a vigor of style and a clarity of expression unique in Russian revolutionary literature."[1]

Olgin's note on "The Proletariat and the Revolution" provides useful background on the Russian political situation that Trotsky's essay addresses: "Prince Svyatopolk-Mirski . . . had promised 'cordial relations' between government and society. In the political jargon, this period of tolerance, lasting from August to the end of the year, was known as the era of 'Spring.' It was a thrilling time, full of political hopes and expectation. Yet, strange enough, the working class was silent. The working class had shown great dissatisfaction in 1902 and especially in summer 1903, when scores of thousands in the southwest and in the south went on a political strike. During the whole of 1904, however, there were almost no mass-manifestations on the part of the workingmen. This gave an occasion for many a liberal to scoff at the representatives of the revolutionary parties who built all their tactics on the expectation of a national revolution. To answer those skeptics and to encourage the active members of the Social-Democratic party, Trotsky wrote this essay. . . . Reading 'The Proletariat

---

1. Leon Trotzky, *Our Revolution: Essays on Working-Class and International Revolution, 1904–1917.* Trans. and ed. Moissaye J. Olgin (New York: Henry Holt, 1918), iv–v.

and the Revolution,' the student of Russian political life has a feeling as if the essay had been written *after* the Revolution, so closely it follows the course of events. Yet, it appeared before January 9th, 1905, i.e., before the first great onslaught of the Petersburg proletariat."

SOURCE: Leon Trotzky, *Our Revolution: Essays on Working-Class and International Revolution, 1904–1917.* Trans. and ed. Moissaye J. Olgin (New York: Henry Holt, 1918), 73–82.

The Proletariat and the Revolution

The proletariat must not only conduct a revolutionary propaganda. The proletariat itself must move towards a revolution.

To move towards a revolution does not necessarily mean to fix a date for an insurrection and to prepare for that day. You never can fix a day and an hour for a revolution. The people have never made a revolution by command.

What *can* be done is, in view of the fatally impending catastrophe, to choose the most appropriate positions, to arm and inspire the masses with a revolutionary slogan, to lead simultaneously all the reserves into the field of battle, to make them practice in the art of fighting, to keep them ready under arms,—and to send an alarm all over the lines when the time has arrived.

Would that mean a series of exercises only, and not a decisive combat with the enemy forces? Would that be mere manœuvers, and not a street revolution?

Yes, that would be mere manœuvers. There is a difference, however, between revolutionary and military manœuvers. Our preparations can turn, at any time and independent of our will, into a real battle which would decide the long drawn revolutionary war. Not only can it be so, it *must* be. This is vouched for by the acuteness of the present political situation which holds in its depths a tremendous amount of revolutionary explosives.

At what time mere manœuvers would turn into a real battle, depends upon the volume and the revolutionary compactness of the masses, upon the atmosphere of popular sympathy which surrounds them and upon the attitude of the troops which the government moves against the people.

Those three elements of success must determine our work of preparation. Revolutionary proletarian masses *are* in existence. We ought to be able to call them into the streets, at a given time, all over the country; we ought to be able to unite them by a general slogan.

All classes and groups of the people are permeated with hatred towards absolutism, and that means with sympathy for the struggle for freedom. We ought to be able to concentrate this sympathy on the proletariat as a revolutionary power which alone can be the vanguard of the people in their fight to save the future of Russia. As to the mood of the army, it hardly kindles the heart of the government with great hopes. There has been many an alarming symptom for the last few years; the army is morose, the army grumbles, there are ferments of dissatisfaction in the army. We ought to do all at our command to make the army detach itself from absolutism at the time of a decisive onslaught of the masses.

Let us first survey the last two conditions, which determine the course and the outcome of the campaign.

We have just gone through the period of "political renovation" opened under the blare of trumpets and closed under the hiss of knouts* —the era of Svyatopolk-Mirski—the result of which is hatred towards absolutism aroused among all the thinking elements of society to an unusual pitch. The coming days will reap the fruit of stirred popular hopes and unfulfilled government's pledges. Political interest has lately taken more definite shape; dissatisfaction has grown deeper and is founded on a more outspoken theoretical basis. Popular thinking, yesterday utterly primitive, now greedily takes to the work of political analysis. All manifestations of evil and arbitrary power are being speedily traced back to the principal cause. Revolutionary slogans no more frighten the people; on the contrary, they arouse a thousandfold echo, they pass into proverbs. The popular consciousness absorbs each word of negation, condemnation or curse addressed towards absolutism, as a sponge absorbs fluid substance. No step of the administration remains unpunished. Each of its blunders is carefully taken account of. Its advances are met with ridicule, its threats breed hatred. The vast apparatus of the liberal press circulates daily thousands of facts, stirring, exciting, inflaming popular emotion.**

---

* *"The hiss of the knout"* which ended the era of "cordial relations" was a statement issued by the government on December 12, 1904, declaring that "all disturbances of peace and order and all gatherings of an anti-governmental character must and will be stopped by all legal means in command of the authorities." The Zemstvo and municipal bodies were advised to keep from political utterings. As to the Socialist parties, and to labor movement in general, they were prosecuted under Svyatopolk-Mirski as severely as under Von Plehve. (*Note by Moissaye J. Olgin.*)

** *"The vast apparatus of the liberal press"* was the only way to reach millions. The revolutionary "underground" press, which assumed towards 1905 unusual proportions, could, after all, reach only a limited number of readers. In times of political unrest, the public became used to read between the lines of the legal press all it needed to feed its hatred of oppression. (*Note by Moissaye J. Olgin.*)

The pent up feelings are seeking an outlet. Thought strives to turn into action. The vociferous liberal press, however, while feeding popular unrest, tends to divert its current into a small channel; it spreads superstitious reverence for "public opinion," helpless, unorganized "public opinion," which does not discharge itself into action; it brands the revolutionary method of national emancipation; it upholds the illusion of legality; it centers all the attention and all the hopes of the embittered groups around the Zemstvo campaign, thus systematically preparing a great debacle for the popular movement. Acute dissatisfaction, finding no outlet, discouraged by the inevitable failure of the legal Zemstvo campaign which has no traditions of revolutionary struggle in the past and no clear prospects in the future, must necessarily manifest itself in an outbreak of desperate terrorism, leaving radical intellectuals in the rôle of helpless, passive, though sympathetic onlookers, leaving liberals to choke in a fit of platonic enthusiasm while lending doubtful assistance.*

This ought not to take place. We ought to take hold of the current of popular excitement; we ought to turn the attention of numerous dissatisfied social groups to one colossal undertaking headed by the proletariat,—to the *National Revolution*.

The vanguard of the Revolution ought to wake from indolence all other elements of the people; to appear here and there and everywhere; to put the questions of political struggle in the boldest possible fashion; to call, to castigate, to unmask hypocritical democracy; to make democrats and Zemstvo liberals clash against each other; to wake again and again, to call, to castigate, to demand a clear answer to the question, *What are you going to do?* to allow no retreat; to compel the legal liberals to admit their own weakness; to alienate from them the democratic elements and help the latter along the way of the revolution. To do this work means to draw the threads of sympathy of all the democratic opposition towards the revolutionary campaign of the proletariat.

We ought to do all in our power to draw the attention and gain the sympathy of the poor non-proletarian city population. During the last mass actions of the proletariat, as in the general strikes of 1903 in the South, nothing was done in this respect, and this was the weakest point of the preparatory work. According to press correspondents, the queerest rumors often circulated among the population as to the intentions of the strikers. The city inhabitants expected attacks on their houses,

---

*By *"legal" press*, *"legal" liberals* are meant the open public press and those liberals who were trying to comply with the legal requirements of absolutism even in their work of condemning the absolutist order. The term "legal" is opposed by the term "revolutionary" which is applied to political actions in defiance of law. (*Note by Moissaye J. Olgin.*)

the store keepers were afraid of being looted, the Jews were in a dread of pogroms. This ought to be avoided. A *political strike, as a single combat of the city proletariat with the police and the army, the remaining population being hostile or even indifferent, is doomed to failure.*

The indifference of the population would tell primarily on the morale of the proletariat itself, and then on the attitude of the soldiers. Under such conditions, the stand of the administration must necessarily be more determined. The generals would remind the officers, and the officers would pass to the soldiers the words of Dragomirov[*]: "Rifles are given for sharp shooting, and nobody is permitted to squander cartridges for nothing."

A *political strike of the proletariat ought to turn into a political demonstration of the population*, this is the first prerequisite of success.

The second important prerequisite is the mood of the army. A dissatisfaction among the soldiers, a vague sympathy for the "revoluters," is an established fact. Only part of this sympathy may rightly be attributed to our direct propaganda among the soldiers. The major part is done by the practical clashes between army units and protesting masses. Only hopeless idiots or avowed scoundrels dare to shoot at a living target. An overwhelming majority of the soldiers are loathe to serve as executioners; this is unanimously admitted by all correspondents describing the battles of the army with unarmed people. The average soldier aims above the heads of the crowd. It would be unnatural if the reverse were the case. When the Bessarabian regiment received orders to quell the Kiev general strike, the commander declared he could not vouch for the attitude of his soldiers. The order, then, was sent to the Cherson regiment, but there was not one half-company in the entire regiment which would live up to the expectations of their superiors.

Kiev was no exception. The conditions of the army must now be more favorable for the revolution than they were in 1903. We have gone through a year of war. It is hardly possible to measure the influence of the past year on the minds of the army. The influence, however, must be enormous. War draws not only the attention of the people, it arouses also the professional interest of the army. Our ships are slow, our guns have a short range, our soldiers are uneducated, our sergeants have neither compass nor map, our soldiers are barefooted, hungry, and freezing, our Red Cross is stealing, our commissariat is stealing,—rumors and facts of this kind leak down to the army and are being eagerly absorbed. Each rumor, as strong acid, dissolves the rust of mental drill. Years of peaceful propaganda could hardly equal in

---

[*]*Dragomirov* was for many years Commander of the Kiev Military region and known by his epigrammatic style. (*Note by Moissaye J. Olgin.*)

their results one day of warfare. The mere mechanism of discipline remains, the faith, however, the conviction that it is right to carry out orders, the belief that the present conditions can be continued, are rapidly dwindling. The less faith the army has in absolutism, the more faith it has in its foes.

We ought to make use of this situation. We ought to explain to the soldiers the meaning of the workingmen's action which is being prepared by the Party. We ought to make profuse use of the slogan which is bound to unite the army with the revolutionary people, *Away with the War!* We ought to create a situation where the officers would not be able to trust their soldiers at the crucial moment. This would reflect on the attitude of the officers themselves.

The rest will be done by the street. It will dissolve the remnants of the barrack-hypnosis in the revolutionary enthusiasm of the people.

The main factor, however, remain the revolutionary masses. True it is that during the war the most advanced elements of the masses, the thinking proletariat, have not stepped openly to the front with that degree of determination which was required by the critical historic moment. Yet it would manifest a lack of political backbone and a deplorable superficiality, should one draw from this fact any kind of pessimistic conclusions.

The war has fallen upon our public life with all its colossal weight. The dreadful monster, breathing blood and fire, loomed up on the political horizon, shutting out everything, sinking its steel clutches into the body of the people, inflicting wound upon wound, causing mortal pain, which for a moment makes it even impossible to ask for the causes of the pain. The war, as every great disaster, accompanied by crisis, unemployment, mobilization, hunger and death, stunned the people, caused despair, but not protest. This is, however, only a beginning. Raw masses of the people, silent social strata, which yesterday had no connection with the revolutionary elements, were knocked by sheer mechanical power of facts to face the central event of present-day Russia, the war. They were horrified, they could not catch their breaths. The revolutionary elements, who prior to the war had ignored the passive masses, were affected by the atmosphere of despair and concentrated horror. This atmosphere enveloped them, it pressed with a leaden weight on their minds. The voice of determined protest could hardly be raised in the midst of elemental suffering. The revolutionary proletariat which had not yet recovered from the wounds received in July, 1903, was powerless to oppose the "call of the primitive."

The year of war, however, passed not without results. Masses, yesterday primitive, to-day are confronted with the most tremendous events. They must seek to understand them. The very duration of the war has produced a desire for reasoning, for questioning as to the meaning of it all. Thus the war, while hampering for a period of time the revolutionary initiative of thousands, has awakened to life the political thought of millions.

The year of war passed not without results, not a single day passed without results. In the lower strata of the people, in the very depths of the masses, a work was going on, a movement of molecules, imperceptible, yet irresistible, incessant, a work of accumulating indignation, bitterness, revolutionary energy. The atmosphere our streets are breathing now is no longer an atmosphere of blank despair, it is an atmosphere of concentrated indignation which seeks for means and ways for revolutionary action. Each expedient action of the vanguard of our working masses would now carry away with it not only all our revolutionary reserves, but also thousands and hundreds of thousands of revolutionary recruits. This mobilization, unlike the mobilization of the government, would be carried out in the presence of general sympathy and active assistance of an overwhelming majority of the population.

In the presence of strong sympathies of the masses, in the presence of active assistance on the part of the democratic elements of the people; facing a government commonly hated, unsuccessful both in big and in small undertakings, a government defeated on the seas, defeated in the fields of battle, despised, discouraged, with no faith in the coming day, a government vainly struggling, currying favor, provoking and retreating, lying and suffering exposure, insolent and frightened; facing an army whose morale has been shattered by the entire course of the war, whose valor, energy, enthusiasm and heroism have met an insurmountable wall in the form of administrative anarchy, an army which has lost faith in the unshakable security of a régime it is called to serve, a dissatisfied, grumbling army which more than once has torn itself free from the clutches of discipline during the last year and which is eagerly listening to the roar of revolutionary voices,—such will be the conditions under which the revolutionary proletariat will walk out into the streets. It seems to us that no better conditions could have been created by history for a final attack. History has done everything it was allowed by elemental wisdom. The thinking revolutionary forces of the country have to do the rest.

A tremendous amount of revolutionary energy has been accumulated. It should not vanish with no avail, it should not be dissipated in scattered engagements and clashes, with no coherence and no definite plan. All efforts ought to be made to concentrate the bitterness, the anger, the protest, the rage, the hatred of the masses, to give those emotions a common language, a common goal, to unite, to solidify all the particles of the masses, to make them feel and understand that they are not isolated, that simultaneously, with the same slogan on the banner, with the same goal in mind, innumerable particles are rising everywhere. If this understanding is achieved, half of the revolution is done.

We have got to summon all revolutionary forces to simultaneous action. How can we do it?

First of all we ought to remember that the main scene of revolutionary events is bound to be the city. Nobody is likely to deny this. It is evident, further, that street demonstrations can turn into a popular revolution only when they are a manifestation of *masses*, i.e., when they embrace, in the first place, the workers of factories and plants. To make the workers quit their machines and stands; to make them walk out of the factory premises into the street; to lead them to the neighboring plant; to proclaim there a cessation of work; to make new masses walk out into the street; to go thus from factory to factory, from plant to plant, incessantly growing in numbers, sweeping police barriers, absorbing new masses that happened to come across, crowding the streets, taking possession of buildings suitable for popular meetings, fortifying those buildings, holding continuous revolutionary meetings with audiences coming and going, bringing order into the movements of the masses, arousing their spirit, explaining to them the aim and the meaning of what is going on; to turn, finally, the entire city into one revolutionary camp, this is, broadly speaking, the plan of action.

The starting point ought to be the factories and plants. That means that street manifestations of a serious character, fraught with decisive events, ought to begin with *political strikes of the masses*.

It is easier to fix a date for a strike, than for a demonstration of the people, just as it is easier to move masses ready for action than to organize new masses.

A political strike, however, not a *local, but a general political strike all over Russia,* —ought to have a general political slogan. This slogan is: *to stop the war and to call a National Constituent Assembly.*

This demand ought to become nation-wide, and herein lies the task for our propaganda preceding the all-Russian general strike. We ought to use all possible occasions to make the idea of a National Constituent Assembly popular among the people. Without losing one moment, we ought to put into operation all the technical means and all the powers of propaganda at our disposal. Proclamations and speeches, educational circles and mass-meetings ought to carry broadcast, to propound and to explain the demand of a Constituent Assembly. There ought to be not one man in a city who should not know that his demand is: a National Constituent Assembly.

The peasants ought to be called to assemble on the day of the political strike and to pass resolutions demanding the calling of a

Constituent Assembly. The suburban peasants ought to be called into the cities to participate in the street movements of the masses gathered under the banner of a Constituent Assembly. All societies and organizations, professional and learned bodies, organs of self-government and organs of the opposition press ought to be notified in advance by the workingmen that they are preparing for an all-Russian political strike, fixed for a certain date, to bring about the calling of a Constituent Assembly. The workingmen ought to demand from all societies and corporations that, on the day appointed for the mass-manifestation, they should join in the demand of a National Constituent Assembly. The workingmen ought to demand from the opposition press that it should popularize their slogan and that on the eve of the demonstration it should print an appeal to the population to join the proletarian manifestation under the banner of a National Constituent Assembly.

We ought to carry on the most intensive propaganda in the army in order that on the day of the strike each soldier, sent to curb the "rebels," should know that he is facing the people who are demanding a National Constituent Assembly.

LEON TROTSKY

"The Events in St. Petersburg"

FEBRUARY 2, 1905

Following the massacre of unarmed strikers by Russian troops on January 22, Trotsky, watching in exile from western Europe, but on his clandestine way back into Russia, announced that "the Revolution has come." Trotsky became the leading figure of the great, though unsuccessful, Revolution of 1905. For his efforts, in 1906 the Russian government sentenced him to lifetime exile in Siberia. He escaped on the way there and continued his writing and revolutionary activities in Europe.

SOURCE: R. W. Postgate, ed., *Revolution from 1789 to 1906* (London: Grant Richards, 1920), 369–370.

The Events in St. Petersburg

The Revolution has come. One move of hers has lifted the people over a whole flight of steps up which in times of peace we should have had to drag a painful and tired journey. The Revolution has come. It has destroyed the plans of many politicians who had dared to make their little political calculations with no regard for their master, the revolutionary people. The Revolution has come. It has destroyed scores of superstitions, and has manifested the power of the programme which is founded on the revolutionary logic of the development of the masses.

The Revolution has come, and the period of our political childhood has passed. Into the archives has gone our traditional liberalism, whose only resource was the belief in a fortunate change of administrative figureheads. Its period of bloom was the meaningless reign of Sviatopolk Mirsky and its ripest fruit was the Ukase of December 27th. But now, January 22nd has come and effaced the Spring. It has put military dictatorship in its place and has promoted to the rank of Governor-General of St. Petersburg that same Trepov who just before had been ejected from the post of Moscow Chief of Police by the same liberal opposition.

213

Liberalism which was not interested in the revolution, which hatched plots behind the scenes, which ignored the masses, which counted only on its own diplomatic genius, has been swept away. We have finished with it for the entire period of the revolution.

Now Liberals of the left wing will follow the people. They will before long attempt to take the people into their own hands. For the people are a power. We must lead them. But they are also a revolutionary power. Therefore, we must master them. Clearly this will be the future tactics of the Osvoboshdenye* group. Our fight for a revolution, our preparatory work for a revolution, must therefore also be a merciless fight against liberalism for influence over the masses, for a leading rôle in the revolution. In this fight we shall have the support of a great power, the simple logic of the Revolution.

The Revolution has come.

The form taken by the uprising of January 22nd could not have been foreseen. A revolutionary priest, placed in a perplexing manner at the head of the working masses for several days, lent to the events the stamp of his personality, his conceptions, and his rank. This form may mislead many an observer as to the real substance of the events. The actual meaning of the events, however, is just that which Social Democracy foresaw. The central figure is the Proletariat. The workers start a strike—they unite—they formulate political demands—they turn out on the streets—they gain the enthusiastic sympathy of the entire population—they engage in battles with the army . . .

The proletariat has arisen. It has chosen an incidental pretext and a casual leader—a self-sacrificing priest. That seemed enough to start with. It was not enough to bring victory.

Victory demands not a romantic method due to a plan based on an illusion, but revolutionary tactics. A simultaneous action of the proletariat of all Russia must be prepared. This is the first condition. No local demonstration has any serious political significance now. After the St. Petersburg uprising, only an all-Russian uprising should take place. Scattered outbursts would only consume the precious revolutionary energy with no results. Wherever spontaneous outbursts occur, as a late echo of the St. Petersburg uprising, they must be made use of to revolutionize and to unite the masses, to popularize among them the idea of an all-Russian uprising as a task of the approaching months, perhaps only weeks.

---

*"Liberators." The Left wing of this Party—Constitutional Monarchist, non-revolutionary—became the Cadet Party, whose tactics were exactly these. (*Note by R. W. Postgate.*)

EMMA GOLDMAN
"The Tragedy of Women's Emancipation"

1910

"One of the most accomplished, magnetic speakers in American history, she crisscrossed the country lecturing on anarchism, the new drama, the new school, the new woman, birth control, crime and punishment. Subject to stubborn and sometimes brutal police and vigilante attempts to silence her, she joyfully waged countless free-speech fights along lines later followed by the Wobblies (Industrial Workers of the World). Her activities moved radicals and even some liberals to action against threats to freedom of expression."[1]

Emma Goldman (1869-1940), born in Russia, came to the United States in 1890. She first delivered this essay as a lecture in Philadelphia in 1904. She collected, revised, and published some of her lectures in December 1910 in *Anarchism and Other Essays*. "History tells us that every oppressed class gained true liberation from its masters through its own efforts," she writes. "It is necessary that woman learn that lesson, that she realize that her freedom will reach as far as her power to achieve her freedom reaches."

SOURCE: Emma Goldman, *Anarchism and Other Essays* (New York: Dover Publications, Inc., 1969), 213–225.

The Tragedy of Women's Emancipation

I begin with an admission: Regardless of all political and economic theories, treating of the fundamental differences between various groups within the human race, regardless of class and race distinctions, regardless of all artificial boundary lines between woman's rights and man's rights, I hold that there is a point where these differentiations may meet and grow into one perfect whole.

---

1. Richard Drinnon, "Introduction." In Emma Goldman, *Anarchism and Other Essays* (New York: Dover Publications, Inc., 1969), vii.

With this I do not mean to propose a peace treaty. The general social antagonism which has taken hold of our entire public life today, brought about through the force of opposing and contradictory interests, will crumble to pieces when the reorganization of our social life, based upon the principles of economic justice, shall have become a reality.

Peace or harmony between the sexes and individuals does not necessarily depend on a superficial equalization of human beings; nor does it call for the elimination of individual traits and peculiarities. The problem that confronts us today, and which the nearest future is to solve, is how to be one's self and yet in oneness with others, to feel deeply with all human beings and still retain one's own characteristic qualities. This seems to me to be the basis upon which the mass and the individual, the true democrat and the true individuality, man and woman, can meet without antagonism and opposition. The motto should not be: Forgive one another; rather, Understand one another. The oft-quoted sentence of Madame de Staël: "To understand everything means to forgive everything," has never particularly appealed to me; it has the odor of the confessional; to forgive one's fellow-being conveys the idea of pharisaical superiority. To understand one's fellow-being suffices. The admission partly represents the fundamental aspect of my views on the emancipation of woman and its effect upon the entire sex.

Emancipation should make it possible for woman to be human in the truest sense. Everything within her that craves assertion and activity should reach its fullest expression; all artificial barriers should be broken, and the road towards greater freedom cleared of every trace of centuries of submission and slavery.

This was the original aim of the movement for woman's emancipation. But the results so far achieved have isolated woman and have robbed her of the fountain springs of that happiness which is so essential to her. Merely external emancipation has made of the modern woman an artificial being, who reminds one of the products of French arboriculture with its arabesque trees and shrubs, pyramids, wheels, and wreaths; anything, except the forms which would be reached by the expression of her own inner qualities. Such artificially grown plants of the female sex are to be found in large numbers, especially in the so-called intellectual sphere of our life.

Liberty and equality for woman! What hopes and aspirations these words awakened when they were first uttered by some of the noblest and bravest souls of those days. The sun in all his light and glory was to rise upon a new world; in this world woman was to be free to direct her own destiny—an aim certainly worthy of the great enthusiasm, courage, perseverance, and ceaseless effort of the tremendous host of pioneer men and women, who staked everything against a world of prejudice and ignorance.

My hopes also move towards that goal, but I hold that the emancipation of woman, as interpreted and practically applied today, has failed to reach that great end. Now, woman is confronted with the necessity of emancipating herself from emancipation, if she really desires to be free. This may sound paradoxical, but is, nevertheless, only too true.

What has she achieved through her emancipation? Equal suffrage in a few States. Has that purified our political life, as many well-meaning advocates predicted? Certainly not. Incidentally, it is really time that persons with plain, sound judgment should cease to talk about corruption in politics in a boarding-school tone. Corruption of politics has nothing to do with the morals, or the laxity of morals, of various political personalities. Its cause is altogether a material one. Politics is the reflex of the business and industrial world, the mottos of which are: "To take is more blessed than to give"; "buy cheap and sell dear"; "one soiled hand washes the other." There is no hope even that woman, with her right to vote, will ever purify politics.

Emancipation has brought woman economic equality with man; that is, she can choose her own profession and trade; but as her past and present physical training has not equipped her with the necessary strength to compete with man, she is often compelled to exhaust all her energy, use up her vitality, and strain every nerve in order to reach the market value. Very few ever succeed, for it is a fact that women teachers, doctors, lawyers, architects, and engineers are neither met with the same confidence as their male colleagues, nor receive equal remuneration. And those that do reach that enticing equality, generally do so at the expense of their physical and psychical well-being. As to the great mass of working girls and women, how much independence is gained if the narrowness and lack of freedom of the home is exchanged for the narrowness and lack of freedom of the factory, sweat-shop, department store, or office? In addition is the burden which is laid on many women of looking after a "home, sweet home"—cold, dreary, disorderly, uninviting—after a day's hard work. Glorious independence! No wonder that hundreds of girls are so willing to accept the first offer of marriage, sick and tired of their "independence" behind the counter, at the sewing or typewriting machine. They are just as ready to marry as girls of the middle class, who long to throw off the yoke of parental supremacy. A so-called independence which leads only to earning the merest subsistence is not so enticing, not so ideal, that one could expect woman to sacrifice everything for it. Our highly praised independence is, after all, but a slow process of dulling and stifling woman's nature, her love instinct, and her mother instinct.

Nevertheless, the position of the working girl is far more natural and human than that of her seemingly more fortunate sister in the more cultured professional walks of life—teachers, physicians, lawyers, engineers, etc., who have to make a dignified, proper appearance, while the inner life is growing empty and dead.

The narrowness of the existing conception of woman's independence and emancipation; the dread of love for a man who is not her social equal; the fear that love will rob her of her freedom and independence; the horror that love or the joy of motherhood will only hinder her in the full exercise of her profession—all these together make of the emancipated modern woman a compulsory vestal, before whom life, with its great clarifying sorrows and its deep, entrancing joys, rolls on without touching or gripping her soul.

Emancipation, as understood by the majority of its adherents and exponents, is of too narrow a scope to permit the boundless love and ecstasy contained in the deep emotion of the true woman, sweetheart, mother, in freedom.

The tragedy of the self-supporting or economically free woman does not lie in too many, but in too few experiences. True, she surpasses her sister of past generations in knowledge of the world and human nature; it is just because of this that she feels deeply the lack of life's essence, which alone can enrich the human soul, and without which the majority of women have become mere professional automatons.

That such a state of affairs was bound to come was foreseen by those who realized that, in the domain of ethics, there still remained many decaying ruins of the time of the undisputed superiority of man; ruins that are still considered useful. And, what is more important, a goodly number of the emancipated are unable to get along without them. Every movement that aims at the destruction of existing institutions and the replacement thereof with something more advanced, more perfect, has followers who in theory stand for the most radical ideas, but who, nevertheless, in their every-day practice, are like the average Philistine, feigning respectability and clamoring for the good opinion of their opponents. There are, for example, Socialists, and even Anarchists, who stand for the idea that property is robbery, yet who will grow indignant if anyone owe them the value of a half-dozen pins.

The same Philistine can be found in the movement for woman's emancipation. Yellow journalists and milk-and-water litterateurs have painted pictures of the emancipated woman that make the hair of the good citizen and his dull companion stand up on end. Every member of the woman's rights movement was pictured as a George Sand in her absolute disregard of morality. Nothing was sacred to her. She had no respect for the ideal relation between man and woman. In short, emancipation stood only for a reckless life of lust and sin; regardless of society, religion, and morality. The exponents of woman's rights were highly indignant at such misrepresentation, and, lacking humor, they exerted all their energy to prove that they were not at all as bad as they were painted, but the very reverse. Of course, as long as woman was the slave of man, she could not be good and pure, but now that she was free and independent she would prove how good she could be and that her influence would have a purifying effect on all institutions in society. True, the movement for woman's rights has broken many old fetters, but it has also forged new ones. The great movement of *true* emancipation has not met with a great race of women who could look liberty in the face. Their narrow, Puritanical vision banished man, as a disturber and doubtful character, out of their emotional life. Man was not to be tolerated at any price, except perhaps as the father of a child, since a child could not very well come to life without a father. Fortunately, the most rigid Puritans never will be strong enough to kill the innate craving for motherhood. But woman's freedom is closely allied with man's freedom, and many of my so-called emancipated sisters seem to overlook the fact that a child born in freedom needs the love and devotion of each human being about him, man as well as woman. Unfortunately, it is this narrow conception of human relations that has brought about a great tragedy in the lives of the modern man and woman.

About fifteen years ago appeared a work from the pen of the brilliant Norwegian Laura Marholm, called *Woman, a Character Study*. She was one of the first to call attention to the emptiness and narrowness of the existing conception of woman's emancipation, and its tragic effect upon the inner life of woman. In her work Laura Marholm speaks of the fate of several gifted women of international fame: the genius Eleonora Duse; the great mathematician and writer Sonya Kovalevskaia; the artist and poet-nature Marie Bashkirtzeff, who died so young. Through each description of the lives of these women of such extraordinary mentality runs a marked trail of unsatisfied craving for a full, rounded, complete, and beautiful life, and the unrest and loneliness resulting from the lack of it. Through these masterly psychological sketches one cannot help but see that the higher the mental development of woman, the less possible it is for her to meet a congenial mate who will see in her, not only sex, but also the human being, the friend, the comrade and strong individuality, who cannot and ought not lose a single trait of her character.

The average man with his self-sufficiency, his ridiculously superior airs of patronage towards the female sex, is an impossibility for woman as depicted in the *Character Study* by Laura Marholm. Equally impossible for her is the man who can see in her nothing more than her mentality and her genius, and who fails to awaken her woman nature.

A rich intellect and a fine soul are usually considered necessary attributes of a deep and beautiful personality. In the case of the modern woman, these attributes serve as a hindrance to the complete assertion of her being. For over a hundred years the old form of marriage, based on the Bible, "till death doth part," has been denounced as an institution that stands for the sovereignty of the man over the woman, of her complete submission to his whims and commands, and absolute dependence on his name and support. Time and again it has been conclusively proved that the old matrimonial relation restricted woman to the function of man's servant and the bearer of his children. And yet we find many emancipated women who prefer marriage, with all its deficiencies, to the narrowness of an unmarried life; narrow and unendurable because of the chains of moral and social prejudice that cramp and bind her nature.

The explanation of such inconsistency on the part of many advanced women is to be found in the fact that they never truly understood the meaning of emancipation. They thought that all that was needed was independence from external tyrannies; the internal tyrants, far more harmful to life and growth—ethical and social conventions—were left to take care of themselves; and they have taken care of themselves. They seem to get along as beautifully in the heads and hearts of the most active exponents of woman's emancipation, as in the heads and hearts of our grandmothers.

These internal tyrants, whether they be in the form of public opinion or what will mother say, or brother, father, aunt, or relative of any sort; what will Mrs. Grundy, Mr. Comstock, the employer, the Board of Education say? All these busybodies, moral detectives, jailers of the human spirit, what will they say? Until woman has learned to defy them all, to stand firmly on her own ground and to insist upon her own unrestricted freedom, to listen to the voice of her nature, whether it call for life's greatest treasure, love for a man, or her most glorious privilege, the right to give birth to a child, she cannot call herself emancipated. How many emancipated women are brave enough to acknowledge that the voice of love is calling, wildly beating against their breasts, demanding to be heard, to be satisfied.

The French writer Jean Reibrach, in one of his novels, *New Beauty*, attempts to picture the ideal, beautiful, emancipated woman. This ideal is embodied in a young girl, a physician. She talks very cleverly and wisely of how to feed infants; she is kind, and administers medicines free to poor mothers. She converses with a young man of her acquaintance about the sanitary conditions of the future, and how various bacilli and germs shall be exterminated by the use of stone walls and floors, and by the doing away with rugs and hangings. She is, of course, very plainly and practically dressed, mostly in black. The young man, who, at their first meeting, was overawed by the wisdom of his emancipated friend, gradually learns to understand her, and recognizes one fine day that he loves her. They are young, and she is kind and beautiful, and though always in rigid attire, her appearance is softened by a spotlessly clean white collar and cuffs. One would expect that he would tell her of his love, but he is not one to commit romantic absurdities. Poetry and the enthusiasm of love cover their blushing faces before the pure beauty of the lady. He silences the voice of his nature, and remains correct. She, too, is always exact, always rational, always well behaved. I fear if they had formed a union, the young man would have risked freezing to death. I must confess that I can see nothing beautiful in this new beauty, who is as cold as the stone walls and floors she dreams of. Rather would I have the love songs of romantic ages, rather Don Juan and Madame Venus, rather an elopement by ladder and rope on a moonlight night, followed by the father's curse, mother's moans, and the moral comments of neighbors, than correctness and propriety measured by yardsticks. If love does not know how to give and take without restrictions, it is not love, but a transaction that never fails to lay stress on a plus and a minus.

The greatest shortcoming of the emancipation of the present day lies in its artificial stiffness and its narrow respectabilities, which produce an emptiness in woman's soul that will not let her drink from the fountain of life. I once remarked that there seemed to be a deeper relationship between the old-fashioned mother and hostess, ever on the alert for the happiness of her little ones and the comfort of those she loved, and the truly new woman, than between the latter and her average emancipated sister. The disciples of emancipation pure and simple declared me a heathen, fit only for the stake. Their blind zeal did not let them see that my comparison between the old and the new was merely to prove that a goodly number of our grandmothers had more blood in their veins, far more humor and wit, and certainly a greater amount of naturalness, kind-heartedness, and simplicity, than the majority of our emancipated professional women who fill the colleges, halls of learning, and various offices. This does not mean a wish to return to the past, nor does it condemn woman to her old sphere, the kitchen and the nursery.

Salvation lies in an energetic march onward towards a brighter and clearer future. We are in need of unhampered growth out of old traditions and habits. The movement for woman's emancipation has so far made but the first step in that direction. It is to be hoped that it will gather strength to make another. The right to vote, or equal civil rights, may be good demands, but true emancipation begins neither at the polls nor in courts. It begins in woman's soul. History tells us that every oppressed class gained true liberation from its masters through its own efforts. It is necessary that woman learn that lesson, that she realize that her freedom will reach as far as her power to achieve her freedom reaches. It is, therefore, far more important for her to begin with her inner regeneration, to cut loose from the weight of prejudices, traditions, and customs. The demand for equal rights in every vocation of life is just and fair; but, after all, the most vital right is the right to love and be loved. Indeed, if partial emancipation is to become a complete and true emancipation of woman, it will have to do away with the ridiculous notion that to be loved, to be sweetheart and mother, is synonymous with being slave or subordinate. It will have to do away with the absurd notion of the dualism of the sexes, or that man and woman represent two antagonistic worlds.

Pettiness separates; breadth unites. Let us be broad and big. Let us not overlook vital things because of the bulk of trifles confronting us. A true conception of the relation of the sexes will not admit of conqueror and conquered; it knows of but one great thing: to give of one's self boundlessly, in order to find one's self richer, deeper, better. That alone can fill the emptiness, and transform the tragedy of woman's emancipation into joy, limitless joy.

LEON TROTSKY ET AL.
The Zimmerwald Manifesto

SEPTEMBER 1915

Trotsky and many other internationalist socialist revolutionaries opposed World War I for pacifist and other reasons. For the meeting of the internationalists in Switzerland, Trotsky drafted this manifesto against the war that won majority support, including Lenin's. "In this unbearable situation, we, the representatives of the Socialist parties, trade unions, or of their minorities, we Germans, French, Italians, Russians, Poles, Letts, Rumanians, Bulgarians, Swedes, Norwegians, Dutch, and Swiss, we who stand not on the ground of national solidarity with the exploiting class, but on the ground of the international solidarity of the proletariat and of the class struggle, have assembled to retie the torn threads of international relations and to call upon the working class to recover itself and to fight for peace."

SOURCE: Leon Trotsky, *Leon Trotsky Speaks*. Ed. Sarah Lovell (New York: Pathfinder Press, 1972), 34–37.

The Zimmerwald Manifesto

Proletarians of Europe!

The war has lasted more than a year. Millions of corpses cover the battlefields. Millions of human beings have been crippled for the rest of their lives. Europe is like a gigantic human slaughterhouse. All civilization, created by the labor of many generations, is doomed to destruction. The most savage barbarism is today celebrating its triumph over all that hitherto constituted the pride of mankind.

Irrespective of the truth as to the direct responsibility for the outbreak of the war, one thing is certain: the war that has produced this chaos is the outcome of imperialism, of the attempt on the part of the capitalist classes of each nation to foster their greed for profit by the exploitation of human labor and of the natural resources of the entire globe.

Economically backward or politically weak nations are thereby subjugated by the great powers who, in this war, are seeking to remake the world map with blood and iron in accord with their exploiting interests. Thus entire nations and countries like Belgium, Poland, the Balkan states, and Armenia are threatened with the fate of being torn asunder, annexed as a whole or in part as booty in the game of compensations.

In the course of the war, its driving forces are revealed in all their vileness. Shred after shred falls the veil with which the meaning of this world catastrophe was hidden from the consciousness of the people. The capitalists of all countries, who are coining the gold of war profits out of the blood shed by the people, assert that the war is for defense of the fatherland, for democracy, and the liberation of oppressed nations. They lie! In actual reality, they are burying the freedom of their own people together with the independence of the other nations on the fields of devastation. New fetters, new chains, new burdens are arising, and it is the proletariat of all countries, of the victorious as well as of the conquered countries, that will have to bear them. Improvement in welfare was proclaimed at the outbreak of the war—want and privation, unemployment and high prices, undernourishment and epidemics are the actual results. The burdens of war will consume the best energies of the peoples for decades, endanger the achievements of social reform, and hinder every step forward.

Cultural devastation, economic decline, political reaction—these are the blessings of this horrible conflict of nations.

Thus the war reveals the naked figure of modern capitalism which has become irreconcilable not only with the interests of the laboring masses, not only with the requirements of historical development, but also with the elementary conditions of human intercourse.

The ruling powers of capitalist society who held the fate of the nations in their hands, the monarchic as well as the republican governments, the secret diplomacy, the mighty business organizations, the bourgeois parties, the capitalist press, the church—all these bear the full weight of responsibility for this war which arose out of the social order fostering them and protected by them, and which is being waged for their interests.

Workers!

Exploited, disfranchised, scorned, they called you brothers and comrades at the outbreak of the war when you were to be led to the slaughter, to death. And now that militarism has crippled you, mutilated you, degraded and annihilated you, the rulers demand that you surrender your interests, your aims, your ideals—in a word, servile subordination to civil peace. They rob you of the possibility of expressing your views, your feelings, your pains; they prohibit you from raising your demands and defending them. The press gagged, political rights and liberties trod upon—this is the way the military dictatorship rules today with an iron hand.

This situation which threatens the entire future of Europe and of humanity cannot and must not be confronted by us any longer without action. The Socialist proletariat has waged a struggle against militarism for decades. With growing concern, its representatives at their national and international congresses occupied themselves with the ever more menacing danger of war growing out of imperialism. At Stuttgart, at Copenhagen, at Basle, the International Socialist congresses indicated the course which the proletariat must follow.

Since the beginning of the war Socialist parties and labor organizations of various countries that helped to determine this course have disregarded the obligations following from this. Their representatives have called upon the working class to give up the class struggle, the only possible and effective method of proletarian emancipation. They have granted credits to the ruling classes for waging the war; they have placed themselves at the disposal of the governments for the most diverse services; through their press and their messengers, they have tried to win the neutrals for the government policies of their countries; they have delivered up to their governments Socialist ministers as hostages for the preservation of civil peace, and thereby they have assumed the responsibility before the working class, before its present and its future, for this war, for its aims and its methods. And just as the individual parties, so the highest of the appointed representative bodies of the Socialists of all countries, the International Socialist Bureau has failed them.

These facts are equally responsible for the fact that the international working class, which did not succumb to the national panic of the first war period or which freed itself from it, has still, in the second year of the slaughter of peoples, found no ways and means of taking up an energetic struggle for peace simultaneously in all countries.

In this unbearable situation, we, the representatives of the Socialist parties, trade unions, or of their minorities, we Germans, French, Italians, Russians, Poles, Letts, Rumanians, Bulgarians, Swedes, Norwegians, Dutch, and Swiss, we who stand not on the ground of national solidarity with the exploiting class, but on the ground of the international solidarity of the proletariat and of the class struggle, have assembled to retie the torn threads of international relations and to call upon the working class to recover itself and to fight for peace.

This struggle is the struggle for freedom, for the reconciliation of peoples, for socialism. It is necessary to take up this struggle for peace, for a peace without annexations or war indemnities. Such a peace, however, is only possible if every thought of violating the rights and liberties of nations is condemned. Neither the occupation of entire countries nor of separate parts of countries must lead to their violent annexation. No annexation, whether open or concealed, and no forcible economic attachment made still more unbearable by political disfranchisement. The right of self-determination of nations must be the indestructible principle in the system of national relationships of peoples.

Proletarians!

Since the outbreak of the war you have placed your energy, your courage, your endurance at the service of the ruling classes. Now you must stand up for your own cause, for the sacred aims of socialism, for the emancipation of the oppressed nations as well as of the enslaved classes, by means of the irreconcilable proletarian class struggle.

It is the task and the duty of the Socialists of the belligerent countries to take up this struggle with full force; it is the task and the duty of the Socialists of the neutral states to support their brothers in this struggle against bloody barbarism with every effective means. Never in world history was there a more urgent, a more sublime task, the fulfillment of which should be our common labor. No sacrifice is too great, no burden too heavy in order to achieve this goal: peace among the people.

Workingmen and workingwomen! Mothers and fathers! Widows and orphans! Wounded and crippled! We call to all of you who are suffering from the war and because of the war: Beyond all borders, beyond the reeking battlefields, beyond the devastated cities and villages—

Proletarians of all countries, unite!

V. I. Lenin
"The Tasks of the Proletariat in the Present Revolution
[The April Theses]"

April 7, 1917

Lenin returned to Russia in April 1917 after the February Revolution and the creation of the Provisional Government. He argued now for the Bolsheviks to take over the reins of the revolution.

Source: V. I. Lenin, *Selected Works*, Volume 2 (New York: International Publishers, 1967), 13–17.

The Tasks of the Proletariat

I did not arrive in Petrograd until the night of April 3, and therefore at the meeting on April 4 I could, of course, deliver the report on the tasks of the revolutionary proletariat only on my own behalf, and with reservations as to insufficient preparation.

The only thing I could do to make things easier for myself—and for *honest* opponents—was to prepare the theses *in writing*. I read them out, and gave the text to Comrade Tsereteli. I read them *twice* very slowly: first at a meeting of Bolsheviks and then at a meeting of both Bolsheviks and Mensheviks.

I publish these personal theses of mine with only the briefest explanatory notes, which were developed in far greater detail in the report.

Theses

1) In our attitude towards the war, which under the new government of Lvov and Co. unquestionably remains on Russia's part a predatory imperialist war owing to the capitalist nature of that government, not the slightest concession to "revolutionary defencism" is permissible.

The class-conscious proletariat can give its consent to a revolutionary war, which would really justify revolutionary defencism, only on condition: (a) that the power pass to the proletariat and the poorest sections of the peasants aligned with the proletariat; (b) that all annexations be renounced in deed and not in word; (c) that a complete break be effected in actual fact with all capitalist interests.

In view of the undoubted honesty of those broad sections of the mass believers in revolutionary defencism who accept the war only as a necessity, and not as a means of conquest, in view of the fact that they are being deceived by the bourgeoisie, it is necessary with particular thoroughness, persistence and patience to explain their error to them, to explain the inseparable connection existing between capital and the imperialist war, and to prove that without overthrowing capital *it is impossible* to end the war by a truly democratic peace, a peace not imposed by violence.

The most widespread campaign for this view must be organised in the army at the front.

Fraternisation.

2) The specific feature of the present situation in Russia is that the country is *passing* from the first stage of the revolution—which, owing to the insufficient class-consciousness and organisation of the proletariat, placed power in the hands of the bourgeoisie—to its *second* stage, which must place power in the hands of the proletariat and the poorest sections of the peasants.

This transition is characterised, on the one hand, by a maximum of legally recognised rights (Russia is *now* the freest of all the belligerent countries in the world); on the other, by the absence of violence towards the masses, and, finally, by their unreasoning trust in the government of capitalists, those worst enemies of peace and socialism.

This peculiar situation demands of us an ability to adapt ourselves to the *special* conditions of Party work among unprecedentedly large masses of proletarians who have just awakened to political life.

3) No support for the Provisional Government; the utter falsity of all its promises should be made clear, particularly of those relating to the renunciation of annexations. Exposure in place of the impermissible, illusion-breeding "demand" that *this* government, a government of capitalists, should *cease* to be an imperialist government.

4) Recognition of the fact that in most of the Soviets of Workers' Deputies our Party is in a minority, so far a small minority, as against *a bloc of all* the petty-bourgeois opportunist elements, from the Popular Socialists and the Socialist-Revolutionaries down to the Organising Committee (Chkheidze, Tsereteli, etc.), Steklov, etc., etc., who have yielded to the influence of the bourgeoisie and spread that influence among the proletariat.

The masses must be made to see that the Soviets of Workers' Deputies are the *only possible* form of revolutionary government, and that therefore our task is, as long as *this* government yields to the influence of the bourgeoisie, to present a patient, systematic, and persistent *explanation* of the errors of their tactics, an explanation especially adapted to the practical needs of the masses.

As long as we are in the minority we carry on the work of criticising and exposing errors and at the same time we preach the necessity of transferring the entire state power to the Soviets of Workers' Deputies, so that the people may overcome their mistakes by experience.

5) Not a parliamentary republic—to return to a parliamentary republic from the Soviets of Workers' Deputies would be a retrograde step—but a Republic of Soviets of Workers', Agricultural Labourers' and Peasants' Deputies throughout the country, from top to bottom.

Abolition of the police, the army and the bureaucracy.*

The salaries of all officials, all of whom are elective and displaceable at any time, not to exceed the average wages of a competent worker.

6) The weight of emphasis in the agrarian programme to be shifted to the Soviets of Agricultural Labourers' Deputies.

Confiscation of all landed estates.

Nationalisation of *all* lands in the country, the land to be disposed of by the local Soviets of Agricultural Labourers' and Peasants' Deputies. The organisation of separate Soviets of Deputies of Poor Peasants. The setting up of a model farm on each of the large estates (ranging in size from 100 to 300 dessiatines, according to local and other conditions, and to the decisions of the local bodies) under the control of the Soviets of Agricultural Labourers' Deputies and for the public account.

7) The immediate amalgamation of all banks in the country into a single national bank, and the institution of control over it by the Soviet of Workers' Deputies.

8) It is not our *immediate* task to "introduce" socialism, but only to bring social production and the distribution of products at once under the *control* of the Soviets of Workers' Deputies.

9) Party tasks:

   a) Immediate convocation of a Party congress;

   b) Alteration of the Party Programme, mainly:

   (1) On the question of imperialism and the imperialist war;

   (2) On our attitude towards the state and *our* demand for a "commune state"**;

---

*I.e., the standing army to be replaced by the arming of the whole people. (*Lenin's note.*)

**I.e., a state of which the Paris Commune was the prototype. (*Lenin's note.*)

(3) Amendment of our out-of-date minimum programme.

(c) Change of the Party's name.*

10) A new International.

We must take the initiative in creating a revolutionary International, an International against the *social-chauvinists* and against the "Centre".**

In order that the reader may understand why I had especially to emphasise as a rare exception the "case" of honest opponents, I invite him to compare the above theses with the following objection by Mr. Goldenberg: Lenin, he said, "has planted the banner of civil war in the midst of revolutionary democracy" (quoted in No. 5 of Mr. Plekhanov's *Yedinstvo*).

Isn't it a gem?

I write, announce and elaborately explain: "In view of the undoubted honesty of those *broad* sections of the *mass* believers in revolutionary defencism . . . in view of the fact that they are being deceived by the bourgeoisie, it is necessary with *particular* thoroughness, persistence and *patience* to explain their error to them. . . ."

Yet the bourgeois gentlemen who call themselves Social-Democrats, who *do not* belong either to the *broad* sections or to the *mass* believers in defencism, with serene brow present my views thus: "The banner [!]† of civil war" (of which there is not a word in the theses and not a word in my speech!) has been planted (!) "in the midst [!!] of revolutionary democracy . . ."

What does this mean? In what way does this differ from riot-inciting agitation, from *Russkaya Volya*?

I write, announce and elaborately explain: "The Soviets of Workers' Deputies are the *only possible* form of revolutionary government, and therefore our task is to present a patient, systematic, and persistent *explanation* of the errors of their tactics, an explanation especially adapted to the practical needs of the masses."

Yet opponents of a certain brand present my views as a call to "civil war in the midst of revolutionary democracy"!

---

*Instead of "Social-Democracy," whose official leaders *throughout* the world have betrayed socialism and deserted to the bourgeoisie (the "defencists" and the vacillating "Kautskyites"), we must call ourselves the *Communist Party*. (*Lenin's note*.)

**The "Centre" in the international Social-Democratic movement is the trend which vacillates between the chauvinists (="defencists") and internationalists, i.e., Kautsky and Co. in Germany, Longuet and Co. in France, Chkheidze and Co. in Russia, Turati and Co. in Italy, MacDonald and Co. in Britain, etc. (*Lenin's note*.)

†Interpolations in square brackets (within passages quoted by Lenin) have been introduced by Lenin, unless otherwise indicated. (*Note by an anonymous Soviet editor*.)

I attacked the Provisional Government for *not* having appointed an early date, or any date at all, for the convocation of the Constituent Assembly, and for confining itself to promises. I argued that *without* the Soviets of Workers' and Soldiers' Deputies the convocation of the Constituent Assembly is not guaranteed and its success is impossible.

And the view is attributed to me that I am opposed to the speedy convocation of the Constituent Assembly!

I would call this "raving," had not decades of political struggle taught me to regard honesty in opponents as a rare exception.

Mr. Plekhanov in his paper called my speech "raving." Very good, Mr. Plekhanov! But look how awkward, uncouth, and slow-witted you are in your polemics. If I delivered a raving speech for two hours, how is it that an audience of hundreds tolerated this "raving"? Further, why does your paper devote a whole column to an account of the "raving"? Inconsistent, highly inconsistent!

It is, of course, much easier to shout, abuse, and howl than to attempt to relate, to explain, to recall *what* Marx and Engels said in 1871, 1872 and 1875 about the experience of the Paris Commune and about the *kind* of state the proletariat needs.

Ex-Marxist Mr. Plekhanov evidently does not care to recall Marxism.

I quoted the words of Rosa Luxemburg, who on August 4, 1914, called *German* Social-Democracy a "stinking corpse." And the Plekhanovs, Goldenbergs and Co. feel "offended." On whose behalf? On behalf of the *German* chauvinists, because they were called chauvinists!

They have got themselves in a mess, these poor Russian social-chauvinists—socialists in word and chauvinists in deed.

Rosa Luxemburg
with Karl Liebknecht, Clara Zetkin and Franz Mehring
A *Call to the Workers of the World*
December 25, 1918

Born in 1871, and raised in Poland, Rosa Luxemburg was repeatedly jailed in various European countries for her work as an important socialist commentator and activist. To help promote worldwide revolution, she advocated mass strikes. In opposition to the leadership of the German Social Democratic Party, which had failed to oppose the war, she and her revolutionary colleagues Karl Liebknecht, Franz Mehring, Clara Zetkin, Julian Marchlewski, Leo Jogiches, and Wilhelm Pieck founded the Spartacus League in 1915. Spartacus became the nucleus of the German Communist Party in December 1918. During an attempted *putsch* against the postwar German government in January 1919 — a violent action of a sort Spartacus had always opposed — Luxemburg and Liebknecht were arrested and murdered by German soldiers.

A *Call to the Workers of the World* was written at the time of the formation of the German Communist Party. It expresses succinctly the revolutionary and internationalist aspirations of Luxemburg and the radical German left.

Source: The Rosa Luxemburg Internet Archive at: **www.marxists.org/archive/luxembur/works/1918/call.html**.

A Call to the Workers of the World

Proletarians! Men and Women of Labor!
Comrades!
The revolution in Germany has come! The masses of the soldiers who for years were driven to slaughter for the sake of capitalistic profits; the masses of workers, who for four years were exploited, crushed, and starved, have revolted. Prussian militarism, that fearful tool of oppression, that scourge of humanity — lies broken on the ground. Its most noticeable representatives, and therewith the most noticeable of

those guilty of this war, the Kaiser and the Crown Prince, have fled from the country. Workers' and Soldiers' Councils have been formed everywhere.

Workers of all countries, we do not say that in Germany all power actually lies in the hands of the working people, that the complete triumph of the proletarian revolution has already been attained. There still sit in the government all those Socialists who in August, 1914, abandoned our most precious possession, the International, who for four years betrayed the German working class and the International.

But, workers of all countries, now the German proletarian himself speaks to you. We believe we have the right to appear before your forum in his name. From the first day of this war we endeavored to do our international duty by fighting that criminal government with all our power and branding it as the one really guilty of the war.

Now at this moment we are justified before history, before the International and before the German proletariat. The masses agree with us enthusiastically, constantly widening circles of the proletariat share the conviction that the hour has struck for a settlement with capitalistic class rule.

But this great task cannot be accomplished by the German proletariat alone; it can only fight and triumph by appealing to the solidarity of the proletarians of the whole world.

Comrades of the belligerent countries, we are aware of your situation. We know full well that your governments, now that they have won the victory, are dazzling the eyes of many strata of the people with the external brilliancy of their triumph. We know that they thus succeed through the success of the murdering in making its causes and aims forgotten.

But we also know that in your countries the proletariat made the most fearful sacrifices of flesh and blood, that it is weary of the dreadful butchery, that the proletarian is now returning to his home, and is finding want and misery there, while fortunes amounting to billions are heaped up in the hands of a few capitalists. He has recognized, and will continue to recognize, that your governments, too, have carried on the war for the sake of the big money bags. And he will further perceive that your governments, when they spoke of "justice and civilization" and of the "protection of small nations," meant capitalist profits as surely as did ours when it talked about the "defence of home"; and that the peace of "justice" and of the "League of Nations" are but a part of the same base brigand that produced the peace of Brest-Litovsk. Here as well as there the same shameless lust for booty, the same desire for oppression, the same determination to exploit to the limit the brutal preponderance of murderous steel.

The Imperialism of all countries knows no "understanding," it knows only one right—capital's profits: it knows only one language—the sword: it knows only one method—violence. And if it is now talking in all countries, in yours as well ours, about the "League of Nations," "disarmament," "rights of small nations," "self-determination of the peoples," it is merely using the customary lying phrases of the rulers for the purpose of lulling to sleep the watchfulness of the proletariat.

Proletarians of all countries! This must be the last war! We owe that to the twelve million murdered victims, we owe that to our children, we owe that to humanity.

Europe has been ruined by this damnable slaughter. Twelve million bodies cover the grewsome scenes of this imperialistic crime. The flower of youth and the best man power of the peoples have been mowed down. Uncounted productive forces have been annihilated. Humanity is almost ready to bleed to death from the unexampled blood-letting of history. Victors and vanquished stand at the edge of the abyss. Humanity is threatened with famine, a stoppage of the entire mechanism of production, plagues, and degeneration.

The great criminals of this fearful anarchy, of this unchained chaos—the ruling classes—are not able to control their own creation. The beast of capital that conjured up the hell of the world war is incapable of banishing it, of restoring real order, of insuring bread and work, peace and civilization, justice and liberty, to tortured humanity.

What is being prepared by the ruling classes as peace and justice is only a new work of brutal force from which the hydra of oppression, hatred and fresh bloody wars raises its thousand heads.

Socialism alone is in a position to complete the great work of permanent peace, to heal the thousand wounds from which humanity is bleeding, to transform the plains of Europe, trampled down by the passage of the apocryphal horseman of war, into blossoming gardens, to conjure up ten productive forces for every one destroyed, to awaken all the physical and moral energies of humanity, and to replace hatred and dissension with internal solidarity, harmony, and respect for every human being.

If representatives of the proletarians of all countries could but clasp hands under the banner of Socialism for the purpose of making peace, then peace would be concluded in a few hours. Then there will be no disputed questions about the left bank of the Rhine, Mesopotamia, Egypt or colonies. Then there will be only one people: the toiling human beings of all races and tongues. Then there will be only one right: the equality of all men. Then there will be only one aim: prosperity and progress for everybody.

Humanity is facing the alternative: Dissolution and downfall in capitalist anarchy, or regeneration through the social revolution. The hour of fate has struck. If you believe in Socialism, it is now time to show it by deeds. If you are Socialists, now is the time to act.

Proletarians of all countries, if we now summon you for a common struggle it is not done for the sake of the German capitalists who, under the label of "German nation," are trying to escape the consequences of their own crimes: it is being done for your sake as well as for ours. Remember that your victorious capitalists stand ready to suppress in blood our revolution, which they fear as they do their own. You yourselves have not become any freer through the "victory," you have only become still more enslaved. If your ruling classes succeed in throttling the proletarian revolution in Germany, and in Russia, then they will turn against you with redoubled violence. Your capitalists hope that victory over us and over revolutionary Russia will give them the power to scourge you with a whip of scorpions.

Therefore the proletariat of Germany looks toward you in this hour. Germany is pregnant with the social revolution, but Socialism can only be realized by the proletariat of the world.

And therefore, we call to you: "Arise for the struggle! Arise for action! The time for empty manifestos, platonic resolutions, and high-sounding words is gone! The hour of action has struck for the International!" We ask you to elect Workers' and Soldiers' Councils everywhere that will seize political power, and together with us, will restore peace.

Not Lloyd George and Poincare, not Sonnino, Wilson, and Ersberger or Scheidemann, must be allowed to make peace. Peace must be concluded under the waving banner of the Socialist world revolution.

Proletarians of all countries! We call upon you to complete the work of Socialist liberation, to give a human aspect to the disfigured world and to make true those words with which we often greeted each other in the old days and which we sang as we parted: "And the Internationale shall be the human race."

V. I. LENIN AND THE PROVISIONAL GOVERNMENT
"Declaration of Rights of the Working and Exploited People"

JANUARY 1918

This document was the occasion for the definitive collapse of the Constituent Assembly, which represented the forces that had made the February Revolution, and the rise of the power of the Congress of Soviets, which represented those·of the more radical and popular October Revolution.

A draft of the Declaration of Rights, which embodied the goals of the Bolsheviks and the left Socialist Revolutionaries (the Bolsheviks' allies in the Congress of Soviets) was prepared by the Bolsheviks in the Provisional Government. "The draft was submitted at the session of the All-Russia Central Executive Committee on January 16, 1918, and was adopted with a few amendments by a unanimous vote. On January 17 the declaration was published in *Izvestia*," says an anonymous Soviet editor. The next day, the first day of the new session of the Constituent Assembly, it was put forward for adoption on behalf of the Provisional Government. "The counter-revolutionary assembly," says the Soviet editor, "refused to discuss it and the Bolsheviks left the assembly" — effectively putting an end to it. The following week, the declaration was adopted by the Third All-Russia Congress of Soviets. Though not exactly "counter-revolutionary," as the Soviet editor would have it, the Constituent Assembly was a largely bourgeois and liberal body, and would not commit itself to the principle of radical social change embodied in the Declaration.

Lenin and the Provisional Government, however, scarcely lived up to the declaration's promises, which include "leaving it to the workers and peasants of each nation [of Russia] to decide independently at their own authoritative Congress of Soviets whether they wish to participate in the federal government and in the other federal Soviet institutions, and on what terms."

SOURCE: Vladimir Ilyich Lenin, *On Proletarian Internationalism* (Moscow: Progress Publishers, 1967), 202–204.

Declaration of Rights

The Constituent Assembly resolves:

I.   1. Russia is hereby proclaimed a Republic of Soviets of Workers', Soldiers' and Peasants' Deputies. All power, centrally and locally, is vested in these Soviets.

2. The Russian Soviet Republic is established on the principle of a free union of free nations, as a federation of Soviet national republics.

II.   Its fundamental aim being to abolish all exploitation of man by man, to completely eliminate the division of society into classes, to mercilessly crush the resistance of the exploiters, to establish a socialist organisation of society and to achieve the victory of socialism in all countries, the Constituent Assembly further resolves:

1. Private ownership of land is hereby abolished. All land together with all buildings, farm implements and other appurtenances of agricultural production is proclaimed the property of the entire working people.

2. The Soviet laws of workers' control and on the Supreme Economic Council are hereby confirmed for the purpose of guaranteeing the power of the working people over the exploiters and as a first step towards the complete conversion of the factories, mines, railways, and other means of production and transport into the property of the workers' and peasants' state.

3. The conversion of all banks into the property of the workers' and peasants' state is hereby confirmed as one of the conditions for the emancipation of the working people from the yoke of capital.

4. For the purpose of abolishing the parasitic sections of society, universal labour conscription is hereby instituted.

5. To ensure the sovereign power of the working people, and to eliminate all possibility of the restoration of the power of the exploiters, the arming of the working people, the creation of a socialist Red Army of workers and peasants and the complete disarming of the propertied classes are hereby decreed.

III.   1. Expressing its firm determination to wrest mankind from the clutches of finance capital and imperialism, which have in this most criminal of wars drenched the world in blood, the Constituent Assembly whole-heartedly endorses the policy pursued by Soviet power of denouncing the secret treaties, organising most extensive fraternisation with the workers and peasants of the armies in the war, and achieving at all costs, by revolutionary means, a democratic peace between the nations, without annexations and indemnities and on the basis of the free self-determination of nations.

2. With the same end in view, the Constituent Assembly insists on a complete break with the barbarous policy of bourgeois civilisation, which has built the prosperity of the exploiters belonging to a few chosen nations on the enslavement of hundreds of millions of working people in Asia, in the colonies in general, and in the small countries.

The Constituent Assembly welcomes the policy of the Council of People's Commissars in proclaiming the complete independence of Finland, commencing the evacuation of troops from Persia, and proclaiming freedom of self-determination for Armenia.

3. The Constituent Assembly regards the Soviet law on the cancellation of the loans contracted by the governments of the tsar, the landowners and the bourgeoisie as a first blow struck at international banking, finance capital, and expresses the conviction that Soviet power will firmly pursue this path until the international workers' uprising against the yoke of capital has completely triumphed.

IV.　Having been elected on the basis of party lists drawn up prior to the October Revolution, when the people were not yet in a position to rise *en masse* against the exploiters, had not yet experienced the full-strength of resistance of the latter in defence of their class privileges, and had not yet applied themselves in practice to the task of building socialist society, the Constituent Assembly considers that it would be fundamentally wrong, even formally, to put itself in opposition to Soviet power.

In essence the Constituent Assembly considers that now, when the people are waging the last fight against their exploiters, there can be no place for exploiters in any government body. Power must be vested wholly and entirely in the working people and their authorised representatives—the Soviets of Workers', Soldiers' and Peasants' Deputies.

Supporting Soviet power and the decrees of the Council of People's Commissars, the Constituent Assembly considers that its own task is confined to establishing the fundamental principles of the socialist reconstruction of society.

At the same time, endeavouring to create a really free and voluntary, and therefore all the more firm and stable, union of the working classes of all the nations of Russia, the Constituent Assembly confines its own task to setting up the fundamental principles of a federation of Soviet Republics of Russia, while leaving it to the workers and peasants of each nation to decide independently at their own authoritative Congress of Soviets whether they wish to participate in the federal government and in the other federal Soviet institutions, and on what terms.

MOHANDAS K. GANDHI
Ahmedabad Speech
APRIL 14, 1919

Born in western India in 1869, Mohandas Karamchand Gandhi ("Mahatma," meaning "great-souled" was a title bestowed on him later by his followers), was the greatest hero of peaceful revolution, inspiring among others the great Martin Luther King, Jr. He earned his law degree in London in 1891 and practiced in South Africa for twenty-one years before returning to India in 1914 as an advocate for *satyagraha* (usually translated as "passive resistance," but literally "truth-force" or "soul-force").

On April 13, 1919, British troops shot 1,500 nonviolent demonstrators for Indian independence, killing four hundred of them. After an outbreak of riots, Gandhi made a speech the next day to the citizens of Ahmedabad in his ashram. He was "ashamed," he told them: "I have said times without number that Satyagraha admits of no violence, no pillage, no incendiarism; and still in the name of Satyagraha we burnt down buildings, forcibly captured weapons, extorted money, stopped trains, cut off telegraph wires, killed innocent people and plundered shops and private houses."

The British authorities repeatedly imprisoned Gandhi for his teaching of *satyagraha*. In spite of this, he led the nationalist movement in India that resulted in independence in August 1947. On January 30, 1948, a Hindu nationalist fanatic assassinated him.

SOURCE: Mohandas K. Gandhi, *Mahatma Gandhi: His Life, Writings and Speeches* (Madras: Ganesh & Co., 1921), 403–409.

Ahmedabad Speech

Brothers,—I mean to address myself mainly to you. Brothers, the events that have happened in course of the last few days have been most disgraceful to Ahmedabad, and as all these things have happened in my name, I am ashamed of them, and those who have been responsible for them have thereby not honoured me but disgraced me. A rapier run through my body could hardly have pained me more. I have said times without number that Satyagraha admits of no violence, no pillage, no incendiarism; and still in the name of Satyagraha we burnt down buildings, forcibly captured weapons, extorted money, stopped trains, cut off telegraph wires, killed innocent people and plundered shops and private houses. If deeds such as these could save me from the prison house or the scaffold I should not like to be so saved. I do wish to say in all earnestness that violence has not secured my discharge. A most brutal rumour was set afloat that Anasuya Bai was arrested. The crowds were infuriated all the more, and disturbance increased. You have thereby disgraced Anasuya Bai and under the cloak of her arrest heinous deeds have been done.

These deeds have not benefited the people in any way. They have done nothing but harm. The buildings burnt down were public property and they will naturally be rebuilt at our expense. The loss due to the shops remaining closed is also our loss. The terrorism prevailing in the city due to Martial Law is also the result of this violence. It has been said that many innocent lives have been lost as a result of the operation of Martial Law. If this is a fact then for that too the deeds described above are responsible. It will thus be seen that the events that have happened have done nothing but harm to us. Moreover they have most seriously damaged the Satyagraha movement. Had an entirely peaceful agitation followed my arrest, the Rowlatt Act would have been out or on the point of being out of the Statute Book to-day. It should not be a matter for surprise if the withdrawal of the Act is now delayed. When I was released on Friday my plan was to start for Delhi again on Saturday to seek re-arrest, and that would have been an accession of strength to the movement. Now, instead of going to Delhi, it remains to me to offer Satyagraha against our own people, and as it is my determination to offer Satyagraha even unto death for securing the withdrawal of the Rowlatt legislation, I think the occasion has arrived when I should offer Satyagraha against ourselves for the violence that has occurred. And I shall do so at the sacrifice of my body, so long as we do not keep perfect peace and cease from violence to person and property. How can I seek imprisonment unless I have absolute confidence that we shall no longer be guilty of such errors? Those desirous of joining the Satyagraha movement or of helping it must entirely abstain from violence. They may not resort to violence even on my being rearrested or on some such events happening. Englishmen and women have been compelled to leave their homes and confine themselves to places of protection in Shahi Bag, because their trust in our harmlessness has received a rude shock. A little thinking should convince us that this is a matter of humiliation for us all. The sooner this state of things stops the better for us. They are our brethren and it is our duty to inspire them with the belief that their persons are as sacred to us as our own and this is what we call *Abhaydan*, the first requisite of true religion. Satyagraha without this is *Duxagraha*.

There are two distinct duties now before us. One is that we should firmly resolve upon refraining from all violence, and the other is that we should repent and do penance for our sins. So long as we don't repent and do not realise our errors and make an open confession of them, we shall not truly change our course. The first step is that those of us who have captured weapons should surrender them. To show that we are really penitent we will contribute each of us not less than eight annas towards helping the families of those who have been killed by our acts. Though no amount of money contribution can altogether undo the results of the furious deeds of the past few days, our contribution will be a slight token of our repentence. I hope and pray that no one will evade this contribution on the plea that he has had no part in those wicked acts. For if such as those who were no party to these deeds had all courageously and bravely gone forward to put down the lawlessness, the mob would have been checked in their career and would have immediately realised the wickedness of their doings. I venture to say that if instead of giving money to the mob out of fear we had rushed out to protect buildings and to save the innocent without fear of death we could have succeeded in so doing. Unless we have this sort of courage, mischief-makers will always try to intimidate us into participating in their misdeeds. Fear of death makes us devoid both of valour and religion. For want of valour is want of religious faith. And having done little to stop the violence we have been all participators in the sins that have been committed. And we ought, therefore, to contribute our mite as a mark of our repentence. Each group can collect its own contributions and send them on to me through its collectors. I would also advise, if it is possible for you, to observe a twenty-four hours fast in slight expiation of these sins. This fast should be observed in private and there is no need for crowds to go to the bathing ghats.

I have thus far drawn attention to what appears to be your duty. I must now consider my own. My responsibility is a million times greater than yours. I have placed Satyagraha before people for their acceptance, and I have lived in your midst for four years. I have also given some contribution to the special service of Ahmedabad. Its citizens are not quite unfamiliar with my views.

It is alleged that I have without proper consideration persuaded thousands to join the movement. That allegation is, I admit, true to a certain extent, but to a certain extent only. It is open to any body to say that but for the Satyagraha campaign there would not have been this violence. For this I have already done a penance, to my mind an unendurable one, namely, that I have had to postpone my visit to Delhi to seek rearrest and I have also been obliged to suggest a temporary restriction of Satyagraha to a limited field. This has been more painful to me than a wound but this penance is not enough, and I have therefore decided to fast for three days, *i.e.*, 72 hours. I hope my fast will pain no one. I believe a seventy-two hours fast is easier for me than a twenty-four hours' fast for you. And I have imposed on me a discipline which I can bear. If you really feel pity for the suffering that will be caused to me, I request that that pity should always restrain you from ever again being party to the criminal acts of which I have complained. Take it from me that we are not going to win Swarajya or benefit our country in the least by violence and terrorism. I am of opinion that if we have to wade through violence to obtain Swarajya and if a redress of grievances were to be only possible by means of ill will for and slaughter of English men I for one would do without that Swarajya and without a redress of those grievances. For me life would not be worth living if Ahmedabad continues to countenance violence in the name of truth. The poet has called Gujarat the "Garvi" (Great and Glorious) Gujarat. The Ahmedabad its capital is the residence of many religious Hindus and Muhammadans. Deeds of public violence in a city like this is like an ocean being on fire. Who can quench that fire? I can only offer myself as a sacrifice to be burnt in that fire, and I therefore ask you all to help in the attainment of the result that I desire out of my fast. May the love that lured you into unworthy acts awaken you to a sense of the reality, and if that love does continue to animate you, beware that I may not have to fast myself to death.

It seems that the deeds I have complained of have been done in an organised manner. There seems to be a definite design about them, and I am sure that there must be some educated and clever man or men behind them. They may be educated, but their education has not enlightened them. You have been misled into doing these deeds by such people. I advise you never to be so misguided, and I would ask them seriously to reconsider their views. To them and to you I commend my book "Hind Swarajya" which as I understand may be printed and published without infringing the law thereby.

Among the millhands the spinners have been on strike for some days. I advise them to resume work immediately and to ask for increase if they want any only after resuming work, and in a reasonable manner. To resort to the use of force to get any increase is suicidal. I would specially advise all millhands to altogether eschew violence. It is their interest to do so and I remind them of the promises made to Anasuya Bai and me that they would ever refrain from violence. I hope that all will now resume work.

PETER KROPOTKIN
"The Russian Revolution and the Soviet Government"
APRIL 28, 1919

While supporting the Russian Revolution, the anarchist Kropotkin (see note above, p. 170) had serious reservations about the Bolsheviks' dictatorial tactics. "Not that there is nothing to oppose in the methods of the Bolshevik government," he writes in this open letter to the "workers of Western Europe." "But all foreign armed intervention necessarily strengthens the dictatorial tendencies of government, and paralyzes the efforts of those Russians who are ready to aid Russia, independently of the government, in the restoration of its life." He encourages the workers to involve themselves in persuading their governments to allow Soviet Russia to solve its own problems. The most serious problem he foresaw is that "this effort to build a communist republic on the basis of a strongly centralized state communism under the iron law of party dictatorship is bound to end in failure." In suggesting remedies, he warned against believing that much influence by any group is possible in the midst of a revolution, which he compared to "a great natural phenomenon . . . such as an earthquake, or, rather, such as a typhoon." What would follow the Soviet government's "horrors" would be, he hoped, a moderated reaction.

SOURCE: Peter Kropotkin, *Anarchism: A Collection of Revolutionary Writings*. Ed. Roger N. Baldwin (Mineola, N.Y.: Dover Publications, Inc., 2002), 252–259.

Letter to the Workers of Western Europe*

Dmitrov, Russia,
April 28, 1919.

I have been asked if I did not have a message for the workers of the western world. Certainly there is plenty to say and learn of the actual events in Russia. As the message would have to be long to cover all, I will indicate only the principal points.

---

*Published first in English in the *Labour Leader* of July 22, 1920, later in the *Temps Nouveaux*, from which this is translated. (*Note by Roger N. Baldwin.*)

First, the workers of the civilized world and their friends in other classes ought to prevail on their governments to abandon entirely the idea of armed intervention in Russia, whether openly or secretly. Russia is undergoing now a revolution of the same extent and importance as England underwent in 1639 to '48, and France in 1789 to '94. Every nation should refuse to play the shameful role played by England, Prussia, Austria and Russia during the French Revolution.

Further, it must be borne in mind that the Russian Revolution—which is trying to build a society in which all productive work, technical ability and scientific knowledge will be entirely communal—is not a mere accident in the struggle of contending parties. It was prepared by almost a century of socialist and communist propaganda, since the days of Robert Owen, Saint Simon and Fourier. And although the effort to introduce the new social system by means of a party dictatorship is apparently condemned to failure, it must be recognized that already the revolution has introduced into our daily lives new conceptions of the rights of labor, its rightful place in society and the duties of each citizen,—and that they will endure.

Not only the workers, but all the progressive forces in the civilized world should put an end to the support given until now to the enemies of the revolution. Not that there is nothing to oppose in the methods of the Bolshevik government. Far from it! But all foreign armed intervention necessarily strengthens the dictatorial tendencies of the government, and paralyzes the efforts of those Russians who are ready to aid Russia, independently of the government, in the restoration of its life.

The evils inherent in a party dictatorship have been accentuated by the conditions of war in which this party maintains its power. This state of war has been the pretext for strengthening dictatorial methods which centralize the control of every detail of life in the hands of the government, with the effect of stopping an immense part of the ordinary activities of the country. The evils natural to state communism have been increased ten-fold under the pretext that all our misery is due to foreign intervention.

I should also point out that if Allied military intervention continues, it will certainly develop in Russia a bitter feeling toward the western nations, a feeling which will be used some day in future conflicts. That bitterness is always developing.

In short, it is high time that the nations of Europe enter into direct relations with the Russian nation. And from this point of view, you—the working class and the progressive elements of all nations—should have your word to say.

A word more on the general question. The re-establishment of relations between the European and American nations and Russia does not mean the supremacy of the Russian nation over the nationalities that composed the Czarist empire. Imperialist Russia is dead and will not be revived. The future of these different provincès lies in a great federation. The natural territories of the various parts of this federation are quite distinct, as those of us familiar with Russian history and ethnography well know. All efforts to reunite under a central control the naturally separate parts of the Russian Empire are predestined to failure. It is therefore fitting that the western nations should recognize the right of independence of each part of the old Russian Empire.

My opinion is that this development will continue. I see the time coming when each part of this federation will be itself a federation of rural communes and free cities. And I believe also that certain parts of western Europe will soon follow the same course.

As to our present economic and political situation, the Russian revolution, being a continuation of the great revolutions of England and France, is trying to reach the point where the French revolution stopped before it succeeded in creating what they called "equality in fact," that is, economic equality.

Unhappily, this effort has been made in Russia under a strongly centralized party dictatorship. This effort was made in the same way as the extremely centralized and Jacobin endeavor of Baboeuf. I owe it to you to say frankly that, according to my view, this effort to build a communist republic on the basis of a strongly centralized state communism under the iron law of party dictatorship is bound to end in failure. We are learning to know in Russia how *not* to introduce communism, even with a people tired of the old régime and opposing no active resistance to the experiments of the new rulers.

The idea of soviets, that is to say, of councils of workers and peasants, conceived first at the time of the revolutionary attempt in 1905, and immediately realized by the revolution of February, 1917, as soon as Czarism was overthrown,—the idea of such councils controlling the economic and political life of the country is a great idea. All the more so, since it necessarily follows that these councils should be composed of all who take a real part in the production of national wealth by their own efforts.

But as long as the country is governed by a party dictatorship, the workers' and peasants' councils evidently lose their entire significance. They are reduced to the passive role formerly played by the "States General," when they were convoked by the king and had to combat an all-powerful royal council.

A council of workers ceases to be free and of any use when liberty of the press no longer exists, and we have been in that condition for two years,—under a pretext that we are in a state of war. But more still. The workers' and peasants' councils lose their significance when the elections are not preceded by a free electoral campaign, and when the elections are conducted under pressure by a party dictatorship. Naturally, the usual excuse is that a dictatorship is inevitable in order to combat the old régime. But such a state of affairs is evidently a step backwards, since the revolution is committed to the construction of a new society on a new economic base. It means the death-knell of the new system.

The methods of overthrowing an already enfeebled government are well known to ancient and modern history. But when it is necessary to create new forms of life, especially new forms of production and exchange, without having examples to imitate; when everything must be constructed anew; when a government which undertakes to furnish every citizen with a lamp and even the match to light it, and then cannot do it even with a limitless number of officials,—that government becomes a nuisance. It develops a bureaucracy so formidable that the French bureaucracy, which requires the help of forty officials to sell a tree broken down by a storm on the national highway, is a mere bagatelle in comparison. That is what we are learning in Russia. And that is what you workers of the west should avoid by every means, since you have at heart the success of a real social reconstruction. Send your delegates here to see how a social revolution is working in real life.

The immense constructive work demanded by a social revolution cannot be accomplished by a central government, even if it had to guide it something more substantial than a few socialist and anarchist hand-books. It has need of knowledge, of brains and of the voluntary collaboration of a host of local and specialized forces which alone can attack the diversity of economic problems in their local aspects. To reject this collaboration and to turn everything over to the genius of party dictators is to destroy the independent centers of our life, the trade unions and the local cooperative organizations, by changing them into bureaucratic organs of the party, as is the case at this time. That is the way *not* to accomplish the revolution, to make its realization impossible. And that is why I consider it my duty to put you on guard against borrowing any such methods. . . .

The late war has brought about new conditions of life for the whole civilized world. Socialism will certainly make considerable progress, and new forms of more independent life will be created based on local autonomy and free initiative. They will be created either peacefully, or by revolutionary means.

But the success of this reconstruction will depend in great part on the possibility of direct cooperation between the different peoples. To achieve that, it is necessary that the working classes of all nations should be directly united and that the idea of a great international of all the workers of the world should be taken up again, but not in the form of a union directed by a single political party, as in the case of the Second and Third Internationals. Such unions have of course plenty of reason to exist, but outside of them, and uniting all, there should be a union of all the workers' organizations of the world, federated to deliver world production from its present subjection to capitalism.

WHAT TO DO?

The revolution we have gone through is the sum total, not of the efforts of separate individuals, *but a natural phenomenon, independent of the human will,* a natural phenomenon similar to a typhoon such as rises suddenly on the coasts of Eastern Asia.

Thousands of causes, in which the work of separate individuals and even of parties has been only a grain of sand, one of the minute local whirlwinds, have contributed to form the great natural phenomenon, the great catastrophe which shall either renew, or destroy; or perhaps both destroy and renew.

All of us prepared this great inevitable change. But it was also prepared by all the previous revolutions of 1793, 1848–1871; by all the writings of the Jacobins, socialists; by all the achievements of science, industry, art and so on. In a word, millions of natural causes have contributed just in the same way as millions of movements of particles of air or water cause the sudden storm which sinks hundreds of ships or destroys thousands of houses—as the trembling of the earth in an earthquake is caused by thousands of small tremors and by the preparatory movements of separate particles.

In general, people do not see events concretely, solidly. They think more in words than in clearly-imagined pictures, and they have absolutely no idea what a revolution is,—of those many millions of causes which have gone to give it its present form,—and they are therefore inclined to exaggerate the importance in the progress of the revolution of their personality and of that attitude which they, their friends and co-thinkers will take up in this enormous upheaval. And of course they are absolutely incapable of understanding how powerless is any individual, whatever his intelligence and experience, in this whirlpool of hundreds of thousands of forces which have been put into motion by the upheaval.

They do not understand that once such a great natural phenomenon has begun, such as an earthquake, or, rather, such as a typhoon, separate individuals are powerless to exercise any kind of influence on the course of events. A party perhaps can do something,—far less than is usually thought,—and on the surface of the oncoming waves, its influence may, perhaps, be very slightly noticeable. But separate small aggregations not forming a fairly large mass are undoubtedly power-less—their powers are certainly *nil.* . . .

It is in this position that I, an anarchist, find myself. But even parties of far greater numbers in Russia at the present moment are in a very similar position.

I will even go farther; the governing party itself is in the same posi-tion. It no longer governs, it is being carried along by the current which it helped to create but which is now already a thousand times stronger than the party itself. . . .

What is then to be done?

We are experiencing a revolution which has advanced not at all along those ways which we had prepared for it, but which we had no time to prepare sufficiently. What is to be done now?

To prevent the revolution? Absurd!

Too late. The revolution will advance in its own way, in the direction of the least resistance, without paying the least attention to our efforts.

At the present moment the Russian revolution is in the following position. It is perpetrating horrors. It is ruining the whole country. In its mad fury it is annihilating human lives. That is why it is a revolution and not a peaceful progress, because it is destroying without regarding what it destroys and whither it goes.

And we are powerless for the present to direct it into another chan-nel, until such time as it will have played itself out. It must wear itself out.

And then? *Then—inevitably will come a reaction.* Such is the law of history, and it is easy to understand why this cannot be otherwise. People imagine that we can change the form of development of a rev-olution. That is a childish illusion. A revolution is such a force that its growth cannot be changed. *And a reaction is absolutely inevitable,* just as a hollow in the water is inevitable after every wave, as weakness is inevitable in a human being after a period of feverish activity.

Therefore the only thing we can do is to use our energy to lessen the fury and force of the oncoming reaction.

But of what can our efforts consist?

To modify the passions—on one as on the other side? Who is likely to listen to us? Even if there exist such diplomats as can do anything in this role, the time for their *début* has not yet come; neither the one nor the other side is as yet disposed to listen to them. I see one thing; we must gather together people *who will be capable of undertaking con-structive work in each and every party after the revolution has worn itself out.* (Italics Kropotkin's.)

. MOHANDAS K. GANDHI
"Satyagraha (Noncoöperation)"
From Speech at Madras

AUGUST 12, 1920

In south India, Gandhi addressed Hindus and Muslims on the practice of
satyagraha, or, as translated in this speech, "noncoöperation." (See note to
Gandhi's Ahmedabad Speech, p. 239)

SOURCE: Mahatma Gandhi, *Freedom's Battle* (Madras: Ganesh & Co., 1921),
207–231.

Satyagraha (Noncoöperation)

What is this noncoöperation, about which you have heard much, and
why do we want to offer this noncoöperation? I wish to go for the time
being into the why. There are two things before this country: the first
and the foremost in the Khilafat question. On this the heart of the
Mussalmans of India has become lascerated. British pledges given after
the greatest deliberation by the Prime Minister of England in the name
of the English nation, have been dragged into the mire. The promises
given to Moslem India on the strength of which, the consideration that
was expected by the British nation was exacted, have been broken, and
the great religion of Islam has been placed in danger. The Mussalmans
hold—and I venture to think they rightly hold—that so long as British
promises remain unfulfilled, so long is it impossible for them to tender
wholehearted fealty and loyalty to the British connection; and if it is to
be a choice for a devout Mussalman between loyalty to the British connection and loyalty to his Code and Prophet, he will not require a second to make his choice,—and he has declared his choice. The
Mussalmans say frankly openly and honourably to the whole world that
if the British Ministers and the British nation do not fulfil the pledges

249

given to them and do not wish to regard with respect the sentiments of 70 millions of the inhabitants of India who profess the faith of Islam, it will be impossible for them to retain Islamic loyalty. It is a question, then for the rest of the Indian population to consider whether they want to perform a neighbourly duty by their Mussalman countrymen, and if they do, they have an opportunity of a lifetime which will not occur for another hundred years, to show their good-will, fellowship and friend-ship and to prove what they have been saying for all these long years that the Mussalman is the brother of the Hindu. If the Hindu regards that before the connection with the British nation comes his natural connection with his Moslem brother, then I say to you that if you find that the Moslem claim is just, that it is based upon real sentiment, and that at its back ground is this great religious feeling, you cannot do oth-erwise than help the Mussalman through and through, so long as their cause remains just, and the means for attaining the end remains equally just, honourable and free from harm to India. These are the plain conditions which the Indian Mussalmans have accepted; and it was when they saw that they could accept the proferred aid of the Hindus, that they could always justify the cause and the means before the whole world, that they decided to accept the proferred hand of fel-lowship. It is then for the Hindus and Mahomedans to offer a united front to the whole of the Christian powers of Europe and tell them that weak as India is, India has still got the capacity of preserving her self-respect, she still knows how to die for her religion and for her self-respect.

That is the Khilafat in a nut-shell; but you have also got the Punjab. The Punjab has wounded the heart of India as no other question has for the past century. I do not exclude from my calculation the Mutiny of 1857. Whatever hardships India had to suffer during the Mutiny, the insult that was attempted to be offered to her during the passage of the Rowlatt legislation and that which was offered after its passage were unparalleled in Indian history. It is because you want justice from the British nation in connection with the Punjab atrocities you have to devise, ways and means as to how you can get this justice. The House of Commons, the House of Lords, Mr. Montagu, the Viceroy of India, every one of them know what the feeling of India is on this Khilafat question and on that of the Punjab; the debates in both the Houses of Parliament, the action of Mr. Montagu and that of the Viceroy have demonstrated to you completely that they are not willing to give the justice which is India's due and which she demands. I suggest that our leaders have got to find a way out of this great difficulty and unless we have made ourselves even with the British rulers in India and unless we have gained a measure of self-respect at the hands of the British rulers in India, no connection, and no friendly intercourse is possible between them and ourselves. I, therefore, venture to suggest this beautiful and unanswerable method of noncoöperation.

I have been told that noncoöperation is unconstitutional. I venture to deny that it is unconstitutional. On the contrary, I hold that noncoöperation is a just and religious doctrine; it is the inherent right of every human being and it is perfectly constitutional. A great lover of the British Empire has said that under the British constitution even a successful rebellion is perfectly constitutional and he quotes historical instances, which I cannot deny, in support of his claim. I do not claim any constitutionality for a rebellion successful or otherwise, so long as that rebellion means in the ordinary sense of the term, what it does mean, namely wresting justice by violent means. On the contrary, I have said it repeatedly to my countrymen that violence whatever end it may serve in Europe, will never serve us in India. My brother and friend Shaukat Ali believes in methods of violence; and if it was in his power to draw the sword against the British Empire, I know that he has got the courage of a man and he has got also the wisdom to see that he should offer that battle to the British Empire. But because he recognises as a true soldier that means of violence are not open to India, he sides with me accepting my humble assistance and pledges his word that so long as I am with him and so long as he believes in the doctrine, so long will he not harbour even the idea of violence against any single Englishman or any single man on earth. I am here to tell you that he has been as true as his word and has kept it religiously. I am here to bear witness that he has been following out this plan of non-violent noncoöperation to the very letter and I am asking India to follow this non-violent noncoöperation. I tell you that there is not a better soldier living in our ranks in British India than Shaukat Ali. When the time for the drawing of the sword comes, if it ever comes, you will find him drawing that sword and you will find me retiring to the jungles of Hindustan. As soon as India accepts the doctrine of the sword, my life as an Indian is finished. It is because I believe in a mission special to India and it is because I believe that the ancients of India after centuries of experience have found out that the true thing for any human being on earth is not justice based on violence but justice based on sacrifice of self, justice based on Yagna and Kurbani, — I cling to that doctrine and I shall cling to it for ever, — it is for that reason I tell you that whilst my friend believes also in the doctrine of violence and has adopted the doctrine of non-violence as a weapon of the weak, I believe in the doctrine of non-violence as a weapon of the strongest. I believe that a man is the strongest soldier for daring to die unarmed with his breast bare before the enemy. So much for the non-violent part of noncoöperation. I, therefore, venture to suggest to my learned countrymen that so long as the doctrine of noncoöperation remains non-violent, so long there is nothing unconstitutional in that doctrine.

I ask further, is it unconstitutional for me to say to the British Government "I refuse to serve you"? Is it unconstitutional for our worthy Chairman to return with every respect all the titles that he has ever held from the Government? Is it unconstitutional for any parent to withdraw his children from a Government or aided school? Is it unconstitutional for a lawyer to say "I shall no longer support the arm of the law so long as that arm of law is used not to raise me but to debase me"? Is it unconstitutional for a civil servant or for a judge to say, "I refuse to serve a Government which does not wish to respect the wishes of the whole people"? I ask, is it unconstitutional for a policeman or for a soldier to tender his resignation when he knows that he is called to serve a Government which traduces its own countrymen"? Is it unconstitutional for me to go to the "krishan," to the agriculturist, and say to him "it is not wise for you to pay any taxes, if these taxes are used by the Government not to raise you but to weaken you"? I hold and I venture to submit, that there is nothing unconstitutional in it. What is more, I have done every one of these things in my life and nobody has questioned the constitutional character of it. I was in Kaira working in the midst of 7 lakhs of agriculturists. They had all suspended the payment of taxes and the whole of India was at one with me. Nobody considered that it was unconstitutional. I submit that in the whole plan of noncoöperation, there is nothing unconstitutional. But I do venture to suggest that it will be highly unconstitutional in the midst of this unconstitutional Government,—in the midst of a nation which has built up its magnificent constitution,—for the people of India to become weak and to crawl on their belly—it will be highly unconstitutional for the people of India to pocket every insult that is offered to them; it is highly unconstitutional for the 70 millions of Mahomedans of India to submit to a violent wrong done to their religion; it is highly unconstitutional for the whole of India to sit still and coöperate with an unjust Government which has trodden under its feet the honour of the Punjab. I say to my countrymen so long as you have a sense of honour and so long as you wish to remain the decendants and defenders of the noble traditions that have been handed to you for generations after generations, it is unconstitutional for you not to noncoöperate and unconstitutional for you to coöperate with a Government which has become so unjust as our Government has become. I am not anti-English; I am not anti-British; I am not anti any Government; but I am anti-untruth—anti-humbug and anti-injustice. So long as the Government spells injustice, it may regard me as its enemy, implacable enemy. I had hoped at the Congress at Amritsar—I am speaking God's truth before you—when I pleaded on bended knees before some of you for coöperation with the Government. I had full hope that the British Ministers who are wise, as a rule, would placate the Mussalman sentiment, that they would do full justice in the matter of the Punjab atrocities; and therefore, I said:—let us return good-will to the hand of fellowship that has been extended to us, which I then believed was extended to us through the Royal proclamation. It was on that account that I pleaded for coöperation. But to-day that faith having gone and obliterated by the acts of the British Ministers, I am here to plead not for futile obstruction in the Legislative Council but for real substantial noncoöperation which would paralyse the mightiest Government on earth. That is what I stand for to-day. Until we have wrung Justice, and until we have wrung our self-respect from unwilling hands and from unwilling pens there can be no coöperation. Our Shastras say and I say so with the greatest deference to all the greatest religious preceptors of India but without fear of contradiction, that our Shastras teach us that there shall be no coöperation between injustice and justice, between an unjust man and a justice-loving man, between truth and untruth. Coöperation is a duty only so long as Government protects your honour, and noncoöperation is an equal duty when the Government instead of protecting robs you of your honour. That is the doctrine of noncoöperation.

I have been told that I should have waited for the declaration of the special Congress which is the mouthpiece of the whole nation. I know that it is the mouthpiece of the whole nation. If it was for me, individual Gandhi, to wait, I would have waited for eternity. But I had in my hands a sacred trust. I was advising my Mussalman countrymen and for the time being I hold their honour in my hands. I dare not ask them to wait for any verdict but the verdict of their own Conscience. Do you suppose that Mussalmans can eat their own words, can withdraw from the honourable position they have taken up? If perchance—and God forbid that it should happen—the Special Congress decides against them, I would still advise my countrymen, the Mussalmans to stand single handed and fight rather than yield to the attempted dishonour to their religion. It is therefore given to the Mussalmans to go to the Congress on bended knees and plead for support. But support or no support, it was not possible for them to wait for the Congress to give them the lead. They had to choose between futile violence, drawing of the naked sword and peaceful non-violent but effective noncoöperation, and they have made their choice. I venture further to say to you that if there is any body of men who feel as I do, the sacred character of noncoöperation, it is for you and me not to wait for the Congress but to act and to make it impossible for the Congress to give any other verdict. After all what is the Congress? The Congress is the collected voice of individuals who form it, and if the individuals go to the Congress with a united voice, that will be the verdict you will gain from the Congress. But if we go to the Congress with no opinion because we have none or because we are afraid to express it, then naturally we await the verdict of the Congress. To those who are unable to make up their mind I say, by all means wait. But for those who have seen the clear light as they see the lights in front of them, for them to wait is a sin. The Congress does not expect you to wait but it expects you to act so that the Congress can gauge properly the national feeling. So much for the Congress.

Among the details of noncoöperation I have placed in the foremost rank the boycott of the councils. Friends have quarrelled with me for the use of the word boycott, because I have disapproved—as I disapprove even now—boycott of British goods or any goods for that matter. But there, boycott has its own meaning and here boycott has its own meaning. I not only do not disapprove but approve of the boycott of the councils that are going to be formed next year. And why do I do it? The people—the masses,—require from us, the leaders, a clear lead. They do not want any equivocation from us. The suggestion that we should seek election and then refuse to take the oath of allegiance, would only make the nation distrust the leaders. It is not a clear lead to the nation. So I say to you, my countrymen, not to fall into this trap. We shall sell our country by adopting the method of seeking election and then not taking the oath of allegiance. We may find it difficult, and I frankly confess to you that I have not that trust in so many Indians making that declaration and standing by it. To-day I suggest to those who honestly hold the view—*viz.* that we should seek election and then refuse to take the oath of allegiance—I suggest to them that they will fall into a trap which they are preparing for themselves and for the nation. That is my view. I hold that if we want to give the nation the clearest possible lead, and if we want not to play with this great nation we must make it clear to this nation that we cannot take any favours, no matter, how great they may be so long as those favours are accompanied by an injustice a double wrong done to India not yet redressed. The first indispensable thing before we can receive any favours from them is that they should redress this double wrong. There is a Greek proverb which used to say "Beware of the Greek but especially beware of them when they bring gifts to you." To-day from those ministers who are bent upon perpetuating the wrong to Islam and to the Punjab, I say we cannot accept gifts but we should be doubly careful lest we may not fall into the trap that they may have devised. I therefore suggest that we must not coquet with the council and must not have anything whatsoever to do with them. I am told that if we, who represent the national sentiment do not seek election, the Moderates who do not represent that sentiment will. I do not agree. I do not know what the Moderates represent and I do not know what the Nationalists represent. I know that there are good sheep and black sheep amongst the Moderates. I know that there are good sheep and black sheep amongst the Nationalists. I know that many Moderates hold honestly the view that it is a sin to resort to non-coöperation. I respectfully agree to differ from them. I do say to them also that they will fall into a trap which they will have devised if they seek election. But that does not affect my situation. If I feel in my heart of hearts that I ought not to go to the councils I ought at least to abide by this decision and it does not matter if ninety-nine other countrymen seek election. That is the only way in which public work can be done, and public opinion can be built. That is the only way in which reforms can be achieved and religion can be conserved. If it is a question of religious honour, whether I am one or among many I must stand upon my doctrine. Even if I should die in the attempt, it is worth dying for, than that I should live and deny my own doctrine. I suggest that it will be wrong on the part of any one to seek election to these Councils. If once we feel that we cannot coöperate with this Government, we have to commence from the top. We are the natural leaders of the people and we have acquired the right and the power to go to the nation and speak to it with the voice of noncoöperation. I therefore do suggest that it is inconsistent with noncoöperation to seek election to the Councils on any terms whatsoever.

I have suggested another difficult matter, viz., that the lawyers should suspend their practice. How should I do otherwise knowing so well how the Government had always been able to retain this power through the instrumentality of lawyers. It is perfectly true that it is the lawyers of to-day who are leading us, who are fighting the country's battles, but when it comes to a matter of action against the Government, when it comes to a matter of paralysing the activity of the Government I know that the Government always look to the lawyers, however fine fighters they may have been, to preserve their dignity and their self-respect. I therefore suggest to my lawyer friends that it is their duty to suspend their practice and to show to the Government that they will no longer retain their offices, because lawyers are considered to be honorary officers of the courts and therefore subject to their disciplinary jurisdiction. They must no longer retain these honorary offices if they want to withdraw coöperation from Government. But what will happen to law and order? We shall evolve law and order through the instrumentality of these very lawyers. We shall promote arbitration courts and dispense justice, pure, simple, home-made justice, swadeshi justice to our countrymen. That is what suspension of practice means.

I have suggested yet another difficulty—to withdraw our children from the Government schools and to ask collegiate students to withdraw from the College and to empty Government aided schools. How could I do otherwise? I want to gauge the national sentiment. I want to know whether the Mahomedans feel deeply. If they feel deeply they will understand in the twinkling of an eye, that it is not right for them to receive schooling from a Government in which they have lost all faith; and which they do not trust at all. How can I, if I do not want to help this Government, receive any help from that Government. I think that the schools and colleges are factories for making clerks and Government servants. I would not help this great factory for manufacturing clerks and servants if I want to withdraw coöperation from that Government. Look at it from any point of view you like. It is not possible for you to send your children to the schools and still believe in the doctrine of noncoöperation.

I have gone further. I have suggested that our title holders should give up their titles. How can they hold on to the titles and honours bestowed by this Government? They were at one time badges of honour when we believed that national honour was safe in their hands. But now they are no longer badges of honour but badges of dishonour and disgrace when we really believe that we cannot get justice from this Government. Every title holder holds his titles and honours as trustee for the nation and in this first step in the withdrawal of coöperation from the Government they should surrender their titles without a moment's consideration. I suggest to my Mahomedan countrymen that if they fail in this primary duty they will certainly fail in noncoöperation unless the masses themselves reject the classes and take up noncoöperation in their own hands and are able to fight that battle even as the men of the French Revolution were able to take the reins of Government in their own hands leaving aside the leaders and marched to the banner of victory. I want no revolution. I want ordered progress. I want no disordered order. I want no chaos. I want real order to be evolved out of this chaos which is misrepresented to me as order. If it is order established by a tyrant in order to get hold of the tyrannical reins of Government I say that it is no order for me but it is disorder. I want to evolve justice out of this injustice. Therefore I suggest to you the passive noncoöperation. If we would only realise the secret of this peaceful and infallible doctrine you will know and you will find that you will not want to use even an angry word when they lift the sword at you and you will not want even to lift your little finger, let alone a stick or a sword.

You may consider that I have spoken these words in anger because I have considered the ways of this Government immoral, unjust, debasing and untruthful. I use these adjectives with the greatest deliberation. I have used them for my own true brother with whom I was engaged in a battle of noncoöperation for full 13 years and although the ashes cover the remains of my brother I tell you that I used to tell him that he was unjust when his plans were based upon immoral foundation. I used to tell him that he did not stand for truth. There was no anger in me. I told him this home truth because I loved him. In the same manner, I tell the British people that I love them, and that I want their association but I want that association on conditions well defined. I want my self-respect and I want my absolute equality with them. If I cannot gain that equality from the British people, I do not want that British connection. If I have to let the British people go and import temporary disorder and dislocation of national business, I will favour that disorder and dislocation than that I should have injustice from the hands of a great nation such as the British nation. You will find that by the time the whole chapter is closed that the successors of Mr. Montagu will give me the credit for having rendered the most distinguished service that I have yet rendered to the Empire, in having offered this noncoöperation and in having suggested the boycott; not of His Royal Highness the Prince of Wales, but of boycott of a visit engineered by the Government in order to tighten its hold on the national neck. I will not allow it even if I stand alone, if I cannot persuade this nation not to welcome that visit but will boycott that visit with all the power at my command. It is for that reason I stand before you and implore you to offer this religious battle, but it is not a battle offered to you by a visionary or a saint. I deny being a visionary. I do not accept the claim of saintliness. I am of the earth, earthy, a common gardener man as much as any one of you, probably much more than you are. I am prone to as many weaknesses as you are. But I have seen the world. I have lived in the world with my eyes open. I have gone through the most fiery ordeals that have fallen to the lot of man. I have gone through this discipline. I have understood the secret of my own sacred Hinduism. I have learnt the lesson that noncoöperation is the duty not merely of the saint but it is the duty of every ordinary citizen, who not knowing much, not caring to know much but wants to perform his ordinary household functions. The people of Europe teach even their masses, the poor people the doctrine of the sword. But the Rishis of India, those who have held the traditions of India have preached to the masses of India the doctrine, not of the sword, not of violence but of suffering, of self-suffering. And unless you and I am prepared to go through this primary lesson we are not ready even to offer the sword and that is the lesson my brother Shaukat Ali has imbibed to teach and that is why he to-day accepts my advice tendered to him in all prayerfulness and in all humility and says "long live noncoöperation." Please remember that even in England the little children were withdrawn from the schools; and colleges in Cambridge and Oxford were closed. Lawyers had left their desks and were fighting in the trenches. I do not present to you the trenches but I do ask you to go through the sacrifice that the men, women and the brave lads of England went through. Remember that you are offering battle to a nation which is saturated with the spirit of sacrifice whenever the occasion arises. Remember that the little band of Boers offered stubborn resistance to a mighty nation. But their lawyers had left their desks. Their mothers had withdrawn their children from the schools and colleges and the children had become the volunteers of the nation. I have seen them with these naked eyes of mine. I am asking my countrymen in India to follow no other gospel than the gospel of self-sacrifice which precedes every battle. Whether you belong to the school of violence or non-violence you will still have to go through the fire of sacrifice, and of discipline. May God grant you, may God grant our leaders, the wisdom, the courage and the true knowledge to lead the nation to its cherished goal. May God grant the people of India the right path, the true vision and the ability and the courage to follow this path, difficult and yet easy, of sacrifice.

Mao Zedong
Manifesto of the Chinese People's Liberation Army
[October 10th Manifesto]

October 10, 1947

From 1927 Mao Zedong [Mao Tse-tung] (1893–1976) helped lead the first Chinese Communist military force, the Red Army, later renamed the People's Liberation Army. Mao's Communists had been fighting the nominal Chinese government, led by Chiang Kai-shek's Nationalists, since the early 1930s; after World War II, from 1946 to 1949, the PLA engaged the Nationalist army in a full-scale civil war. This selection, part of the Communists' propaganda campaign, is known as the October 10th Manifesto. "It analyzed the political situation in China . . . raised the slogan 'Overthrow Chiang Kai-shek and liberate all China!' and announced the eight basic policies of the Chinese People's Liberation Army, which were also those of the Communist Party of China," writes an anonymous Chinese editor. On October 1, 1949, after the PLA took Peking, Mao established by declaration the People's Republic of China.

SOURCE: Mao Tse-tung, *Selected Military Writings of Mao Tse-tung*. (Peking: Foreign Languages Press, 1966), 335–340.

October 10th Manifesto

The Chinese People's Liberation Army, having smashed Chiang Kai-shek's offensive, has now launched a large-scale counter-offensive. Our armies on the southern front are advancing on the Yangtse River valley, and our armies on the northern front are advancing on the Chinese Changchun Railway and the Peiping-Liaoning Railway. Wherever our troops go, the enemy flees pell-mell before us and the people give thunderous cheers. The whole situation has fundamentally changed as compared with a year ago.

The aim of our army in this war, as proclaimed time and again to the nation and the world, is the liberation of the Chinese people and of the

Chinese nation. And today, our aim is to carry out the urgent demand of the people of the whole country, that is, to overthrow the arch-criminal of the civil war, Chiang Kai-shek, and form a democratic coalition government in order to attain the general goal of liberating the people and the nation.

For eight long years the Chinese people fought heroically against Japanese imperialism for their own liberation and national independence. After the Japanese surrender the people longed for peace, but Chiang Kai-shek wrecked all their peace efforts and forced the disaster of an unprecedented civil war on them. Hence the people of all strata throughout the country had no alternative but to unite to overthrow Chiang Kai-shek.

Chiang Kai-shek's present policy of civil war is no accident but is the inevitable outcome of the policy against the people he and his reactionary clique have consistently followed. As far back as 1927, Chiang Kai-shek, devoid of all gratitude, betrayed the revolutionary alliance between the Kuomintang and the Communist Party and betrayed the revolutionary Three People's Principles and the Three Great Policies of Sun Yat-sen; then he set up a dictatorship, capitulated to imperialism, fought ten years of civil war and brought on the aggression of the Japanese bandits. In the Sian Incident of 1936, the Communist Party of China returned good for evil and helped Generals Chang Hsueh-liang and Yang Hu-cheng in reaching the decision to set Chiang Kai-shek free in the hope that he would repent, turn over a new leaf and join in the fight against the Japanese aggressors. But once again he proved devoid of all gratitude; he was passive against the Japanese invaders, active in suppressing the people and extremely hostile to the Communist Party. The year before last (1945), Japan surrendered and the Chinese people once more forgave Chiang Kai-shek, demanding that he should stop the civil war he had already started, put democracy into practice and unite with all parties and groups for peace and national reconstruction. But no sooner had the truce agreement been signed, the resolutions of the Political Consultative Conference adopted and the four pledges proclaimed than the utterly faithless Chiang Kai-shek went back on his word completely. Time and again the people showed themselves forbearing and conciliatory for the sake of the common good, but, aided by U.S. imperialism, Chiang Kai-shek was determined to launch an unprecedented all-out offensive against the people, in utter disregard of the fate of the country and the nation. From January last year (1946), when the truce agreement was announced, up to the present, Chiang Kai-shek has mobilized more than 220 brigades of his regular troops and nearly a million miscellaneous troops and launched large-scale attacks against the Liberated

Areas which the Chinese people wrested from Japanese imperialism after bloody battles; he has seized successively the cities of Shenyang, Fushun, Penki, Szepingkai, Changchun, Yungchi, Chengteh, Chining, Changchiakou, Huaiyin, Hotse, Linyi, Yenan and Yentai and vast rural areas. Wherever Chiang Kai-shek's troops go, they murder and burn, rape and loot, carry out the policy of the three atrocities and behave exactly like the Japanese bandits. In November last year Chiang Kai-shek convened the bogus National Assembly and proclaimed the bogus constitution. In March this year he expelled the representatives of the Communist Party from the Kuomintang areas. In July he issued an order of general mobilization against the people. Towards the just movement of the people in different parts of the country against civil war, against hunger and against U.S. imperialist aggression and towards the struggle for existence waged by the workers, peasants, students, townspeople, government employees and teachers, Chiang Kai-shek's policy is one of repression, arrest and massacre. Towards our country's minority nationalities, his policy is one of Han chauvinism, of persecution and repression by every possible means. In all the areas under Chiang Kai-shek's rule corruption is rife, secret agents run amuck, taxes are innumerable and crushing, prices are skyrocketing, the economy is bankrupt, all business languishes, conscription and the grain levy are imposed and voices of discontent are heard everywhere; all this has plunged the overwhelming majority of the people throughout the country into an abyss of suffering. Meanwhile the financial oligarchs, corrupt officials, local tyrants and bad gentry, all headed by Chiang Kai-shek, have amassed vast fortunes. Chiang Kai-shek and his like made these fortunes by using their dictatorial powers to extort taxes and levies and promote their private interests under the guise of serving the public. To maintain his dictatorship and carry on the civil war, Chiang Kai-shek has not hesitated to sell out our country's sovereign rights to foreign imperialism, to collude with the U.S. armed forces so that they should remain in Tsingtao and elsewhere and to procure advisers from the United States to take part in directing the civil war and training troops to slaughter his own fellow-countrymen. Aircraft, tanks, guns and ammunition for the civil war are shipped from the United States in great quantities. Funds for the civil war are borrowed from the United States on a large scale. In return for its favours, Chiang Kai-shek has presented U.S. imperialism with military bases and the rights of air flight and navigation, concluded a commercial treaty of enslavement, etc.—acts of treason many times worse than those of Yuan Shih-kai. In a word, Chiang Kai-shek's twenty-year rule has been traitorous, dictatorial and against the people. Today, the overwhelming majority of the people throughout the country, north and south, young and old, know his towering crimes and hope that our army will quickly launch the counter-offensive, overthrow Chiang Kai-shek and liberate all China.

We are the army of the Chinese people and in all things we take the will of the Chinese people as our will. The policies of our army represent the urgent demands of the Chinese people and chief among them are the following:

(1) Unite workers, peasants, soldiers, intellectuals and businessmen, all oppressed classes, all people's organizations, democratic parties, minority nationalities, overseas Chinese and other patriots; form a national united front; overthrow the dictatorial Chiang Kai-shek government; and establish a democratic coalition government.

(2) Arrest, try, and punish the civil war criminals headed by Chiang Kai-shek.

(3) Abolish the Chiang Kai-shek dictatorship, carry out the system of people's democracy and guarantee freedom of speech, of the press, of assembly and of association for the people.

(4) Abolish the rotten institutions of the Chiang Kai-shek regime, clear out all corrupt officials and establish clean government.

(5) Confiscate the property of the four big families of Chiang Kai-shek, T. V. Soong, H. H. Kung and the Chen brothers, and the property of the other chief war criminals; confiscate bureaucrat-capital, develop the industry and commerce of the national bourgeoisie, improve the livelihood of workers and employees, and give relief to victims of calamities and to poverty-stricken people.

(6) Abolish the system of feudal exploitation and put into effect the system of land to the tillers.

(7) Recognize the right to equality and autonomy of the minority nationalities within the borders of China.

(8) Repudiate the traitorous foreign policy of the dictatorial Chiang Kai-shek government, abrogate all the treasonable treaties and repudiate all the foreign debts contracted by Chiang Kai-shek during the civil war period. Demand that the U.S. government withdraw its troops stationed in China, which are a menace to China's independence, and oppose any foreign country's helping Chiang Kai-shek to carry on civil war or trying to revive the forces of Japanese aggression. Conclude treaties of trade and friendship with foreign countries on the basis of equality and reciprocity. Unite in a common struggle with all nations which treat us as equals.

The above are the basic policies of our army. They will be put into practice at once wherever our army goes. These policies conform with the demands of more than 90 per cent of the people in our country.

Our army does not reject all Chiang Kai-shek's personnel but adopts a policy of dealing with each case on its merits. That is, the chief criminals shall be punished without fail, those who are accomplices under duress shall go unpunished and those who perform deeds of merit shall be rewarded. As for Chiang Kai-shek, the archcriminal who started the civil war and who has committed most heinous crimes, and as for all his hardened accomplices who have trampled the people underfoot and are branded as war criminals by the broad masses, our army will hunt them down, even to the four corners of the earth, and will surely bring them to trial and punishment. Our army warns all officers and men in Chiang Kai-shek's army, all officials in his government and all members of his party whose hands are not yet stained with the blood of innocent people that they should strictly refrain from joining these criminals in their evil-doing. Those who have been doing evil should immediately stop, repent and start anew and break with Chiang Kai-shek, and we will give them a chance to make amends for their crimes by good deeds. Our army will not kill or humiliate any of Chiang Kai-shek's army officers and men who lay down their arms, but will accept them into our service if they are willing to remain with us or send them home if they wish to leave. As for those Chiang Kai-shek troops who rise in revolt and join our army and those who work for our army openly or in secret, they shall be rewarded.

In order to overthrow Chiang Kai-shek and form a democratic coalition government at an early date, we call on our fellow-countrymen in all walks of life to co-operate actively with us in cleaning up the reactionary forces and setting up a democratic order wherever our army goes. In places we have not yet reached, they should take up arms on their own, resist press-ganging and the grain levy, distribute the land, repudiate debts and take advantage of the enemy's gaps to develop guerrilla warfare.

In order to overthrow Chiang Kai-shek and form a democratic coalition government at an early date, we call on the people in the Liberated Areas to carry through the land reform, consolidate the foundations of democracy, develop production, practise economy, strengthen the people's armed forces, eliminate the remaining strongholds of the enemy and support the fighting at the front.

All comrade commanders and fighters of our army! We are shouldering the most important, the most glorious task in the history of our country's revolution. We should make great efforts to accomplish our task. Our efforts will determine the day when our great motherland will emerge from darkness into light and our beloved fellow-countrymen will be able to live like human beings and to choose the government they wish. All officers and fighters of our army must improve their military art, march forward courageously towards certain victory in the war and resolutely, thoroughly, wholly and completely wipe out all enemies. They must all raise their level of political consciousness, learn the two skills of wiping out the enemy forces and arousing the masses, unite intimately with the masses and rapidly build the new Liberated Areas into stable areas. They must heighten their sense of discipline and resolutely carry out orders, carry out our policy, carry out the Three Main Rules of Discipline and the Eight Points for Attention—with army and people united, army and government united, officers and soldiers united, and the whole army united—and permit no breach of discipline. All our officers and fighters must always bear in mind that we are the great People's Liberation Army, we are the troops led by the great Communist Party of China. Provided we constantly observe the directives of the Party, we are sure to win.

Down with Chiang Kai-shek!

Long live New China!

CHE GUEVARA

"Colonialism is Doomed"

Speech before the General Assembly of the United Nations

DECEMBER 11, 1964

The short, dramatic, and tragic life of Ernesto "Che" Guevara de la Serna (1928–1967) has made him a folk hero. Born in Buenos Aires, Argentina, he became a doctor and through his medical work across South America realized the extent of the continent's economic and political injustice. While working in Mexico, he became allied with the Cuban revolutionaries Fidel and Raul Castro. He became a Cuban citizen after the Cuban Revolution of 1959, and was an important and popular spokesperson for Cuba. He left Cuba in 1965 to promote revolutionary activity in Africa and South America. In October 1967, having organized guerilla units in Bolivia, he was captured and killed by the Bolivian army.

His speech to the United Nations General Assembly in 1964 attacked American foreign and internal policies and asked for the UN's help in coercing American policy changes around the world and particularly in the Caribbean. Among these changes were "Cessation of the economic blockade and all economic and trade pressures by the United States in all parts of the world against our country."

SOURCE: Cuban Ministry of External Relations, Information Department. Official OAS translation. On the Che Guevara Internet Archive at: www.marxists.org/archive/guevara/1966/12/11.htm.

Colonialism is Doomed

The Cuban delegation to this assembly has pleasure, first of all, in fulfilling the pleasant duty of welcoming three new nations to the large number of nations whose representatives are discussing the problems of the world. We therefore greet through their Presidents and Prime Ministers the people of Zambia, Malawi, and Malta, and express the hope that from the outset these countries will be added to the group of non-aligned countries which struggle against imperialism, colonialism, and neocolonialism.

We also wish to convey our congratulations to the President of this assembly whose elevation to so high a post is of special significance since it reflects this new historic stage of resounding triumphs for the peoples of Africa, until recently subject to the colonial system of imperialism, and who, today, for the great part in the legitimate exercise of self-determination, have become citizens of sovereign states. The last hour of colonialism has struck, and millions of inhabitants of Africa, Asia, and Latin America rise to meet a new life, and assert their unrestricted right to self-determination and to the independent development of their nations.

We wish you, Mr President, the greatest success in the tasks entrusted to you by member states.

Cuba comes here to state its position on the most important controversial issues and will do so with the full sense of responsibility which the use of this rostrum implies, while at the same time responding to the unavoidable duty of speaking out, clearly and frankly.

We should like to see this assembly shake itself out of complacency and move forward. We should like to see the committees begin their work and not stop at the first confrontation. Imperialism wishes to convert this meeting into an aimless oratorical tournament, instead of using it to solve the grave problems of the world. We must prevent their doing so. This assembly should not be remembered in the future only by the number nineteen which identifies it. We feel that we have the right and the obligation to try to make this meeting effective because our country is a constant point of friction; one of the places where the principles supporting the rights of small nations to sovereignty are tested day by day, minute by minute; and at the same time our country is one of the barricades of freedom in the world, situated a few steps away from United States imperialism, to show with its actions, its daily example, that peoples can liberate themselves, can keep themselves free, in the existing conditions of the world.

Of course, there is now a socialist camp which becomes stronger day by day and has more powerful weapons of struggle. But additional conditions are required for survival: the maintenance of internal cohesion, faith in one's destiny, and the irreversible decision to fight to the death for the defense of one's country and revolution. These conditions exist in Cuba.

Of all the burning problems to be dealt with by this assembly, one which has special significance for us and whose solution we feel must be sought first, so as to leave no doubt in the minds of anyone, is that of peaceful coexistence among states with different economic and social Systems. Much progress has been made in the world in this field. But imperialism, particularly United States imperialism, has tried to make the world believe that peaceful coexistence is the exclusive right of the great powers on earth. We repeat what our President said in Cairo, and which later took shape in the Declaration of the Second Conference of Heads of State or Government of Non-Aligned Countries: that there cannot be peaceful coexistence only among the powerful if we are to ensure world peace. Peaceful coexistence must be practiced by all states, independent of size, of the previous historic relations that linked them, and of the problems that may arise among some of them at a given moment."

At present the type of peaceful coexistence to which we aspire does not exist in many cases. The kingdom of Cambodia, merely because it maintained a neutral attitude and did not submit to the machinations of United States imperialism, has been subjected to all kinds of treacherous and brutal attacks from the Yankee bases in South Vietnam.

Laos, a divided country, has also been the object of imperialist aggression of every kind. The conventions concluded at Geneva have been violated, its peoples have been massacred from the air, and part of its territory is in constant danger from cowardly attacks by imperialist forces.

The Democratic Republic of Vietnam, which knows of the histories of aggressions as few people on earth, once again has seen its frontier violated, its installations attacked by enemy bomber and fighter planes, its naval posts attacked by the United States warships violating territorial waters.

At this moment, there hangs over the Democratic Republic of Vietnam the threat that the United States warmongers may openly extend to its territory the war that, for many years, they have been waging against the people of South Vietnam.

The Soviet Union and the People's Republic of China have given serious warning to the United States. Not only the peace of the world is in danger in this situation, but also the lives of millions of human beings in this part of Asia are being constantly threatened and subjected to the whim of the United States invader.

Peaceful coexistence has also been put to the test in a brutal manner in Cyprus, due to pressures from the Turkish Government and NATO, compelling the people and the government of Cyprus to make a firm and heroic stand in defense of their sovereignty.

In all these parts of the world imperialism attempts to impose its version of what coexistence should be. It is the oppressed peoples in alliance with the socialist camp which must show them the meaning of true coexistence, and it is the obligation of the United Nations to support them.

We must also say that it is not only in relations between sovereign states that the concept of peaceful coexistence must be clearly defined. As Marxists we have maintained that peaceful coexistence among nations does not encompass coexistence between the exploiters and the exploited, the oppressor and the oppressed.

Furthermore, a principle proclaimed by this Organization is that of the right to full independence of all forms of colonial oppression. That is why we express our solidarity with the colonial peoples of so-called Portuguese Guinea, Angola, and Mozambique, who have been massacred for the crime of demanding their freedom, and we are prepared to help them to the extent of our ability in accordance with the Cairo Declaration.

We express our solidarity with the people of Puerto Rico and its great leader, Pedro Albizu Campos, who has been set free in another act of hypocrisy, at the age of seventy-two, after spending a lifetime in jail, now paralytic and almost without the ability to speak. Albizu Campos is a symbol of the still unredeemed but indomitable America. Years and years of prison, almost unbearable pressures in jail, mental torture, solitude, total isolation from his people and his family, the insolence of the conqueror and lackeys in the land of his birth—nothing at all broke his will. The delegation of Cuba, on behalf of its people, pays a tribute of admiration and gratitude to a patriot who bestows honor upon America.

The North Americans, for many years, have tried to convert Puerto Rico into a reflection of hybrid culture—the Spanish language with an English inflection, the Spanish language with hinges on its backbone, the better to bend before the United States soldier. Puerto Rican soldiers have been used as cannon-fodder in imperialist wars, as in Korea, and even been made to fire at their own brothers, as in the massacre perpetrated by the United States Army a few months ago against the helpless people of Panamane of the most recent diabolical acts carried out by Yankee imperialism. Yet despite that terrible attack against its will and its historic destiny, the people of Puerto Rico have preserved their culture, their Latin character, their national feelings, which in themselves give proof of the implacable will for independence that exists among the masses on the Latin American island.

We must also point out that the principle of peaceful coexistence does not imply a mockery of the will of the peoples, as is happening in the case of so-called British Guiana, where the government of Prime Minister Cheddi Jagan has been the victim of every kind of pressure and maneuver, while the achievement of independence has been delayed by the search for methods that would allow for the flouting of the will of the people while ensuring the docility of a Government different from the present one, put in by underhanded tactics, and then to grant an important "freedom" to this piece of American soil. Whatever roads Guiana may be compelled to follow to obtain independence, the moral and militant support of Cuba goes to its people.

Furthermore, we must point out that the islands of Guadaloupe and Martinique have been fighting for a long time for their autonomy without obtaining it. This state of affairs must not continue.

Once again we raise our voice to put the world on guard against what is happening in South Africa. The brutal policy of apartheid is being carried out before the eyes of the whole world. The peoples of Africa are being compelled to tolerate in that continent the concept, still official, of the superiority of one race over another and in the name of that racial superiority the murder of people with impunity. Can the United Nations do nothing to prevent this? I should like specifically to refer to the painful case of the Congo, unique in the history of the modern world, which shows how, with absolute impunity, with the most insolent cynicism, the rights of peoples can be flouted. The prodigious wealth of the Congo, which the imperialist nations wish to maintain under their control, is the direct reason for this. In his speech on his first visit to the United Nations, our comrade Fidel Castro said that the whole problem of coexistence among peoples was reduced to the undue appropriation of another's wealth. He said, "When this philosophy of despoilment disappears, the philosophy of war will have disappeared."

The philosophy of despoilment not only has not ceased, but rather it is stronger than ever, and that is why those who used the name of the United Nations to commit the murder of Lumumba, today, in the name of the defense of the white race, are assassinating thousands of Congolese. How can one forget how the hope that Patrice Lumumba placed in the United Nations was betrayed? How can one forget the machinations and maneuvers which followed in the wake of the occupation of that country by United Nations troops under whose auspices the assassins of this great African patriot acted with impunity? How can we forget that he who flouted the authority of the United Nations in the Congo, and not exactly for patriotic reasons, but rather by virtue of conflicts between imperialists, was Moise Tshombe, who initiated the secession in Katanga with Belgian support? And how can one justify, how can one explain, that at the end of all the United Nations activities there, Tshombe, dislodged from Katanga, returned as lord and master of the Congo? Who can deny the abject role that the imperialists compelled the United Nations to play?

To sum up, dramatic mobilizations were made to avoid the secession of Katanga, but today that same Katanga is in power! The wealth of the Congo is in imperialist hands and the expenses must be paid by honest nations. The merchants of war certainly do good business. That is why the government of Cuba supports the just attitude of the Soviet Union in refusing to pay the expenses of this crime.

And as if this were not enough, we now have flung in our faces recent events which have filled the world with horror and indignation. Who are the perpetrators? Belgian paratroopers transported by United States planes, who took off from British bases. We remember as if it were yesterday that we saw a small country in Europe, a civilized and industrious country, the kingdom of Belgium, invaded by the hordes of Hitler. We learned with bitterness that these people were being massacred by the German imperialists, and our sympathy and affection went out to them. But the other side of the imperialist coin many did not then perceive. Perhaps the sons of Belgian patriots who died defending their country are now assassinating thousands of Congolese in the name of the white race, just as they suffered under the German heel because their blood was not purely Aryan. But the scales have fallen from our eyes and they now open upon new horizons, and we can see what yesterday, in our conditions of colonial servitude, we could not observe—that "Western civilization" disguises under its showy front a scene of hyenas and jackals. That is the only name that can be applied to those who have gone to fulfill "humanitarian" tasks in the Congo. Bloodthirsty butchers who feed on helpless people! That is what imperialism does to men; that is what marks the "white" imperialists.

The free men of the world must be prepared to avenge the crime committed in the Congo. It is possible that many of those soldiers who were converted into "supermen" by imperialist machinery, believe in good faith that they are defending the rights of a superior race, but in this assembly those peoples whose skins are darkened by a different sun, colored by different pigments, constitute the majority, and they fully and clearly understand that the difference between men does not lie in the color of their skins, but in the ownership of the means of production and in the relationship of production.

The Cuban delegation extends greetings to the peoples of Southern Rhodesia and Southwest Africa, oppressed by white colonialist minorities, to the peoples of Basutoland, Bechuanaland, Swaziland, French Somaliland, the Arabs of Palestine, Aden, and the Protectorates, Oman, and to all peoples in conflict with imperialism and colonialism; and we reaffirm our support.

I express also the hope that there will be a just solution to the conflict facing our sister republic of Indonesia in its relations with Malaysia.

One of the essential items before this conference is general and complete disarmament. We express our support of general and complete disarmament. Furthermore, we advocate the complete destruction of thermonuclear devices and the holding of a conference of all the nations of the world toward the fulfillment of this aspiration of all people. In his statement before this assembly, our Prime Minister said that arms races have always led to war. There are new atomic powers in the world, and the possibilities of a confrontation are grave.

We feel that a conference is necessary to obtain the total destruction of thermonuclear weapons and as a first step, the total prohibition of tests. At the same time there must be clearly established the obligation of all states to respect the present frontiers of other states and to refrain from indulging in any aggression even with conventional weapons.

In adding our voice to that of all peoples of the world who plead for general and complete disarmament, the destruction of all atomic arsenals, the complete cessation of thermonuclear devices and atomic tests of any kinds, we feel it necessary to stress, furthermore, that the territorial integrity of nations must be respected and the armed hand of imperialism, no less dangerous with conventional weapons, must be held back. Those who murdered thousands of defenseless citizens in the Congo did not use the atomic weapons. They used conventional weapons, and it was these conventional weapons, used by imperialists, which caused so many deaths.

Even if the measures advocated here were to become effective, thus making it unnecessary to say the following, we must still point out that we cannot adhere to any regional pact for denuclearization so long as the United States maintains aggressive bases on our territory, in Puerto Rico and in Panama, and in other American states where it feels it has the right to station them without any restrictions on conventional or nuclear weapons.

However, we feel we must be able to provide for our own defense in the light of the recent resolution of the Organization of American States against Cuba, which on the basis of the Treaty of Rio might permit aggression.

If such a conference to which we have just referred should achieve all these objectives—which unfortunately, would be rather difficult to do—it would be one of the most important developments in the history of mankind. To ensure this, the People's Republic of China must be represented, and that is why such a conference must be held. But it would be much simpler for the peoples of the world to recognize the undeniable truth that the People's Republic of China exists, that its rulers are the only representatives of the Chinese people, and to give it the place it deserves, which is, at present, usurped by a clique who control the province of Taiwan with United States aid.

The problem of the representation of China in the United Nations cannot, in any way, be considered as a case of a new admission to the organization, but rather as the restitution of their legitimate rights to the people of the People's Republic of China.

We repudiate strongly the concept of "two Chinas." The Chiang Kai-shek clique of Taiwan cannot remain in the United Nations. It must be expelled and the legitimate representative of the Chinese people put in.

We warn, also, against the insistence of the United States Government on presenting the problem of the legitimate representation of China in the United Nations as an "important question" so as to require a two-thirds majority of members present and voting.

The admission of the People's Republic of China to the United Nations is, in fact, an important question for the entire world, but not for the mechanics of the United Nations where it must constitute a mere question of procedure.

Thus will justice be done, but almost as important as attaining justice would be the fact that it would be demonstrated, once and for all, that this august Assembly uses its eyes to see with, its ears to hear with, and its tongue to speak with; and has definite standards in making its decisions.

The proliferation of atomic weapons among the member States of NATO, and especially the possession of these devices of mass destruction by the Federal Republic of Germany, would make the possibility of an agreement on disarmament even more remote, and linked to such an agreement is the problem of the peaceful reunification of Germany. So long as there is no clear understanding, the existence of two Germanies must be recognized: that of the Democratic Republic of Germany and the Federal Republic. The German problem can only be solved with the direct participation of the Democratic Republic of Germany with full rights in negotiations.

We shall touch lightly on the questions of economic development and international trade which take up a good part of the agenda. In this year, 1964, the Conference of Geneva was held, where a multitude of matters related to these aspects of international relations was dealt with. The warnings and forecasts of our delegation were clearly confirmed to the misfortune of the economically dependent countries.

We wish only to point out that insofar as Cuba is concerned, the United States of America has not implemented the explicit recommendations of that conference, and recently the United States

Government also prohibited the sale of medicine to Cuba, thus divesting itself once and for all, of the mask of humanitarianism with which it attempted to disguise the aggressive nature of its blockade against the people of Cuba.

Furthermore, we once more state that these colonial machinations, which impede the development of the peoples, are not only expressed in political relations. The so-called deterioration of the terms of trade is nothing less than the result of the unequal exchange between countries producing raw materials and industrial countries which dominate markets and impose a false justice on an inequitable exchange of values.

So long as the economically dependent peoples do not free themselves from the capitalist markets, and as a bloc with the socialist countries, impose new terms of trade between the exploited and the exploiters, there will be no sound economic development, and in certain cases there will be retrogression, in which the weak countries will fall under the political domination of imperialists and colonialists.

Finally, it must be made clear that in the area of the Caribbean, maneuvers and preparations for aggression against Cuba are taking place; off the coast of Nicaragua above all, in Costa Rica, in the Panama Canal Zone, in the Vieques Islands of Puerto Rico, in Florida, and possibly in other parts of the territory of the United States, and also, perhaps, in Honduras, Cuban mercenaries are training, as well as mercenaries of other nationalities, with a purpose that cannot be peaceful.

After an open scandal, the government of Costa Rica, it is said, has ordered the elimination of all training fields for Cuban exiles in that country. No one knows whether this attitude is sincere, or whether it is simply a maneuver, because the mercenaries training there were about to commit some offense. We hope that full cognizance will be taken of the actual existence of those bases for aggression, which we denounced long ago, and that the world will think about the international responsibility of the government of a country which authorizes and facilitates the training of mercenaries to attack Cuba.

We must point out that news of the training of mercenaries at different places in the Caribbean and the participation of the United States Government in such acts is news that appears openly in United States newspapers. We know of no Latin American voice that has been lifted officially in protest against this. This shows the cynicism with which the United States moves its pawns.

The shrewd foreign ministers of the OAS had eyes to "see" Cuban emblems and find "irrefutable proof" in the Yankee weapons in Venezuela, but do not see the preparations for aggression in the United States, just as they did not hear the voice of President Kennedy, who explicitly declared himself to be the aggressor against Cuba at Playa Giron. In some cases it is a blindness provoked by the hatred of the ruling classes of the Latin American people against our revolution; in others, and these are even more deplorable, it is the result of the blinding light of Mammon.

As everyone knows, after the terrible upheaval called the "Caribbean crisis," the United States undertook certain given commitments with the Soviet Union which culminated in the withdrawal of certain types of weapons that the continued aggressions of that country—such as the mercenary attack against Playa Giron and threats of invasion against our country—had compelled us to install in Cuba as a legitimate act of defense.

The Americans claimed, furthermore, that the United Nations should inspect our territory, which we refused and refuse emphatically since Cuba does not recognize the right of the United States, or of anyone else in the world, to determine what type of weapons Cuba may maintain within its borders.

In this connection, we would only abide by multilateral agreements, with equal obligations for all the parties concerned. Fidel Castro declared that "so long as the concept of sovereignty exists as the prerogative of nations and of independent peoples, and as a right of all peoples, we shall not accept the exclusion of our people from that right; so long as the world is governed by these principles, so long as the world is governed by those concepts which have universal validity because they are universally accepted by peoples, we shall not accept the attempt to deprive us of any of those rights and we shall renounce none of those rights."

The Secretary-General of the United Nations, U Thant, understood our reasons. Nevertheless, the United States presumed to establish a new prerogative, an arbitrary and illegal one; that of violating the air space of any small country. Thus, we see flying over our country U-2 aircraft and other types of espionage apparatus which fly over our airspace with impunity. We have issued all the necessary warnings for the cessation of the violation of our airspace as well as the provocations of the American navy against our sentry posts in the zone of Guantanamo, the "buzzing" by aircraft over our ships or ships of other nationalities in international waters, the piratical attacks against ships sailing under different flags, and the infiltration of spies, saboteurs and weapons in our island.

We want to build socialism; we have declared ourselves partisans of those who strive for peace; we have declared ourselves as falling within the group of non-aligned countries, although we are Marxist-Leninists, because the non-aligned countries, like ourselves, fight imperialism.

We want peace; we want to build a better life for our people, and that is why we avoid answering, so far as possible, the planned provocations of the Yankee. But we know the mentality of United States rulers; they want to make us pay a very high price for that peace. We reply that price cannot go beyond the bounds of dignity.

And Cuba reaffirms once again the right to maintain on its territory the weapons it wishes and its refusal to recognize the right of any power on earth—no matter how powerful—to violate our soil, our territorial waters, or our airspace.

If, in any assembly, Cuba assumes obligations of a collective nature, it will fulfill them to the letter. So long as this does not happen, Cuba maintains all its rights, just as any other nation.

In the face of the demands of imperialism our Prime Minister posed the five necessary points for the existence of a sound peace in the Caribbean. They are as follows:

Cessation of the economic blockade and all economic and trade pressure by the United States in all parts of the world against our country.

Cessation of all subversive activities, launching and landing of weapons, and explosives by air and sea, organization of mercenary invasions, infiltration of spies and saboteurs, all of which acts are carried out from the territory of the United States and some accomplice countries.

Cessation of piratical attacks carried out from existing bases in the United States and Puerto Rico.

Cessation of all the violations of our airspace and our territorial waters by aircraft and warships of the United States.

Withdrawal from the Guantanamo naval base and restitution of the Cuban territory occupied by the United States.

None of these fundamental demands has been met, and our forces are still being provoked from the naval base at Guantanamo. That base has become a nest of thieves and the point from which they are introduced into our territory.

We would bore this assembly were we to give a detailed account of the large number of provocations of all kinds. Suffice it to say that including the first day of December, the number amounts to 1,323 in 1964 alone. The list covers minor provocations such as violation of the dividing line, launching of objects from the territory controlled by the North Americans, the commission of acts of sexual exhibitionism by North Americans of both sexes, verbal insults, others which are graver such as shooting off small-caliber weapons, the manipulation of weapons directed against our territory and offenses against our national emblem. The more serious provocations are those of crossing the dividing line and starting fires in installations on the Cuban side, seventy-eight rifle shots this year and the death of Ramon Lopez Pena, a soldier, from two shots fired from the United States post three and a half kilometers from the coast on the northern boundary.

This grave provocation took place at 19:07 hours on July 19, 1964, and our Prime Minister publicly stated on July 26 that if the event were to recur, he would give orders for our troops to repel the aggression. At the same time orders were given for the withdrawal of the advance line of Cuban forces to positions farther away from the dividing line and construction of the necessary housing.

One thousand three hundred and twenty-three provocations in 340 days amount to approximately four per day. Only a perfectly disciplined army with a morale such as ours could resist so many hostile acts without losing its self-control.

Forty-seven countries which met at the Second Conference of Heads of State or Government of the nonaligned countries at Cairo unanimously agreed that:

"Noting with concern that foreign military bases are, in practice, a means of bringing pressure on nations and retarding their emancipation and development, based on their own ideological, political, economic and cultural ideas . . . declares its full support to the countries which are seeking to secure the evacuation of foreign bases on their territory and calls upon all States maintaining troops and bases in other countries to remove them forthwith.

The Conference considers that the maintenance at Guantanamo (Cuba) of a military base of the United States of America, in defiance of the will of the Government and people of Cuba and in defiance of the provisions embodied in the Declaration of the Belgrade Conference, constitutes a violation of Cuba's sovereignty and territorial integrity.

Noting that the Cuban Government expresses its readiness to settle its dispute over the base at Guantanamo with the United States on an equal footing, the Conference urges the United States Government to negotiate the evacuation of their base with the Cuban Government."

The government of the United States has not responded to the above request of the Cairo Conference and presumes to maintain indefinitely its occupation by force of a piece of our territory from which it carries out acts of aggression such as those we mentioned earlier.

The Organization of American States—also called by some people the United States Ministry of Colonies—condemned us vigorously, although it had excluded us from its midst, and ordered its members to break off diplomatic and trade relations with Cuba. The OAS authorized aggression against our country at any time and under any pretext and violated the most fundamental international laws, completely disregarding the United Nations. Uruguay, Bolivia, Chile, and Mexico opposed that measure, and the government of the United States of Mexico refused to comply with the sanctions that had been approved.

Since then we have no relations with any Latin American countries other than Mexico; thus the imperialists have carried out one of the stages preliminary to a plan of direct aggression.

We want to point out once again that our concern over Latin America is based on the ties that link us; the language we speak, our culture, and the common master we shared. But we have no other reason for desiring the liberation of Latin America from the colonial yoke of the United States. If any of the Latin American countries here decides to [resume relations it must be on the] basis of equality and not with the assumption that it is a gift to our government that we be recognized as a free country in the world, because we won the recognition of our freedom with our blood in the days of our struggles for liberation. We acquired it with our blood in the defense of our shores against Yankee invasion.

Although we reject any attempt to attribute to us interference in the internal affairs of other countries, we cannot deny that we sympathize with those people who strive for their freedom, and we must fulfill the obligation of our government and people to state clearly and categorically to the world that we morally support and feel as one with people everywhere who struggle to make a reality of the rights of full sovereignty proclaimed in the United Nations Charter.

It is the United States of America which intervenes. It has done so throughout the history of America. Since the end of the last century Cuba has known very well the truth of the matter; but it is known, too, by Venezuela, Nicaragua, Central America in general, Mexico, Haiti, and Santo Domingo. In recent years, besides our peoples, Panama has also known direct aggression, when the marines of the Canal opened fire against the defenseless people; Santo Domingo, whose coast was violated by the Yankee fleet to avoid an outbreak of the righteous fury of the people after the death of Trujillo; and Colombia, whose capital was taken by assault as a result of a rebellion provoked by the assassination of Gaitan.

There are masked interventions through military missions which participate in internal repression, organizing forces designed for that purpose in many countries, and also in coups d'etat which have been so frequently repeated on the American continent during the past few years. Specifically, United States forces took part in the repression of the peoples of Venezuela, Colombia, and Guatemala, who carry on an armed struggle for their freedom. In Venezuela not only do the Americans advise the army and the police, but they also direct acts of genocide from the air against the peasant population in vast rebel-held areas, and the United States companies established there exert pressures of every kind to increase direct interference.

The imperialists are preparing to repress the peoples of America and are setting up an "international" [network] of crime. The United States interfered in America while invoking the "defense of free institutions." The time will come when this assembly will acquire greater maturity and demand guarantees from the United States Government for the lives of the Negro and Latin American population who reside in that country, most of whom are native-born or naturalized United States citizens.

How can they presume to be the "guardians of liberty" when they kill their own children and discriminate daily against people because of the color of their skin; when they not only free the murderers of colored people, but even protect them, while punishing the colored population because they demand their legitimate rights as free men? We understand that today the assembly is not in a position to ask for explanations of these acts, but it must be clearly established that the government of the United States is not the champion of freedom, but rather the perpetrator of exploitation and oppression of the peoples of the world, and of a large part of its own population.

To the equivocating language with which some delegates have painted the case of Cuba and the Organization of American States, we reply with blunt words, that the governments pay for their treason.

Cuba, a free and sovereign state, with no chains binding it to anyone, with no foreign investments on its territory, with no proconsuls orienting its policy, can speak proudly in this assembly, proving the justice of the phrase by which we will always be known, "Free Territory of America."

Our example will bear fruit in our continent, as it is already doing to a certain extent already in Guatemala, Colombia, and Venezuela. The imperialists no longer have to deal with a small enemy, a contemptible force, since the people are no longer isolated.

As laid down in the Second Declaration of Havana:

"No people of Latin America is weak, because it is part of a family of 200 million brothers beset by the same miseries, who harbor the same feelings, have the same enemy, while they all dream of the same better destiny and have the support of all honest men and women in the world.

Future history will be written by the hungry masses of Indians, of landless peasants, of exploited workers; it will be written by the progressive masses, by the honest and brilliant intellectuals who abound in our unfortunate lands of Latin America, by the struggle of the masses and of ideas; an epic that will be carried forward by our peoples who have been ill-treated and despised by imperialism, our peoples who have until now gone unrecognized but who are awakening. We were considered an impotent and submissive flock; but now they are afraid of that flock, a gigantic flock of 200 million Latin Americans, which is sounding a warning note to the Yankee monopolist capitalists.

The hour of vindication, the hour it chose for itself, is now striking from one end to the other of the continent. That anonymous mass, that colored America, sombre, adamant, which sings throughout the continent the same sad, mournful song; now that mass is beginning definitely to enter into its own history, it is beginning to write it with its blood, to suffer and to die for it. Because now, in the fields, and in the mountains of America, in its plains and in its forests, in the solitude, and in the bustle of cities, on the shores of the great oceans and rivers, it is beginning to shape a world full of quickening hearts, who are ready to die for what is theirs, to conquer their rights which have been flouted for almost 500 years. History will have to tell the story of the poor of America, of the exploited of Latin America, who have decided to begin to write for themselves, forever, their own odyssey. We see them already walking along those roads, on foot, day after day, in long and endless marches, hundreds of kilometers, until they reach the ruling "Olympus" and wrest back their rights. We see them armed with stones, with sticks, with machetes, here, there, everywhere, daily occupying their lands, and taking root in the land that is theirs and defending it with their lives; we see them carrying banners, their banners running in the wind in the mountains and on the plains. And that wave of heightening fury, of just demands, of rights that have been flouted, is rising throughout Latin America, and no one can stem that tide; it will grow day by day because it is made up of the great multitude in every respect, those who with their work create the riches of the earth, and turn the wheel of history, those who are now awakening from their long, stupefying sleep.

For this great humanity has said "enough" and has started to move forward. And their march, the march of giants, cannot stop, will not stop until they have conquered their true independence, for which many have already died, and not uselessly. In any event, those who die will die like those in Cuba, at Playa Giron; they will die for their never-to-be-renounced, their only true independence."

This new will of a whole continent, America, shows itself in the cry proclaimed daily by our masses as the irrefutable expression of their decision to fight, to grasp and deter the armed hand of the invader. It is a cry that has the understanding and support of all the peoples of the world and especially of the socialist camp, headed by the Soviet Union. That cry is: "Our country or death."

Vaclav Havel, Jan Patocka, et al.

Charter 77

January 1, 1977

Charter 77, a clever and pointed manifesto signed by 230 Czech intellectuals including the playwright (and future president of the Czech Republic) Vaclav Havel (b. 1936) and the philosopher Jan Patocka (1907–1977), made a public claim to the rights ostensibly guaranteed by the Czechoslovak Socialist Republic to all Czechs. The Charter points out that "basic human rights in our country exist, regrettably, on paper only." Charter 77 was also the collective name for the signatories, "a free informal, open community of people of different convictions, different faiths, and different professions united by the will to strive, individually and collectively, for the respect of civic and human rights in our own country and throughout the world." *Charter 77* was published in western Europe, and resulted in the arrest of some of the signatories, including Patocka, who died after police interrogation. The Czechoslovak Socialist Republic collapsed in the "Velvet Revolution" of 1989, a revolution led by members of Charter 77.

SOURCE: Library of Congress, Federal Research Division at: **www.memory.loc.gov/frd/cs/czechoslovakia/cs_appnd.html**.

Charter 77

In the Czechoslovak Register of Laws No. 120 of October 13, 1976, texts were published of the International Covenant on Civil and Political Rights, and of the International Covenant on Economic, Social and Cultural Rights, which were signed on behalf of our republic in 1968, reiterated at Helsinki in 1975 and came into force in our country on March 23, 1976. From that date our citizens have enjoyed the rights, and our state the duties, ensuing from them.

The human rights and freedoms underwritten by these covenants constitute features of civilized life for which many progressive movements have striven throughout history and whose codification could greatly assist humane developments in our society.

We accordingly welcome the Czechoslovak Socialist Republic's accession to those agreements.

Their publication, however, serves as a powerful reminder of the extent to which basic human rights in our country exist, regrettably, on paper alone.

The right to freedom of expression, for example, guaranteed by Article 19 of the first-mentioned covenant, is in our case purely illusory. Tens of thousands of our citizens are prevented from working in their own fields for the sole reason that they hold views differing from official ones, and are discriminated against and harassed in all kinds of ways by the authorities and public organizations. Deprived as they are of any means to defend themselves, they become victims of a virtual apartheid.

Hundreds of thousands of other citizens are denied that "freedom from fear" mentioned in the preamble to the first covenant, being condemned to the constant risk of unemployment or other penalties if they voice their own opinions.

In violation of Article 13 of the second-mentioned covenant, guaranteeing everyone the right to education, countless young people are prevented from studying because of their own views or even their parents'. Innumerable citizens live in fear of their own, or their children's right to education being withdrawn if they should ever speak up in accordance with their convictions.

Any exercise of the right to "seek, receive and impart information and ideas of all kinds, regardless of frontiers, either orally, in writing or in print" or "in the form of art" specified in Article 19, Clause 2 of the first covenant is followed by extra-judicial and even judicial sanctions, often in the form of criminal charges, as in the recent trial of young musicians.

Freedom of public expression is inhibited by the centralized control of all the communication media and of publishing and cultural institutions. No philosophical, political or scientific view or artistic activity that departs ever so slightly from the narrow bounds of official ideology or aesthetics is allowed to be published; no open criticism can be made of abnormal social phenomena; no public defense is possible against false and insulting charges made in official propaganda—the legal protection against "attacks on honor and reputation" clearly guaranteed by Article 17 of the first covenant is in practice non-existent: false accusations cannot be rebutted, and any attempt to secure compensation or correction through the courts is futile; no open debate is allowed in the domain of thought and art.

Many scholars, writers, artists and others are penalized for having legally published or expressed, years ago, opinions which are condemned by those who hold political power today.

Freedom of religious confession, emphatically guaranteed by Article 18 of the first covenant, is continually curtailed by arbitrary official action; by interference with the activity of churchmen, who are constantly threatened by the refusal of the state to permit them the exercise of their functions, or by the withdrawal of such permission; by financial or other transactions against those who express their religious faith in word or action; by constraints on religious training and so forth.

One instrument for the curtailment or in many cases complete elimination of many civic rights is the system by which all national institutions and organizations are in effect subject to political directives from the machinery of the ruling party and to decisions made by powerful individuals.

The constitution of the republic, its laws and legal norms do not regulate the form or content, the issuing or application of such decisions; they are often only given out verbally, unknown to the public at large and beyond its powers to check; their originators are responsible to no one but themselves and their own hierarchy; yet they have a decisive impact on the decision-making and executive organs of government, justice, trade unions, interest groups and all other organizations, of the other political parties, enterprises, factories, institutions, offices and so on, for whom these instructions have precedence even before the law.

Where organizations or individuals, in the interpretation of their rights and duties, come into conflict with such directives, they cannot have recourse to any non-party authority, since none such exists. This constitutes, of course, a serious limitation of the right ensuing from Articles 21 and 22 of the first-mentioned covenant, which provides for freedom of association and forbids any restriction on its exercise, from Article 25 on the right to take part in the conduct of public affairs, and from Article 26 stipulating equal protection by the law without discrimination.

This state of affairs likewise prevents workers and others from exercising the unrestricted right to establish trade unions and other organizations to protect their economic and social interests, and from freely enjoying the right to strike provided for in Clause 1 of Article 8 in the second-mentioned covenant.

Further civic rights, including the explicit prohibition of "arbitrary interference with privacy, family, home or correspondence" (Article 17 of the first covenant), are seriously vitiated by the various forms of interference in the private life of citizens exercised by the Ministry of the Interior, for example by bugging telephones and houses, opening mail, following personal movements, searching homes, setting up networks of neighborhood informers (often recruited by illicit threats or promises) and in other ways.

The ministry frequently interferes in employers' decisions, instigates acts of discrimination by authorities and organizations, brings weight to bear on the organs of justice and even orchestrates propaganda campaigns in the media. This activity is governed by no law and, being clandestine, affords the citizen no chance to defend himself.

In cases of prosecution on political grounds the investigative and judicial organs violate the rights of those charged and those defending them, as guaranteed by Article 14 of the first covenant and indeed by Czechoslovak law. The prison treatment of those sentenced in such cases is an affront to their human dignity and a menace to their health, being aimed at breaking their morale.

Clause 2, Article 12 of the first covenant, guaranteeing every citizen the right to leave the country, is consistently violated, or under the pretense of "defense of national security" is subjected to various unjustifiable conditions (Clause 3). The granting of entry visas to foreigners is also treated arbitrarily, and many are unable to visit Czechoslovakia merely because of professional or personal contacts with those of our citizens who are subject to discrimination.

Some of our people—either in private, at their places of work or by the only feasible public channel, the foreign media—have drawn attention to the systematic violation of human rights and democratic freedoms and demanded amends in specific cases. But their pleas have remained largely ignored or been made grounds for police investigation.

Responsibility for the maintenance of rights in our country naturally devolves in the first place on the political and state authorities. Yet not only on them: everyone bears his share of responsibility for the conditions that prevail and accordingly also for the observance of legally enshrined agreements, binding upon all individuals as well as upon governments.

It is this sense of co-responsibility, our belief in the importance of its conscious public acceptance and the general need to give it new and more effective expression that led us to the idea of creating Charter 77, whose inception we today publicly announce.

Charter 77 is a loose, informal and open association of people of various shades of opinion, faiths and professions united by the will to strive individually and collectively for the respecting of civic and human rights in our own country and throughout the world—rights accorded to all men by the two mentioned international covenants, by the Final Act of the Helsinki conference and by numerous other international documents opposing war, violence and social or spiritual oppression, and which are comprehensively laid down in the UN Universal Charter of Human Rights.

Charter 77 springs from a background of friendship and solidarity among people who share our concern for those ideals that have inspired, and continue to inspire, their lives and their work.

Charter 77 is not an organization; it has no rules, permanent bodies or formal membership. It embraces everyone who agrees with its ideas and participates in its work. It does not form the basis for any oppositional political activity. Like many similar citizen initiatives in various countries, West and East, it seeks to promote the general public interest.

It does not aim, then, to set out its own platform of political or social reform or change, but within its own field of impact to conduct a constructive dialogue with the political and state authorities, particularly by drawing attention to individual cases where human and civic rights are violated, to document such grievances and suggest remedies, to make proposals of a more general character calculated to reinforce such rights and machinery for protecting them, to act as an intermediary in situations of conflict which may lead to violations of rights, and so forth.

By its symbolic name Charter 77 denotes that it has come into being at the start of a year proclaimed as Political Prisoners' Year—a year in which a conference in Belgrade is due to review the implementation of the obligations assumed at Helsinki.

As signatories, we hereby authorize Professor Dr. Jan Patocka, Dr. Vaclav Havel and Professor Dr. Jiri Hajek to act as the spokesmen for the Charter. These spokesmen are endowed with full authority to represent it vis-a-vis state and other bodies, and the public at home and abroad, and their signatures attest to the authenticity of documents issued by the Charter. They will have us and others who join us as their colleagues taking part in any needful negotiations, shouldering particular tasks and sharing every responsibility.

We believe that Charter 77 will help to enable all citizens of Czechoslovakia to work and live as free human beings.

DOVER · THRIFT · EDITIONS

FICTION

FLATLAND: A ROMANCE OF MANY DIMENSIONS, Edwin A. Abbott. 96pp. 0-486-27263-X

SHORT STORIES, Louisa May Alcott. 64pp. 0-486-29063-8

WINESBURG, OHIO, Sherwood Anderson. 160pp. 0-486-28269-4

PERSUASION, Jane Austen. 224pp. 0-486-29555-9

PRIDE AND PREJUDICE, Jane Austen. 272pp. 0-486-28473-5

SENSE AND SENSIBILITY, Jane Austen. 272pp. 0-486-29049-2

LOOKING BACKWARD, Edward Bellamy. 160pp. 0-486-29038-7

BEOWULF, Beowulf (trans. by R. K. Gordon). 64pp. 0-486-27264-8

CIVIL WAR STORIES, Ambrose Bierce. 128pp. 0-486-28038-1

WUTHERING HEIGHTS, Emily Brontë. 256pp. 0-486-29256-8

THE THIRTY-NINE STEPS, John Buchan. 96pp. 0-486-28201-5

TARZAN OF THE APES, Edgar Rice Burroughs. 224pp. (Not available in Europe or United Kingdom.) 0-486-29570-2

ALICE'S ADVENTURES IN WONDERLAND, Lewis Carroll. 96pp. 0-486-27543-4

THROUGH THE LOOKING-GLASS, Lewis Carroll. 128pp. 0-486-40878-7

MY ÁNTONIA, Willa Cather. 176pp. 0-486-28240-6

O PIONEERS!, Willa Cather. 128pp. 0-486-27785-2

FIVE GREAT SHORT STORIES, Anton Chekhov. 96pp. 0-486-26463-7

TALES OF CONJURE AND THE COLOR LINE, Charles Waddell Chesnutt. 128pp. 0-486-40426-9

FAVORITE FATHER BROWN STORIES, G. K. Chesterton. 96pp. 0-486-27545-0

THE AWAKENING, Kate Chopin. 128pp. 0-486-27786-0

A PAIR OF SILK STOCKINGS AND OTHER STORIES, Kate Chopin. 64pp. 0-486-29264-9

HEART OF DARKNESS, Joseph Conrad. 80pp. 0-486-26464-5

LORD JIM, Joseph Conrad. 256pp. 0-486-40650-4

THE SECRET SHARER AND OTHER STORIES, Joseph Conrad. 128pp. 0-486-27546-9

THE "LITTLE REGIMENT" AND OTHER CIVIL WAR STORIES, Stephen Crane. 80pp. 0-486-29557-5

THE OPEN BOAT AND OTHER STORIES, Stephen Crane. 128pp. 0-486-27547-7

THE RED BADGE OF COURAGE, Stephen Crane. 112pp. 0-486-26465-3

MOLL FLANDERS, Daniel Defoe. 256pp. 0-486-29093-X

ROBINSON CRUSOE, Daniel Defoe. 288pp. 0-486-40427-7

A CHRISTMAS CAROL, Charles Dickens. 80pp. 0-486-26865-9

THE CRICKET ON THE HEARTH AND OTHER CHRISTMAS STORIES, Charles Dickens. 128pp. 0-486-28039-X

A TALE OF TWO CITIES, Charles Dickens. 304pp. 0-486-40651-2

THE DOUBLE, Fyodor Dostoyevsky. 128pp. 0-486-29572-9

THE GAMBLER, Fyodor Dostoyevsky. 112pp. 0-486-29081-6

NOTES FROM THE UNDERGROUND, Fyodor Dostoyevsky. 96pp. 0-486-27053-X

THE ADVENTURE OF THE DANCING MEN AND OTHER STORIES, Sir Arthur Conan Doyle. 80pp. 0-486-29558-3

THE HOUND OF THE BASKERVILLES, Arthur Conan Doyle. 128pp. 0-486-28214-7

THE LOST WORLD, Arthur Conan Doyle. 176pp. 0-486-40060-3

DOVER·THRIFT·EDITIONS

FICTION

A JOURNAL OF THE PLAGUE YEAR, Daniel Defoe. 192pp. 0-486-41919-3
SIX GREAT SHERLOCK HOLMES STORIES, Sir Arthur Conan Doyle. 112pp. 0-486-27055-6
SHORT STORIES, Theodore Dreiser. 112pp. 0-486-28215-5
SILAS MARNER, George Eliot. 160pp. 0-486-29246-0
JOSEPH ANDREWS, Henry Fielding. 288pp. 0-486-41588-0
THIS SIDE OF PARADISE, F. Scott Fitzgerald. 208pp. 0-486-28999-0
"THE DIAMOND AS BIG AS THE RITZ" AND OTHER STORIES, F. Scott Fitzgerald. 0-486-29991-0
MADAME BOVARY, Gustave Flaubert. 256pp. 0-486-29257-6
THE REVOLT OF "MOTHER" AND OTHER STORIES, Mary E. Wilkins Freeman. 128pp. 0-486-40428-5
A ROOM WITH A VIEW, E. M. Forster. 176pp. (Available in U.S. only.) 0-486-28467-0
WHERE ANGELS FEAR TO TREAD, E. M. Forster. 128pp. (Available in U.S. only.) 0-486-27791-7
THE IMMORALIST, André Gide. 112pp. (Available in U.S. only.) 0-486-29237-1
HERLAND, Charlotte Perkins Gilman. 128pp. 0-486-40429-3
"THE YELLOW WALLPAPER" AND OTHER STORIES, Charlotte Perkins Gilman. 80pp. 0-486-29857-4
THE OVERCOAT AND OTHER STORIES, Nikolai Gogol. 112pp. 0-486-27057-2
CHELKASH AND OTHER STORIES, Maxim Gorky. 64pp. 0-486-40652-0
GREAT GHOST STORIES, John Grafton (ed.). 112pp. 0-486-27270-2
DETECTION BY GASLIGHT, Douglas G. Greene (ed.). 272pp. 0-486-29928-7
THE MABINOGION, Lady Charlotte E. Guest. 192pp. 0-486-29541-9
"THE FIDDLER OF THE REELS" AND OTHER SHORT STORIES, Thomas Hardy. 80pp. 0-486-29960-0
THE LUCK OF ROARING CAMP AND OTHER STORIES, Bret Harte. 96pp. 0-486-27271-0
THE HOUSE OF THE SEVEN GABLES, Nathaniel Hawthorne. 272pp. 0-486-40882-5
THE SCARLET LETTER, Nathaniel Hawthorne. 192pp. 0-486-28048-9
YOUNG GOODMAN BROWN AND OTHER STORIES, Nathaniel Hawthorne. 128pp. 0-486-27060-2
THE GIFT OF THE MAGI AND OTHER SHORT STORIES, O. Henry. 96pp. 0-486-27061-0
THE ASPERN PAPERS, Henry James. 112pp. 0-486-41922-3
THE BEAST IN THE JUNGLE AND OTHER STORIES, Henry James. 128pp. 0-486-27552-3
DAISY MILLER, Henry James. 64pp. 0-486-28773-4
THE TURN OF THE SCREW, Henry James. 96pp. 0-486-26684-2
WASHINGTON SQUARE, Henry James. 176pp. 0-486-40431-5
THE COUNTRY OF THE POINTED FIRS, Sarah Orne Jewett. 96pp. 0-486-28196-5
THE AUTOBIOGRAPHY OF AN EX-COLORED MAN, James Weldon Johnson. 112pp. 0-486-28512-X
DUBLINERS, James Joyce. 160pp. 0-486-26870-5
A PORTRAIT OF THE ARTIST AS A YOUNG MAN, James Joyce. 192pp. 0-486-28050-0
THE METAMORPHOSIS AND OTHER STORIES, Franz Kafka. 96pp. 0-486-29030-1
THE MAN WHO WOULD BE KING AND OTHER STORIES, Rudyard Kipling. 128pp. 0-486-28051-9
YOU KNOW ME AL, Ring Lardner. 128pp. 0-486-28513-8
SELECTED SHORT STORIES, D. H. Lawrence. 128pp. 0-486-27794-1
THE CALL OF THE WILD, Jack London. 64pp. 0-486-26472-6
FIVE GREAT SHORT STORIES, Jack London. 96pp. 0-486-27063-7
THE SEA-WOLF, Jack London. 248pp. 0-486-41108-7
WHITE FANG, Jack London. 160pp. 0-486-26968-X
DEATH IN VENICE, Thomas Mann. 96pp. (Available in U.S. only.) 0-486-28714-9
THE NECKLACE AND OTHER SHORT STORIES, Guy de Maupassant. 128pp. 0-486-27064-5
BARTLEBY AND BENITO CERENO, Herman Melville. 112pp. 0-486-26473-4
THE OIL JAR AND OTHER STORIES, Luigi Pirandello. 96pp. 0-486-28459-X
THE GOLD-BUG AND OTHER TALES, Edgar Allan Poe. 128pp. 0-486-26875-6
TALES OF TERROR AND DETECTION, Edgar Allan Poe. 96pp. 0-486-28744-0

DOVER · THRIFT · EDITIONS

FICTION

THE QUEEN OF SPADES AND OTHER STORIES, Alexander Pushkin. 128pp. 0-486-28054-3

THE STORY OF AN AFRICAN FARM, Olive Schreiner. 256pp. 0-486-40165-0

FRANKENSTEIN, Mary Shelley. 176pp. 0-486-28211-2

THE JUNGLE, Upton Sinclair. 320pp. (Available in U.S. only.) 0-486-41923-1

THREE LIVES, Gertrude Stein. 176pp. (Available in U.S. only.) 0-486-28059-4

THE BODY SNATCHER AND OTHER TALES, Robert Louis Stevenson. 80pp. 0-486-41924-X

THE STRANGE CASE OF DR. JEKYLL AND MR. HYDE, Robert Louis Stevenson. 64pp. 0-486-26688-5

TREASURE ISLAND, Robert Louis Stevenson. 160pp. 0-486-27559-0

GULLIVER'S TRAVELS, Jonathan Swift. 240pp. 0-486-29273-8

THE KREUTZER SONATA AND OTHER SHORT STORIES, Leo Tolstoy. 144pp. 0-486-27805-0

THE WARDEN, Anthony Trollope. 176pp. 0-486-40076-X

FATHERS AND SONS, Ivan Turgenev. 176pp. 0-486-0073-5

ADVENTURES OF HUCKLEBERRY FINN, Mark Twain. 224pp. 0-486-28061-6

THE ADVENTURES OF TOM SAWYER, Mark Twain. 192pp. 0-486-40077-8

THE MYSTERIOUS STRANGER AND OTHER STORIES, Mark Twain. 128pp. 0-486-27069-6

HUMOROUS STORIES AND SKETCHES, Mark Twain. 80pp. 0-486-29279-7

AROUND THE WORLD IN EIGHTY DAYS, Jules Verne. 160pp. 0-486-41111-7

CANDIDE, Voltaire (François-Marie Arouet). 112pp. 0-486-26689-3

GREAT SHORT STORIES BY AMERICAN WOMEN, Candace Ward (ed.). 192pp. 0-486-28776-9

"THE COUNTRY OF THE BLIND" AND OTHER SCIENCE-FICTION STORIES, H. G. Wells. 160pp. (Not available in Europe or United Kingdom.) 0-486-29569-9

THE ISLAND OF DR. MOREAU, H. G. Wells. 112pp. (Not available in Europe or United Kingdom.) 0-486-29027-1

THE INVISIBLE MAN, H. G. Wells. 112pp. (Not available in Europe or United Kingdom.) 0-486-27071-8

THE TIME MACHINE, H. G. Wells. 80pp. (Not available in Europe or United Kingdom.) 0-486-28472-7

THE WAR OF THE WORLDS, H. G. Wells. 160pp. (Not available in Europe or United Kingdom.) 0-486-29506-0

ETHAN FROME, Edith Wharton. 96pp. 0-486-26690-7

SHORT STORIES, Edith Wharton. 128pp. 0-486-28235-X

THE AGE OF INNOCENCE, Edith Wharton. 288pp. 0-486-29803-5

THE PICTURE OF DORIAN GRAY, Oscar Wilde. 192pp. 0-486-27807-7

JACOB'S ROOM, Virginia Woolf. 144pp. (Not available in Europe or United Kingdom.) 0-486-40109-X

MONDAY OR TUESDAY: Eight Stories, Virginia Woolf. 64pp. (Not available in Europe or United Kingdom.) 0-486-29453-6

NONFICTION

POETICS, Aristotle. 64pp. 0-486-29577-X

POLITICS, Aristotle. 368pp. 0-486-41424-8

NICOMACHEAN ETHICS, Aristotle. 256pp. 0-486-40096-4

MEDITATIONS, Marcus Aurelius. 128pp. 0-486-29823-X

THE LAND OF LITTLE RAIN, Mary Austin. 96pp. 0-486-29037-9

THE DEVIL'S DICTIONARY, Ambrose Bierce. 144pp. 0-486-27542-6

THE ANALECTS, Confucius. 128pp. 0-486-28484-0

CONFESSIONS OF AN ENGLISH OPIUM EATER, Thomas De Quincey. 80pp. 0-486-28742-4

THE SOULS OF BLACK FOLK, W. E. B. Du Bois. 176pp. 0-486-28041-1

DOVER · THRIFT · EDITIONS

NONFICTION

NARRATIVE OF THE LIFE OF FREDERICK DOUGLASS, Frederick Douglass. 96pp. 0-486-28499-9

SELF-RELIANCE AND OTHER ESSAYS, Ralph Waldo Emerson. 128pp. 0-486-27790-9

THE LIFE OF OLAUDAH EQUIANO, OR GUSTAVUS VASSA, THE AFRICAN, Olaudah Equiano. 192pp. 0-486-40661-X

THE AUTOBIOGRAPHY OF BENJAMIN FRANKLIN, Benjamin Franklin. 144pp. 0-486-29073-5

TOTEM AND TABOO, Sigmund Freud. 176pp. (Not available in Europe or United Kingdom.) 0-486-40434-X

LOVE: A Book of Quotations, Herb Galewitz (ed.). 64pp. 0-486-40004-2

PRAGMATISM, William James. 128pp. 0-486-28270-8

THE STORY OF MY LIFE, Helen Keller. 80pp. 0-486-29249-5

TAO TE CHING, Lao Tze. 112pp. 0-486-29792-6

GREAT SPEECHES, Abraham Lincoln. 112pp. 0-486-26872-1

THE PRINCE, Niccolò Machiavelli. 80pp. 0-486-27274-5

THE SUBJECTION OF WOMEN, John Stuart Mill. 112pp. 0-486-29601-6

SELECTED ESSAYS, Michel de Montaigne. 96pp. 0-486-29109-X

UTOPIA, Sir Thomas More. 96pp. 0-486-29583-4

BEYOND GOOD AND EVIL: Prelude to a Philosophy of the Future, Friedrich Nietzsche. 176pp. 0-486-29868-X

THE BIRTH OF TRAGEDY, Friedrich Nietzsche. 96pp. 0-486-28515-4

COMMON SENSE, Thomas Paine. 64pp. 0-486-29602-4

SYMPOSIUM AND PHAEDRUS, Plato. 96pp. 0-486-27798-4

THE TRIAL AND DEATH OF SOCRATES: Four Dialogues, Plato. 128pp. 0-486-27066-1

A MODEST PROPOSAL AND OTHER SATIRICAL WORKS, Jonathan Swift. 64pp. 0-486-28759-9

CIVIL DISOBEDIENCE AND OTHER ESSAYS, Henry David Thoreau. 96pp. 0-486-27563-9

WALDEN; OR, LIFE IN THE WOODS, Henry David Thoreau. 224pp. 0-486-28495-6

NARRATIVE OF SOJOURNER TRUTH, Sojourner Truth. 80pp. 0-486-29899-X

THE THEORY OF THE LEISURE CLASS, Thorstein Veblen. 256pp. 0-486-28062-4

DE PROFUNDIS, Oscar Wilde. 64pp. 0-486-29308-4

OSCAR WILDE'S WIT AND WISDOM: A Book of Quotations, Oscar Wilde. 64pp. 0-486-40146-4

UP FROM SLAVERY, Booker T. Washington. 160pp. 0-486-28738-6

A VINDICATION OF THE RIGHTS OF WOMAN, Mary Wollstonecraft. 224pp. 0-486-29036-0